International Governance

A volume in the series

Cornell Studies in Political Economy

EDITED BY PETER J. KATZENSTEIN

A full list of titles in the series appears at the end of the book.

International Governance

PROTECTING THE ENVIRONMENT
IN A STATELESS SOCIETY

ORAN R. YOUNG

CORNELL UNIVERSITY PRESS

Ithaca and London

First published 1994 by Cornell University Press.

Printed in the United States of America

⊚ The paper in this book meets the minimum requirements of the American National Standard for Information Sciences—Permanence of Paper for Printed Library Materials, ANSI Z39.48-1984.

Library of Congress Cataloging-in-Publication Data

Young, Oran R.
    International governance : protecting the environment in a stateless society / Oran R. Young.
        p.   cm.—(Cornell studies in political economy)
    Includes bibliographical references and index.
    ISBN 0-8014-2972-2.—ISBN 0-8014-8176-7 (pbk.)
    1. Environmental policy—International cooperation.   2. Natural resources—International cooperation.   3. Social ecology—International cooperation.   I. Title.   II. Series.
GE170.Y68   1994
363.7'0526—dc20   94-11846

To Gail

who has found the courage to be her own person

and the wisdom to respect the identity of others

Contents

Preface

This book is a successor to *International Cooperation: Building Regimes for Natural Resources and the Environment* (Cornell University Press, 1989). Much like its predecessor, it came into being as a series of essays that I have endeavored to integrate into a coherent whole rather than simply collect as somewhat related pieces. This volume builds on its predecessor analytically, reflecting the evolution of my thinking about international institutions over the last five years. Among the most important developments to arise from my continuing encounter with a range of international governance systems and regimes are (1) a realization that the study of international regimes needs to be set more broadly in the context of the "new institutionalism" within the social sciences, (2) the emergence of the concept of institutional bargaining as a way of thinking about the creation of international regimes, (3) the articulation of the idea of effectiveness as an element essential to the study of international governance systems, and (4) a growing concern with the task of integrating the work of those who study international regimes with the contributions of students of international law and organization.

The essential message of this book arises out of the distinction between governance systems, which are social institutions or sets of rules guiding the behavior of those engaged in identifiable social practices, and governments, which are organizations or material entities established to administer the provisions of governance systems. This distinction leads directly to the conclusion that, under a variety of conditions, the operations of governments are not only insufficient to ensure that growing demands for governance are met but also may be unnecessary for the provision of governance. This realization is truly liberating. It does not lead to a blanket rejection of arguments about the importance of governments or international organizations in efforts to fulfill the demand for governance. But it does allow us to think seriously about the idea of governance without government, and it encourages a critical assessment of the essential nature of those organizations that may prove useful in administering various governance systems. This is a perspective, in my judgment, whose significance ranges far beyond the normal boundaries of the field of international relations. In this era of disillusionment with the performance of governments in a wide variety of settings, it is high time to reexamine the basic issues that come into focus with the distinction between governance and government.

I have had the extraordinary benefit over the last five years of being able to refine my thinking about such matters through a constant dialogue with superb colleagues both in this country and abroad. In part, this contact has occurred as a by-product of the large research teams I have been privileged to lead dealing first with an effort to formulate and test a selection of hypotheses about the process of regime formation and later with a similar effort to deepen our understanding of what it means to speak of the effectiveness of international institutions and what methods are appropriate to the study of institutional effectiveness. These teams have brought together analysts from five countries willing to invest their time and energy in complex programs of collaborative research. The first program resulted in a published volume: Oran R. Young and Gail Osherenko, eds., *Polar Politics: Creating International Environmental Regimes* (Cornell University Press, 1993). The second is expected to produce a similar publication in the near future. I am particularly grateful to Gail Osherenko and Marc Levy, my closest collaborators in the management of these research teams, but I have learned a great deal from each and every one of the participants.

Partly, the dialogue has developed out of a general recognition that roughly comparable work on international regimes or governance systems has been going on at several research centers in this country and abroad and that we should work consciously to increase the comparability of our findings. This realization led us to organize an event at Dartmouth's Minary Center during November 1991, now known as the Regimes Summit, in which senior researchers from Harvard University, the University of Washington, the University of Oslo, the Fridtjof Nansen Institute in Oslo, and the University of Tübingen, as well as Dartmouth College, came together to compare notes regarding their work on international regimes and to prepare the way for the development of a regimes data base. This project resulted in a module in the newly established research program of the International Institute for Applied Systems Analysis (IIASA) on the implementation and effectiveness of international environmental commitments. I have profited from my contact with all the participants in the Regimes Summit and especially with Marc Levy and Michael Zurn.

Of course, none of this would have been possible without adequate financial support, and it is a pleasure to record my debts. Above all, the Ford Foundation has supported my research teams and generously allowed us to use some of its funds to cover ongoing expenses of the Institute of Arctic Studies at Dartmouth. The MacArthur Foundation contributed funding for much of the analysis of Arctic cases that continues to crop up in my published work. Many other organizations in Canada, England, Norway, Russia, and the United States provided support by allowing staff members to participate in the research teams working on regime formation and regime effectiveness. I will not attempt to list them all, but I deeply appreciate their contributions. Finally, I am grateful to the John Sloan Dickey Endowment for International Understanding and to its longtime director, Leonard Rieser, for investing in me and my work at Dartmouth. It has been a privilege for me to serve as the acting director of the Dickey Endowment during 1992–1993 following Leonard's retirement. It is a pleasure as well to be able to report that my successor, Martin Sherwin, is now in office, which will allow me to concentrate in a more focused manner on my continuing studies of governance.

Finally, it is my pleasure to acknowledge a growing debt to individuals who have helped to maintain order in my life and who have put up with my desire to continue a life of scholarship even as I have become increasingly involved in science policy and program administration. My secretaries, Nicki Maynard, Margaret Brannen, and Marcella Logue, have played an essential role in this regard. Even more important have been the good-natured tolerance of my daughter, Naomi Young, and the intellectual and emotional support of my wife, Gail

Osherenko. To Gail, who is occupied with the evolution of her own career as a scholar and writer, I become more grateful with each passing year; this book is dedicated—again—to her.

ORAN R. YOUNG

Wolcott, Vermont

International Governance

The "New Institutionalism" in International Relations

The rise of "neoliberal institutionalism" in international relations is one element in a broader intellectual movement that spans the principal social science disciplines and has had more impact in several other fields of study than it has in international relations.[1] Economists now recognize the "new institutional economics" as a major stream of analysis within their discipline;[2] several recent Nobel prizes in economics have gone to scholars whose research centers on the role of property rights, decision rules, and electoral systems as determinants of collective outcomes in a variety of social settings.[3] For their part, political scientists are "rediscovering institutions,"[4] and sociologists have picked up on this theme under the rubric of the "new institutionalism."[5]

---

[1] The phrase is Robert O. Keohane's, in "Neoliberal Institutionalism: A Perspective on World Politics," chap. 1 in *International Institutions and State Power* (Boulder: Westview, 1990). See also Joseph S. Nye, "Neorealism and Neoliberalism," *World Politics* 40 (January 1988), 235–251; Andrew Moravcsik, "Liberalism and International Relations Theory," unpublished paper dated September 1991; and Mark W. Zacher and Richard A. Matthew, "Liberal International Theory: Common Threads, Divergent Strands," paper prepared for the 1992 annual meeting of the American Political Science Association.

[2] Eirik G. Furubotn and Rudolf Richter, eds., *The New Institutional Economics* (College Station: Texas A & M University Press, 1991); and Thrainn Eggertsson, *Economic Behavior and Institutions* (Cambridge, Eng.: Cambridge University Press, 1989).

[3] The prizes awarded to James Buchanan, Ronald Coase, and Herbert Simon are prime examples. Other recipients, including Kenneth Arrow and Gary Becker, have also done work involving institutional issues.

[4] James G. March and Johan P. Olsen, *Rediscovering Institutions: The Organizational Basis of Politics* (New York: Free Press, 1989).

[5] Walter W. Powell and Paul J. DiMaggio, eds., *The New Institutionalism in Organizational Analysis* (Chicago: University of Chicago Press, 1991).

What are the defining features of this intellectual movement? Why has it emerged at the present time? What are its prospects for taking root and flourishing over the next decade or two? Is it more or less likely to yield results of lasting significance in international relations than in other fields? The answers to these questions will help in providing a larger intellectual framework for the studies of the new institutionalism in international relations set forth in this book.

It is important to observe, at the outset, that the movement I am discussing involves institutionalism with a difference. Those associated with this movement have no interest in reverting to the formal/legal institutionalism that occupied a central place in the discipline of political science before the behavioral revolution of the 1950s and 1960s.[6] We are all painfully aware that many formal instruments purporting to establish institutional arrangements are dead letters. Worse, we know that some institutions are hollow shells exploited by authoritarian leaders to mask oppressive and destructive practices carried out in the name of the state. Nor are today's economists attracted to the earlier economic institutionalism of Commons, Mitchell, and Veblen, long since rejected by a discipline committed to the development of parsimonious models capable of accounting for behavior in a wide range of social settings.[7] If the new institutionalism is to make a lasting mark in the social sciences, it will need to differentiate between effective institutions likely to generate predictable consequences in a variety of settings and arrangements that are institutions in name only.

Equally important is the realization that the new institutionalism is not simply a call for more sophisticated analyses of organizations—including private enterprises, public agencies, and international organizations—either through studies of the behavior of individuals operating within organizational settings or through analyses of the roles organizations themselves play in society. New developments in the field of organization theory (for example, studies dealing with organizational design, bureaucratic politics, and organizational cultures) undoubtedly constitute significant contributions to the social sciences, especially when treated as correctives to the formalistic as-

---

[6] Harry Eckstein, "A Perspective on Comparative Politics, Past and Present," in Harry Eckstein and David E. Apter, eds., *Comparative Politics* (New York: Free Press, 1963), 3–32.

[7] Terence W. Hutchison, "Institutionalist Economics Old and New," in Furubotn and Richter, eds., *New Institutional Economics*, 35–44.

sumptions about organizations embedded in many models of interactive decision making.[8] As I shall suggest, an important agenda of questions concerns the relationships between institutions and organizations. But none of these questions can be addressed in a rigorous manner in the absence of an explicit account of the concept of social institutions as the new institutionalists use it.

Institutions, then, are sets of rules of the game or codes of conduct that serve to define social practices, assign roles to the participants in these practices, and guide the interactions among occupants of these roles. Structures of property rights, on this account, are institutions. So also are electoral systems used to choose representatives in political systems. Institutions can and frequently do vary along many dimensions, including numbers and types of members, functional scope, geographical domain, degree of formalization, and stage of development. Beyond this, functionally specific institutions are often nested or embedded into broader or more general institutional arrangements in the sense that they assume the operation of the rules of the game associated with the broader arrangements.[9] Nonetheless, all institutions are social artifacts created by human beings—consciously or unconsciously[10]—to cope with problems of coordination and cooperation that arise as a result of interdependencies among the activities of distinct individuals or social groups.[11]

The distinction between institutions and organizations is now easy to clarify. Whereas institutions are sets of rules of the game or codes of conduct defining social practices, organizations are material enti-

[8] Oliver Williamson, *Markets and Hierarchies* (New York: Free Press, 1975); Graham T. Allison, *Essence of Decision* (Boston: Little, Brown, 1971); James E. Alt and Kenneth A. Shepsle, eds., *Perspectives on Positive Political Economy* (Cambridge, Eng.: Cambridge University Press, 1990), Part II; and Jay R. Galbraith, Edward E. Lawler III and Associates, *Organizing for the Future: The New Logic for Managing Complex Organizations* (San Francisco: Jossey-Bass, 1993).

[9] John Gerard Ruggie, "International Regimes, Transactions, and Change: Embedded Liberalism in the Postwar Economic Order," in Stephen D. Krasner, ed., *International Regimes* (Ithaca: Cornell University Press, 1983), 195–231; and Ruggie, "Embedded Liberalism Revisited: Institutions and Progress in International Economic Relations," in Emanuel Adler and Beverly Crawford, eds., *Progress in Postwar International Relations* (New York: Columbia University Press, 1991), 201–234.

[10] Economists, used to dealing with markets, often think of institutions as spontaneous or self-generating arrangements in the sense that they are "the product of the action of many men but . . . not the result of human design" (Friedrich A. Hayek, *Rules and Order*, vol. 1 of *Law, Legislation and Liberty* [Chicago: University of Chicago Press, 1973], 37).

[11] Oran R. Young, *International Cooperation: Building Regimes for Natural Resources and the Environment* (Ithaca: Cornell University Press, 1989), 81–84.

ties possessing offices, personnel, budgets, equipment, and, more often than not, legal personality. Put another away, organizations are actors in social practices. Institutions affect the behavior of these actors by defining social practices and spelling out codes of conduct appropriate to them, but they are not actors in their own right. As James March and Herbert Simon pointed out long ago in their seminal work on organizations, the United States Steel Corporation (now USX), the Red Cross, the New York State Highway Department, and the corner grocery store are all organizations in this sense.[12] By contrast, the complex structures of property rights that govern most of the activities these organizations engage in are institutions. As these examples make clear, the purpose of drawing a distinction between institutions and organizations is not to argue that one is more important than the other but to open up a large and important research agenda focusing on the relationships between institutions and organizations.

What accounts for the rise of the new institutionalism in the major social science disciplines as well as in international relations? The answer to this question, I now believe, involves at least three separate sets of considerations. Recent decades have witnessed a remarkable surge in the demand for institutions to cope with both broadening and deepening interdependencies. Once unrelated activities of numerous individuals and social groups now impinge on each other in significant ways. For instance, the destruction of moist tropical forests in Brazil is likely to have major consequences for residents of the Northern Hemisphere, and the thinning of the stratospheric ozone layer resulting from the widespread use of chlorofluorocarbons (CFCs) will affect large groups of people who are neither producers nor consumers of these chemicals. At the same time, the links among those who have been interacting with each other for some time are becoming tighter. Nowhere is this interaction more apparent than in the complex issues surrounding international trade and the recent links between trade and environment.[13] It is no cause for surprise that a growing agenda of institutional issues is demanding attention.

These problems are complicated by a loss of confidence, at least in

---

[12] James G. March and Herbert A. Simon, *Organizations* (New York: Wiley, 1958), 1.
[13] Jim McNeil et al., *Beyond Interdependence: The Meshing of the Earth's Economy with the Earth's Ecology* (New York: Oxford University Press, 1991); and Hilary F. French, "Costly Tradeoffs: Reconciling Trade and the Environment," *Worldwatch Paper 113* (Washington, D.C.: Worldwatch Institute, 1993).

some influential circles, in the standard institutional tools that have made up our repertoire in recent times. Specifically, serious doubts have arisen about both familiar structures of private property rights and well-known forms of public regulation as solutions to many of our emerging concerns. For example, many observers have come to see existing structures of private property rights as a major source of environmental problems. Conversely, we have become increasingly aware of the deficiencies of familiar command-and-control-style public regulation in altering the behavior of individuals and organizations that has caused environmental problems.[14] I do not mean to imply that these standard institutional tools are bankrupt and should be discarded in favor of some new set of social practices. Private property and public regulation will undoubtedly be with us for the foreseeable future. But coupled with the growing demand for institutions to cope with new interdependencies, these doubts about the standard institutional tools have precipitated a striking increase of interest in rethinking the spectrum of institutional arrangements available to solve coordination and cooperation problems.

Interest in the new institutionalism has also been fueled by some striking successes that have rewarded the initial efforts of those who have emerged as leaders of the movement. In the hands of economists, in particular, much of this work has centered on the role of structures of property rights as determinants of collective outcomes in social settings. Ronald Coase and his successors, for example, have demonstrated some important propositions about the consequences of liability rules for both the allocation of resources and the distribution of benefits.[15] A major outgrowth of this stream of analysis is the growing interest in transaction costs and other social frictions as determinants of collective outcomes.[16] Allen Kneese and others have traced a variety of environmental problems to externalities attributable to incentives resulting from prevailing structures of private property.[17] The appropriate response, on this account, lies in altering

[14] R. W. Hahn and R. N. Stavins, "Market Based Environmental Regulation," *Ecology Law Quarterly* 18 (1991), 1–42.

[15] The seminal work is Ronald H. Coase, "The Problem of Social Cost," *Journal of Law and Economics* 3 (October 1960), 1–44. The development of this stream of analysis can be followed in the *Journal of Law and Economics*, which Coase edited for many years.

[16] Henry G. Manne, ed., *The Economics of Legal Relationships: Readings in the Theory of Property Rights* (St. Paul: West Publishing, 1975), Part 2.

[17] Allen V. Kneese and Blair T. Bower, *Managing Water Quality: Economics, Technology, Institutions* (Baltimore: Johns Hopkins University Press, 1968); and J. H. Dales, *Pollution, Property and Prices* (Toronto: University of Toronto Press, 1968).

the rules of the game either by redefining or by placing restrictions on property rights.[18] Scott Gordon identified the situation that has become familiar to most of us as Garrett Hardin's "tragedy of the commons."[19] Interestingly, a rapidly growing group of writers representing several disciplines have since produced evidence to suggest that other institutional arrangements—especially codes of conduct governing the behavior of those operating in a common property environment—will often eliminate or alleviate the tragedy of the commons without requiring the replacement of common property with some fundamentally different structure of property rights.[20]

Similar observations are in order about studies centered on the role of decision rules as determinants of the social choices that electorates or legislatures make. Anthony Downs, for instance, initiated a line of spatial models of voting by showing how in the American electoral system candidates' or parties' positions on major issues tend to converge.[21] Building on this foundation, others have sought to explain the striking differences in American and European voting behavior based on the effects of their respective electoral systems.[22] James Buchanan and Gordon Tullock, writing on the calculus of consent, initiated important work on the impact of consensus rules versus majoritarian rules on the processes as well as the outcomes of social choice.[23] In so doing, they have drawn our attention to the trade-offs between welfare losses sustained by losers in majoritarian systems and the rising transaction costs associated with movement toward the pole of unanimity. More recently, Kenneth Shepsle has sought to general-

[18] Manne, ed., *Economics of Legal Relationships,* Part 3; and Robert Dorfman and Nancy S. Dorfman, eds., *Economics of the Environment,* 2d ed. (New York: Norton, 1977), Part III.

[19] H. Scott Gordon, "The Economic Theory of a Common Property Resource: The Fishery," *Journal of Political Economy* 62 (April 1954), 124–142. For the evocative tragedy of the commons formulation see Garrett Hardin, "The Tragedy of the Commons," *Science* 162 (December 1968), 1343–1348.

[20] Bonnie M. McCay and James M. Acheson, eds., *The Question of the Commons: The Culture and Ecology of Communal Resources* (Tucson: University of Arizona Press, 1987); Fikret Berkes, ed., *Common Property Resources: Ecology and Community-Based Sustainable Development* (London: Belhaven Press, 1989); Elinor Ostrom, *Governing the Commons: The Evolution of Institutions for Collective Action* (Cambridge, Eng.: Cambridge University Press, 1990); and Daniel W. Bromley, ed., *Making the Commons Work: Theory, Practice, and Policy* (San Francisco: Institute for Contemporary Studies, 1992).

[21] Anthony Downs, *An Economic Theory of Democracy* (New York: Harper & Row, 1957).

[22] These developments are clearly exemplified in the pages of *Public Choice,* the journal of the Public Choice Society.

[23] James M. Buchanan and Gordon Tullock, *The Calculus of Consent* (Ann Arbor: University of Michigan Press, 1962).

ize these concerns by introducing the overarching idea of structure-induced equilibrium and observing that the new institutionalism seeks "to explain characteristics of social outcomes on the basis not only of agent preferences and optimizing behavior, but also on the basis of institutional features."[24] In the world of research, as in other realms, nothing succeeds like success, and it seems apparent that these initial achievements have joined the growth of demand for institutions and the loss of confidence in standard institutional tools as driving forces behind the movement I have been discussing.

What are the prospects for the new institutionalism in the foreseeable future? Is this movement likely to have a lasting impact in the various social sciences or is it destined to end up as another in a long line of intellectual fashions, influential while it lasts but lacking in staying power? In my judgment, the answers to these questions will turn on the capacity of the new institutionalism to achieve success in its basic program of accounting for a sizable proportion of the variance in collective outcomes on the basis of the operation of institutions. It is not necessary for institutional analyses to account for all of the variance in these outcomes, thereby crowding out arguments that point to ideas, including cultural constructs, and material conditions, including demographic and technological forces, as determinants of collective outcomes.[25] Nor is it necessary to accept some of the grander claims associated with the new institutionalism, such as the role Douglass North and Robert P. Thomas ascribe to changing structures of property rights in their account of the rise of the West, to acknowledge the importance of this movement as a force to be reckoned with in the social sciences.[26] In fact, there are good reasons to conclude that once we accept the proposition that social institutions are significant drivers of collective outcomes, we will then want to turn our attention to studies of the interactions between and among institutions, ideas, and material conditions in our efforts to account for much of what takes places in a wide range of social settings.

[24] Kenneth A. Shepsle, "Studying Institutions: Some Lessons from the Rational Choice Approach," *Journal of Theoretical Politics* 1 (1989), 135.

[25] For a helpful discussion of the roles of ideas, institutions, and material conditions as social drivers see Robert W. Cox, "Social Forces, States and World Orders: Beyond International Relations Theory," in Robert O. Keohane, ed., *Neorealism and Its Critics* (New York: Columbia University Press, 1986), 204–254.

[26] Douglass C. North and Robert P. Thomas, *The Rise of the Western World: A New Economic History* (Cambridge, Eng.: Cambridge University Press, 1973); and Douglass C. North, *Institutions, Institutional Change and Economic Performance* (Cambridge, Eng.: Cambridge University Press, 1990).

The need to prove our point regarding the significance of institutions as determinants of collective outcomes poses, in my view, three separate challenges.[27] First, we need to set clear-cut boundaries on the range of effects that we associate with the operation of institutions. In general, it seems desirable to devote the bulk of our attention to direct effects or, in other words, situations in which causal chains linking the operation of an institution to the relevant outcomes are short. Otherwise, we will find ourselves trading in tenuous claims that are difficult or impossible to evaluate. Next, we need to develop a repertoire of tools to identify causal connections between institutions and outcomes. It is not enough to observe that an institution is created and that certain outcomes follow shortly thereafter; the danger of ending up with spurious correlations is too great for that. Although it is highly unlikely that we will discover a simple litmus test to deal with this challenge, it is not unreasonable to expect the development of a set of analytic tools to be used in building consensual knowledge regarding such matters.

Above all, we need to investigate the behavioral mechanisms through which institutions produce their effects and thereby influence collective outcomes. In the final analysis, it is the interactive behavior of agents (whether individuals or organizations) that leads to the outcomes we wish to understand. Because the social sciences employ a number of distinct models to explain such behavior, it is appropriate to focus on each of these models in turn and to ask how the operation of institutions can be expected to guide behavior modeled in these ways. Until we understand the causal connections involved in these impacts, arguments regarding the significance of institutions as determinants of collective outcomes cannot progress beyond the level of correlational accounts.[28]

Nowhere are these analytic challenges more critical or more imposing than in the field of international relations. Students of domestic societies generally agree that institutions are important even when they do not stop to examine what is actually involved in making such a

---

[27] For a more detailed discussion of these issues see Marc Levy, Gail Osherenko, and Oran R. Young, "The Effectiveness of International Regimes: A Design for Large-Scale Collaborative Research," unpublished paper dated 4 December 1991; and Marc Levy and Oran Young, "Memorandum to Members of the Effectiveness Research Team," unpublished paper dated 14 January 1993.

[28] On the epistemological issues involved in this sort of causal analysis see David Dessler, "The Causal Analysis of International Environmental Institutions," unpublished paper dated 23 April 1992.

claim. By contrast, those who write on international relations and especially those who style themselves realists or neorealists often deny that institutions are significant determinants of collective outcomes in international society. They typically explain such outcomes as resulting from the exercise of power, and they are inclined to regard institutional arrangements (generally known as regimes or governance systems among students of international affairs) as epiphenomena that reflect underlying power relations and that can and often do change as these deeper power relations shift.[29] There is a sense, therefore, in which it may be appropriate to treat international society as a hard case for proponents of the new institutionalism. If institutional arguments can be used to explain a significant proportion of the variance in collective outcomes in this social setting, the more general claims of the new institutionalism will receive a substantial boost.

The chapters that follow should be read in this light. Not only do I set the study of international institutions in the broader analytic context provided by the work of the new institutionalists in a variety of fields, but I seek also to contribute to the larger program of the new institutionalism by showing the power of institutional explanations in accounting for collective outcomes under the conditions prevailing in international society. Although the arguments presented are generic, I turn repeatedly to examples relating to natural resources and the environment in search of both analytic inspiration and an empirical testbed for efforts to validate my arguments. In the process, I have become increasingly convinced of the virtues of this choice. There is nothing sacred about environmental issues; others can and will make use of different issue areas in their efforts both to develop and to critique the new institutionalism. At this juncture, however, I am persuaded that issues pertaining to natural resources and the environment constitute a rewarding domain in which to explore the role of social institutions; there can be no doubt about the growing significance of this issue area in its own right.

Chapter 1 relates the recent literature on international regimes and governance systems to the broader dialogue initiated by those who have been developing the new institutionalism in other fields of study.

[29] Perhaps the most celebrated expression of this view is Susan Strange, "*Cave! hic dragones:* A Critique of Regime Analysis," in Krasner ed., *International Regimes,* 337–354. But see also Robert Gilpin, *The Political Economy of International Relations* (Princeton: Princeton University Press, 1987).

In doing so, it both standardizes the usage of key concepts employed in this book and provides an analytic vantage point from which to track and assess the rapid growth of interest in the concept of international governance. The chapter also offers an introduction to the environment as an increasingly central issue area at the international level. Chapters 2–8 are divided into three parts, one devoted to illustrative cases intended to provide the reader with a substantive basis for thinking about international governance systems; the second focusing on theoretical issues arising from the idea of governance without government; and the third discussing relationships between the new institutionalism in international relations and the more traditional concerns of those whose work deals with international organizations and international law.

The first of the case studies, contained in Chapter 2, deals with the effort to devise a global climate regime, which yielded the framework Convention on Climate Change signed in June 1992 at the United Nations Conference on Environment and Development (UNCED) but will continue throughout the foreseeable future. This case, centering on an international commons of growing concern to a wide array of constituencies, directs attention to questions concerning the creation or formation of international governance systems. Chapter 3 examines a collection of shared natural resources that are regional or subregional in scope; it shifts the focus from regime formation to a series of questions relating to the effectiveness and the robustness of international governance systems once they are put in place.

Using these cases as an intellectual springboard, the chapters of Part Two probe several theoretical issues that are central to our understanding of international governance systems. Chapter 4 lays out my current thinking about institutional bargaining as the process through which the creation of governance systems occurs in international society. Chapter 5 provides a more extended account of the problems facing those seeking to exercise power in the context of institutional bargaining. As the chapter makes clear, there is an essential difference between structural power or power in the material sense and bargaining leverage in efforts to reach agreement on the terms of international governance systems. Chapter 6 then turns to a discussion of the effectiveness of governance systems in international society. Expanded efforts to improve our understanding of effectiveness are essential to the future of the new institutionalism, and the chapter seeks to lay the groundwork for these efforts by clarifying the conceptual and methodological issues facing those endeavoring to advance our knowledge of the effectiveness of international governance systems.

The chapters that make up Part Three are devoted to the links between the study of international governance systems and the more familiar concerns of those who study international organizations and international law. Chapter 7 begins by sharpening the distinction between international governance systems treated as social institutions and international organizations; it then examines the roles that international organizations play in creating and administering governance systems. Chapter 8 shifts the focus to international law; it asks what it means to describe specific governance systems as legal regimes and seeks, in the process, to find ways to bridge the two cultures of law and the social sciences in the study of international governance. In the end, I adopt and endeavor to defend the view that students of international law and organization have much to contribute to the pursuit of knowledge about international governance systems.

CHAPTER ONE

International Environmental Governance

We have entered a period of profound change in our thinking
about governance in international society that offers an exciting new
research agenda for students of international affairs and an opportunity to bridge the gap that has long separated the main streams of
research in the fields of international relations, international law, and
political science. In this volume, I explore the implications of this
development with particular reference to international environmental affairs, seeking in the process to explain how environmental matters have made their way onto the international agenda and why they
can be expected to retain a prominent place there for years to come.[1]
But the underlying argument is generic; it should attract the attention of those whose substantive concerns center on matters of security,
economics, and human rights as well as those addressing environmental matters.

Throughout much of the twentieth century, a broad spectrum of
students of international affairs argued that the politically decentralized or anarchical character of international society is a defect to be

This chapter originated as a presentation at IIASA '92, An International Conference on the Challenges to Systems Analysis in the Nineties and Beyond, Laxenburg,
Austria, 12–13 May 1992. An earlier version appeared as Oran R. Young, "International Environmental Governance: Building Institutions in an Anarchical Society," in International Institute for Applied Systems Analysis, *Science and Sustainability: Selected Papers
on IIASA's 20th Anniversary* (Vienna: IIASA, 1992), 245–268.

[1] On the rapid rise of environmental issues on the international agenda see Jim
MacNeill, "The Greening of International Relations," *International Journal* 45 (Winter
1989–1990), 1–35.

remedied as quickly as possible through the creation of organizations capable of governing at the international level.[2] Prescriptions for achieving this goal have varied widely, ranging from the contractarian vision of those who have advocated the pursuit of "world peace through world law" to the incrementalism of those who propose to rely on the processes of spillover articulated in functionalist or neofunctionalist thinking.[3] But all concur in the conclusion that we cannot hope to secure peace or achieve order, much less promote justice or other valued ends, at the international level in the absence of governmental organizations. This view has led students of international affairs to look to experience with domestic systems as a source of inspiration, whereas conversely students of politics at the domestic level have seldom thought to study international society as a source of helpful ideas about governance.[4]

Changes affecting this line of thought, stimulated by developments of the last decade or two, are now beginning to coalesce into an alternative picture of international governance. In part, this is a consequence of the growing realization that domestic political systems, much like markets, often fail in ways that can and do lead to inefficiencies and to unfortunate outcomes measured in terms of other values such as sustainability and equity. Under the rubric of government failure, for example, analysts are now exploring an array of problems centering on institutional arthritis resulting from progressive bureaucratization, the capture of public agencies by special interests, the impact of repressive measures carried out in the name of the state, and ultimately the breakdown of order eventuating in civil strife.[5] Simply establishing a government or a collection of governmental organizations, we have learned from painful experience, offers no assurance that the function of governance will be fulfilled

[2] I do not mean to imply that all students of international relations share these views. For a particularly prominent exception see Hedley Bull, *The Anarchical Society: A Study of Order in World Politics* (New York: Columbia University Press, 1977).

[3] For a well-known expression of the "world peace through world law" perspective see Grenville Clark and Louis B. Sohn, *World Peace through World Law* (Cambridge, Mass.: Harvard University Press, 1960). A sophisticated account of the logic of functionalism and neofunctionalism can be found in Ernst B. Haas, *Beyond the Nation-State: Functionalism and International Organization* (Stanford: Stanford University Press, 1964).

[4] On the role of the domestic analogy in studies of international relations see Hidemi Suganami, *The Domestic Analogy and World Order Proposals* (Cambridge, Eng.: Cambridge University Press, 1989).

[5] Charles Wolf, Jr., *Markets or Governments: Choosing between Imperfect Alternatives* (Cambridge, Mass.: MIT Press, 1988).

13

effectively, efficiently, and equitably; it may impose terrible costs at both the individual and the societal levels.[6]

Equally important is the growing realization that the achievement of governance does not invariably require the creation of material entities or formal organizations of the sort we ordinarily associate with the concept of government. Once we set aside our preoccupation with structures of government, it is apparent that governance is by no means lacking in international society, despite the conspicuous absence of a material entity possessing the power and authority to handle the functions of government for this society as a whole.[7] This realization suggests an array of important topics for research on the part of students of international relations. How is it possible to achieve governance without government in the sort of social setting exemplified by international society?[8] Does success in such endeavors depend on the presence of certain conditions or the absence of others? Are some strategies more likely to prove effective than others in the pursuit of governance without government?

This line of analysis not only raises questions about the conventional wisdom concerning international governance, but it also opens up the prospect that experience with governance systems at the international level may offer insights of value to those principally concerned with problems of governance at the domestic level. It even suggests intriguing links between the concerns of students of international governance and the research of those who focus on the prospects for avoiding the tragedy of the commons in small-cale, stateless societies and who speak increasingly of governing the commons.[9] For the first time, therefore, we have entered an era in which there is a solid basis

[6] On the problem of "failed" states see Gerald B. Helman and Steven R. Ratner, "Saving Failed States," *Foreign Policy* 89 (Winter 1992–1993), 3–20.

[7] For a sophisticated argument that this is true even in security affairs see Dorothy V. Jones, *Code of Peace: Ethics and Security in a World of Warlord States* (Chicago: University of Chicago Press, 1991).

[8] The concept of "governance without government" is developed at length in James N. Rosenau and Ernst-Otto Czempiel, eds., *Governance without Government: Order and Change in World Politics* (New York: Cambridge University Press, 1992). See also Charles P. Kindleberger, *The International Economic Order: Essays on Financial Crisis and International Public Goods* (Cambridge, Mass.: MIT Press, 1988), chap. 9.

[9] Elinor Ostrom, *Governing the Commons: The Evolution of Institutions for Collective Action* (Cambridge, Eng.: Cambridge University Press, 1990); and Robert Keohane, Michael McGinnis, and Elinor Ostrom, eds., *Proceedings of a Conference on Linking Local and Global Commons, 23–25 April 1992* (Cambridge, Mass.: Harvard University Center for International Affairs and Indiana University Workshop in Political Theory and Policy Analysis, 1993).

for students of politics at every level of social organization to interact with each other in a mutually beneficial fashion.

GOVERNANCE WITHOUT GOVERNMENT

Governance arises as a social or societal concern whenever the members of a group find that they are interdependent in the sense that the actions of each impinge on the welfare of the others.[10] Interdependence is likely to become a source of conflict when the efforts of individual members of the group to achieve their goals interfere with or impede the efforts of others to pursue their own ends. It will be seen as a basis for cooperation, on the other hand, when opportunities arise to enhance social welfare by taking steps to coordinate the actions of the individual members of the group. More generically, interdependence gives rise to collective-action problems in the sense that actors left to their own devices in an interdependent world frequently suffer joint losses as a result of conflict or are unable to reap joint gains because of an inability to cooperate. In general, moreover, the higher the level of interdependence among the members of the group, the more pervasive and complex these collective-action problems become.[11]

At the most general level, governance involves the establishment and operation of social institutions (in the sense of rules of the game that serve to define social practices, assign roles, and guide interactions among the occupants of these roles) capable of resolving conflicts, facilitating cooperation, or, more generally, alleviating collective-action problems in a world of interdependent actors.[12] There is nothing in this way of framing the issue that presupposes the

[10] Though the basic idea is generic, this formulation is Lockean in character; see John Locke, *Two Treaties of Government*, ed. Peter Laslett (Cambridge, Eng.: Cambridge University Press, 1967). For a sophisticated discussion of interdependence at the level of international society, see Robert O. Keohane and Joseph S. Nye, *Power and Interdependence*, 2d ed. (Glenview: Scott, Foresman, 1989).

[11] For a sophisticated survey of these problems see Russell Hardin, *Collective Action* (Baltimore: Johns Hopkins University Press, 1982).

[12] This perspective on social institutions reflects the work of those, like North and Thomas, who have been major contributors to "neoinstitutional economics." For an excellent survey consult Thrainn Eggertsson, *Economic Behavior and Institutions* (Cambridge, Eng.: Cambridge University Press, 1990). For an application of this school of thought to international relations see Beth V. Yarborough and Robert M. Yarborough, "International Institutions and the New Economics of Organizations," *International Organization* 44 (Spring 1990), 235–259.

15

need to create material entities or organizations (that is, governments) to administer the rules of the game that arise to handle the function of governance. In some general sense, in fact, the burden of proof must always lie with those who argue that the achievement of governance requires the establishment of a government. This is so because the maintenance and operation of any government or public agency is costly, both in purely material terms (for example, the revenues required to run government agencies) and in terms of more intangible values (for example, the restrictions on individual liberties imposed by governments).

Approached in this way, the initially counterintuitive idea of governance without government is easy enough to grasp. It refers to the role that social institutions or governance systems, in contrast to organizations or material entities, play in solving the collective-action problems that pervade social relations under conditions of interdependence.[13] The general proposition that groups of interdependent actors can and sometimes do succeed in providing themselves with governance in the absence of government or, in any case, with no more than rudimentary organizations is now well established.[14] The literature on common property regimes, which has expanded rapidly over the last decade as a counter to the intuitively appealing notion of the tragedy of the commons, has proved this point.[15] Today, sophisticated analysts are trying to determine the conditions under which governance without government can succeed rather than prolonging unproductive debates about the need to establish centralized public agencies to solve collective-action problems arising from interactions among interdependent actors.[16]

The establishment of this general proposition raises a host of new questions of interest to students of politics in general and to students of international relations more particularly. Although governance

[13] For an extended discussion of the differences between institutions and organizations see Oran R. Young, *International Cooperation: Building Regimes for Natural Resources and the Environment* (Ithaca: Cornell University Press, 1989), chap. 2.

[14] This is the principal finding of the new literature on common property resources. For a survey of this literature consult David Feeny, Fikret Berkes, Bonnie J. McCay, and James M. Acheson, "The Tragedy of the Commons: Twenty-Two Years Later," *Human Ecology* 18 (1990), 1–19.

[15] See Bonnie M. McCay and James M. Acheson, eds., *The Question of the Commons: The Culture and Ecology of Communal Resources* (Tucson: University of Arizona Press, 1987); and Fikret Berkes, ed., *Common Property Resources: Ecology and Community-Based Sustainable Development* (London: Belhaven Press, 1989).

[16] Ostrom, *Governing the Commons;* and Kenneth A. Oye, ed., *Cooperation under Anarchy* (Princeton: Princeton University Press, 1986).

systems unencumbered with public agencies sometimes circumvent or solve specific collective-action problems (for example, the tragedy of the commons), is there nonetheless a price to be paid for relying on these governance systems when we come to values such as maximizing social welfare or ensuring robustness in the sense of a capacity to adapt to changing social or material circumstances?[17] Having articulated a clear distinction between governance systems in the sense of social institutions and governments in the sense of material entities or organizations, can we now begin to explore interactions and linkages between the two? Are there roles for organizations, for example, in establishing governance systems in a variety of issue areas?[18] Can organizations that are issue-specific and more modest in scope than what we think of as governments play constructive roles in the administration or operation of governance systems? Do governance systems go through recognizable life cycles that tend to rely increasingly on organizations with the passage of time? Is it normal for the resultant organizations to build linkages among issue areas so that they eventually come to resemble our conventional idea of government? Are the prospects for governance without government tied to particular characteristics of the broader social setting so that arrangements that are successful in some settings (for example, small-scale, traditional societies) are not likely to prove viable in others (for example, international society)?

Given these observations, it will come as no surprise that governance systems in international society, as in other social settings, can and do vary substantially along several dimensions. They may, for example, differ from each other in their functional scope, their geographical domain, their membership composition, their degree of formalization, their stage of development, and the nature of their administrative apparatus (if any). It follows, as well, that there will be a multiplicity of governance systems or institutional arrangements aimed at solving collective-action problems in the large, multifaceted social setting that is contemporary international society. Despite (or perhaps because of) the absence of a central government in this social setting, individual governance systems will impinge on each other

[17] For a review of the recent literature on common property resources that discusses this question consult Barry C. Field, "The Economics of Common Property," *Natural Resources Journal* 30 (1990), 239–252.

[18] For a discussion of such roles see Oran R. Young, "International Organizations Perspective," chap. 14 in Gunnar Sjosted, ed., *International Environmental Negotiations* (Newburg Park, Ca.: Sage Publications, 1993).

with some regularity. They may do so by nesting specific governance systems or regimes (for instance, the various regional seas arrangements) within broader or more comprehensive social institutions (for instance, the overarching law of the sea).[19] Or it may simply mean that linkages among the problem sets addressed by various governance systems create interdependencies (with the attendant prospects of conflict or cooperation) among the activities associated with the governance systems themselves.

Lest we jump from these observations to the comforting conclusion that governance without government offers a simple or easy way out of the environmental (and other) problems that now threaten to engulf us at the international level, some critical caveats are in order. Governance systems are not easy to establish; those engaged in interactive relationships commonly fail to solve collective-action problems, even when the mutual losses to be avoided or the joint gains to be reaped from doing so are substantial. Nor is there any guarantee that governance systems once established will perform as intended or achieve the measure of robustness required to sustain them.

When we turn to the complex environmental problems that confront us now (for instance, climate change or the loss of biological diversity), moreover, the barriers to the achievement of effective governance are far more severe than they appear to be in the simple scenarios commonly used to illustrate the basic logic of collective action.[20] It is often difficult to frame the problems to be solved appropriately, much less to design and operate governance systems that are both acceptable to all the major actors involved and likely to prove effective in practice. Negotiations aimed at establishing international governance systems can easily become stalemated over distributive issues, and the logic of two-level games makes it clear that those endeavoring to work out the provisions of governance systems will often face problems in selling the arrangements they come up with to influential constituencies back home.[21] In some cases, states and other actors lack the capacity to implement the provisions of governance

[19] On the Mediterranean as a regional sea consult Peter M. Haas, *Saving the Mediterranean: The Politics of International Environmental Cooperation* (New York: Columbia University Press, 1990). For a discussion of similar relationships involving trade see Jagdish Bhagwati, *The World Trading System at Risk* (Princeton: Princeton University Press, 1991).

[20] The seminal modern work is Mancur Olson, Jr., *The Logic of Collective Action* (Cambridge, Mass.: Harvard University Press, 1965).

[21] Robert D. Putnam, "Diplomacy and Domestic Politics: The Logic of Two-Level Games," *International Organization* 42 (Summer 1988), 427–460.

systems they have agreed to in international negotiations, while in other cases public agencies responsible for implementing these provisions at the domestic level experience powerful incentives to cut corners on fulfilling requirements they have accepted in principle. Hence there is a need for systematic analyses of experience with governance systems at the international level to identify determinants of success or failure in efforts to establish international institutions and, above all, to pinpoint the factors that explain why some governance systems prove more effective than others in solving the problems that motivate their creation.[22]

ENVIRONMENTAL PROBLEM SETS

To pursue this research agenda with specific reference to international environmental matters it is helpful to begin by classifying environmental problem sets or, in other words, clusters of interactive situations in which groups of interdependent actors are likely to suffer mutual losses or fail to reap joint gains in the absence of effective governance systems. There are many ways to classify environmental issues that transcend the boundaries of national jurisdictions. Such issues may deal with physical systems (for example, the atmosphere or the hydrosphere), with biological systems (for example, the living resources of the oceans), or with coupled land, ocean, and atmosphere systems (for example, the climate system). They may involve concerns that are geographically restricted (for example, the Mediterranean Basin) or global in scope (for example, the depletion of stratospheric ozone). They may affect only a limited number of actors (for example, the range states involved in efforts to protect migratory birds), or they may evoke concern throughout international society (for example, the universal concern for the protection of great whales). In addressing questions of governance, however, there is much to be said for grouping international environmental problem sets into four broad clusters: commons, shared natural resources, transboundary externalities, and linked issues.

---

[22] On the study of institutional effectiveness see Oran R. Young, "The Effectiveness of International Institutions: Hard Cases and Critical Variables," in Rosenau and Czempiel, eds., *Governance without Government;* and especially Marc Levy, Gail Osherenko, and Oran R. Young, "The Effectiveness of International Regimes: A Design for Large-Scale Collaborative Research," unpublished paper dated 4 December 1991.

International Commons

Commons are physical or biological systems that lie wholly or large-ly outside the jurisdiction of any of the individual members of a society but that are valued resources for many segments of society. International commons of current interest include Antarctica, the high seas, deep seabed minerals, the electromagnetic spectrum, the geostationary orbit, the stratospheric ozone layer, the global climate system, and outer space.[23] As these examples suggest, commons may be geographically limited, as in the cases of Antarctica and deep sea-bed minerals, global in scope, as in the case of the climate system, or even more comprehensive, as in the case of outer space. The category of international commons of interest from a policy perspective ex-pands over time as a result of the introduction of new technologies allowing humans to gain access to previously inaccessible areas or to engage in previously infeasible activities; it may also shrink as a conse-quence of efforts to extend the jurisdictional reach of the individual members of international society. The electromagnetic spectrum and the geostationary orbit, for instance, have come into focus as signifi-cant commons during this century with the advent and diffusion of modern communications systems.[24] Marine areas adjacent to the coastlines of states, in contrast, have lost many of the attributes of commons as a result of the extension of coastal state jurisdiction to offshore areas and, more particularly, the establishment of exclusive economic zones in broad coastal bands.

Three broad options are available to those concerned with the gov-ernance of international commons: world government, national juris-diction, and restricted common property.[25] Those who, like Garrett Hardin, are preoccupied with the tragedy of the commons often pre-scribe mutual coercion mutually agreed upon as the best means of avoiding or coming to terms with the dangers they associate with

[23] For an introductory account see Marvin S. Soroos, "The International Commons: A Historical Perspective," *Environmental Review* 12 (Spring 1988), 1–23.

[24] Donna A. Demac, ed., *Tracing New Orbits: Cooperation and Competition in Global Satellite Development* (New York: Columbia University Press, 1986).

[25] For broad discussions concerning the governance of commons see Peter S. Thacher, "Alternative Legal and Institutional Approaches to Global Change," *Colorado Journal of International Environmental Law and Policy* 1 (Summer 1990), 101–126; Thacher, "Global Security and Risk Management" (Geneva: World Federation of United Nations Associations, n.d.), and Nazli Choucri, ed., *Global Commons: Environ-mental Challenges and International Responses* (Cambridge, Mass.: MIT Press, 1993).

human uses of the commons.[26] At the international level, this coercion would entail the establishment of a world government with the authority to make and the power to enforce rules relating to the use of commons areas. The idea of extending national jurisdiction—opting for a strategy of enclosure—by contrast, flows from the premise that the tragedy of the commons is a consequence of inappropriate assignments of property rights, a problem that can be avoided by engineering a shift from common property to some alternative under which property rights (or at least grants of management authority) are accorded to individual members of the group.[27] In international society, this would require extending the jurisdiction or management authority of individual states to areas that are now treated as commons. For its part, restricted common property is a form of response that features the retention of common property arrangements coupled with the introduction of systems of rules to guide the behavior of the individual members of the ownership group. The practical application of this option at the international level centers on the formation of resource regimes, an approach that has elicited growing interest among those who see fundamental drawbacks in the other options, at least as applied to international society.[28]

Shared Natural Resources

Shared natural resources are physical or biological systems that extend into or across the jurisdictions of two or more members of international society. They may involve nonrenewable resources (for example, pools of oil that underlie areas subject to the jurisdiction of adjacent or opposite states), renewable resources (for example, straddling stocks of fish or migratory stocks of wild animals), or complex ecosystems that transcend the boundaries of national jurisdictions (for example, regional seas or river basins). While it is natural to focus on shared resources of interest to adjacent or neighboring states, such

[26] For a collection that includes Hardin's original essay, "The Tragedy of the Commons," together with a selection of other essays written from the same point of view see Garrett Hardin and John Baden, eds., *Managing the Commons* (San Francisco: W. H. Freeman, 1977).

[27] Systems of this sort loom large in the new literature on common property resources. For a case study dealing with marine resources see Oran R. Young, "Fishing by Permit: Restricted Common Property in Practice," *Ocean Development and International Law* 13 (1983), 121–170.

[28] Young, *International Cooperation*.

resources may also link states that are far removed from each other geographically, as in the case of migratory birds that traverse long distances and pass through numerous jurisdictions in the course of their annual cycles. Similarly, shared natural resources may impinge on the commons as well as on the jurisdictional zones of two or more states, depending upon the attributes of the resources themselves and the prevailing jurisdictional boundaries. Many marine mammals, for example, move through waters under the jurisdiction of several coastal states as well as waters that are part of the high seas, despite the creation of exclusive economic zones. As this observation makes clear, moreover, the groupings of actors concerned with shared natural resources may expand or contract as jurisdictional boundaries in international society shift. Changes in national jurisdictions, for example, have caused some fish stocks to drop out of the category of shared natural resources and others to move into the category of straddling stocks.

The obvious solution to problems of shared resources is to establish joint management regimes. Just as unitization has become a well-known and richly nuanced practice used in domestic societies for the management of oil pools and other nonrenewable resources extending across property lines, the idea of setting up joint development zones for analogous situations is gaining currency at the international level.[29] Similarly, there is considerable experience with management regimes for renewable resources extending across jurisdictional boundaries (for example, the migratory bird arrangements) and flow resources shared by two or more states (for example, the Great Lakes water quality regime in North America or the Rhine River regime in Europe).[30] But these experiences do not mean that the management of shared resources is a simple matter. As the case of river basins makes clear, sharp conflicts of interest have occurred among the relevant states which make it difficult to devise any regime that can solve the underlying problem, much less be equitable to all parties concerned.[31] When recent shifts in jurisdictional arrangements have giv-

---

[29] On the application of the idea of joint development zones at the international level see Elliot L. Richardson, "Jan Mayen in Perspective," *American Journal of International Law* 82 (July 1988), 443–458.

[30] For an extended account of arrangements involving wildlife see Simon Lyster, *International Wildlife Law* (Cambridge, Eng.: Grotius Publishers, 1985).

[31] Genady N. Golubev, "Availability and Quality of Fresh-Water Resources: Perspective from the North," in Oran R. Young, George J. Demko, and Kilaparti Ramakrishna, eds., *Global Environmental Change and International Governance* (forthcoming).

en rise to shared resources, legitimate questions have arisen also concerning the extent to which other states can deploy the principle of the common heritage of mankind as a basis for claiming some right to share in any proceeds accruing from the exploitation of these resources.

Transboundary Externalities

Transboundary externalities arise when activities that occur wholly within the jurisdiction of individual states produce results that affect the welfare of those residing in other jurisdictions. Sometimes the externalities center on intangible effects arising from moral interdependencies. The destruction of world heritage sites, such as the temples of Angkor Wat or the city of Dubrovnik, detracts from the welfare of people everywhere, even if they derive only vicarious benefits from the existence of the sites.[32] Similarly, people everywhere now express genuine concern about the consequences of tragic environmental accidents (for example, Chernobyl or Bhopal), apart from any natural transboundary consequences they may have. In other cases, the externalities in question involve material interdependencies and tangibly affect the welfare of those located elsewhere. A striking case that has become a matter of widespread concern involves the stakes of the rest of the world (measured in values such as the potential for the development of new drugs) in the loss of biological diversity caused by the destruction of moist tropical forests in Brazil and a small number of other countries. As economists are fond of pointing out, externalities may have positive as well as negative effects on the welfare of others; careful observers will no doubt be able to point to cases of positive externalities occurring at the level of international society. When it comes to problems of international environmental governance, however, it is apparent that the focus of attention is increasingly on the dangers of negative externalities.

Dealing with transboundary externalities in international society raises two issues of fundamental importance to those concerned with governance systems. Do the members of international society acting as a group have the authority to intervene in the domestic affairs of

---

[32] These resources possess what economists have come to regard as amenity value in contrast to commodity value. See John V. Krutilla and Anthony C. Fisher, *The Economics of Natural Environments: Studies in the Valuation of Amenity and Commodity Resources* (Baltimore: Johns Hopkins University Press, 1975).

individual states, regardless of the wishes of the governments of such states, when events occurring within their jurisdictions pose severe threats to the well-being of others or to international society as a whole?[33] Although we are often willing to accept such interventions when the activities in question threaten international peace and security, doing so in the case of environmental threats raises profound concerns in the minds of those committed to traditional conceptions of sovereignty at the international level.[34] Nevertheless, the threats to human welfare now arising in conjunction with environmental issues—from the geographically focused impact of the Bhopal disaster to the prospect of worldwide changes in climate—are raising serious concerns about sovereignty that will become more insistent with the passage of time.[35]

There are as well important questions regarding liability on the part of states for the negative effects on others of activities taking place within their jurisdictions. Basing their thinking on general propositions (for instance, the polluter pays principle), some will undoubtedly argue that there is a need for the development of a more effective code of environmental liability rules in international society. But this approach cannot solve all the problems. As many of those now struggling to come to terms with the environmental problems of the developing countries and the former socialist countries are discovering, the most effective way to enhance environmental protection for one's own population or ecosystems may be to join forces with polluters to assist them, both financially and technologically, to alter their polluting practices.

Linked Issues

Issues relevant to environmental governance arise when efforts to devise social institutions to deal with environmental concerns have

[33] See Kenneth W. Piddington, "Sovereignty and the Environment: Part of the Solution or Part of the Problem?" *Environment* 31 (September 1989), 18–20, 35–39. On this and related questions now being raised under the rubric of environmental security see Richard Ullman, "Redefining Security," *International Security* 8 (Summer 1983), 129–153; and Jessica Tuchman Mathews, "Redefining Security," *Foreign Affairs* 68 (1989), 162–167.

[34] See Francisco R. Sagasti and Michael E. Colby, "Eco-development Perspectives in Developing Countries," in Choucri, ed., *Global Commons*, 175–203.

[35] Ronnie D. Lipschutz and Ken Conca, eds., *Environmental Dramas on a Hundred Thousand Stages: Society, Politics, and Global Ecological Interdependence* (New York: Columbia University Press, 1993).

unintended consequences affecting other regimes and vice versa. Perhaps the most striking and potentially controversial issues of this type coming into focus today involve links between efforts to protect the environment and to promote economic development within countries along with links between efforts to promote trade among countries and initiatives aimed at protecting or enhancing environmental quality.[36]

Does the protection of the stratospheric ozone layer or the global climate system require developing countries to forgo the use of products or resources (for instance, fossil fuels) that have played key roles in the development of the advanced, industrial societies? Does the maintenance of biological diversity compel states such as Brazil, Indonesia, and Malaysia to eschew strategies that may seem attractive to advocates of rapid economic growth? Similarly, does participation in a free trade regime (for example, the arrangement set forth in the North American Free Trade Agreement) also require member states to take steps to homogenize their environmental standards? Or are individual members at liberty to attract industries to locate within their borders with promises of less stringent environmental rules as well as cheaper labor? Are states free to impose restrictions on imports from other countries whose production involves practices they consider unacceptable on environmental grounds (for example, catching tuna in nets that also kill dolphins)? Or are such actions restraints on trade deemed impermissible under the terms of the governance system articulated in the General Agreement on Tariffs and Trade (GATT)?[37]

In decentralized political systems, in which governance without government is the rule rather than the exception, difficulties involving linkages of this sort are unavoidable. The higher the level of interdependence in the system, the more troublesome such issues are likely to become. No doubt, this fact constitutes an important part of the rationale articulated in many social settings for the establishment of governments, over and above the creation of governance systems. But even in this connection, caveats are in order. As innumerable

[36] For some striking illustrations see Andrew Hurrell, "Brazil and the International Politics of Amazonian Deforestation," in Andrew Hurrell and Benedict Kingsbury, eds., *The International Politics of the Environment: Actors, Interests and Institutions* (Oxford: Oxford University Press, 1992), 398–429.

[37] For a thoughtful discussion of the GATT and efforts to protect the environment see Steve Charnovitz, "GATT and the Environment: Examining the Issues," *International Environmental Affairs* 4 (Summer 1992), 203–233.

painful experiences with intergovernmental relations and interagency coordination within governments attest, the creation of a government offers no assurance that these linkage problems will be resolved efficiently, much less equitably. Nor can we simply assume that such problems will prove unyielding when governance systems are not accompanied by the formal organizations of government. Current efforts to come to terms with the linkages between environment and trade are particularly intriguing in this regard. Although this problem set has recently become a focus of considerable controversy between environmentalists and advocates of free trade, it would be premature to conclude that acceptable accommodations cannot be negotiated without establishing some form of government to handle the issues at stake.[38]

ANALYZING INTERNATIONAL GOVERNANCE SYSTEMS

What do we want to know about past, present, and future governance systems in international society? What are the prospects for applying our general knowledge of governance to environmental problems to help practitioners responsible for establishing such systems or operating them on a day-to-day basis? In addressing these questions, it will help to begin by standardizing the usage of several key terms employed throughout this book. Thus an institution is a set of rules or conventions (both formal and informal) that define a social practice, assign roles to individual participants in the practice, and guide interactions among the occupants of these roles.[39] A governance system is an institution that specializes in making collective choices on matters of common concern to the members of a distinct social group. Although the distinction is not a sharp one, a regime is a governance system intended to deal with a more limited set of issues or a single issue area.[40] Organizations, by contrast, are material entities possessing budgets, personnel, offices, equipment, and legal personality. Governments are organizations established to make and implement collective choices in specific social settings.

[38] Hilary F. French, "Costly Tradeoffs: Reconciling Trade and the Environment," *Worldwatch Paper 113* (Washington, D.C.: Worldwatch Institute, 1993).

[39] A social practice, then, is a complex of activities taking place within the framework of a social institution. In this sense, we can speak of the exchange behavior occurring within markets or the interactions occurring within families as social practices. Unlike institutions per se, social practices have a behavioral component that is subject to direct observation.

[40] It follows that all regimes are governance systems and all governance systems are social institutions but not vice versa.

Building on these distinctions, we can identify the principal concerns of students of international governance. Though it is often difficult, in reality, to separate out aspects or elements of such multidimensional phenomena, it is helpful for purposes of analysis to divide the research agenda into issues involving regime formation, the administration of governance systems, the effectiveness of institutional arrangements, and institutional stability and change.

Regime Formation

The provisions of international governance systems are ordinarily articulated explicitly in constitutional contracts that may, but need not, be codified in legally binding instruments such as conventions or treaties.[41] Efforts to (re)form governance systems involve processes of institutional bargaining in which the participants seek to reach agreement on the terms of these constitutional contracts.[42] Unlike legislative bargaining, which focuses on building winning coalitions to meet the requirements of a majoritarian rule, institutional bargaining in international society normally operates under a consensus rule that gives the participants an incentive to put together packages of provisions that will prove attractive to as many interests as possible. The resultant bargaining is saved from certain failure or the conclusion of toothless agreements by the absence of perfect information and the expectation that governance systems will remain in place over indefinite periods of time. These features of institutional bargaining introduce an element of "good" uncertainty in the sense that they give the participants incentives to engage in integrative rather than distributive bargaining and to deal with the resultant veil of uncertainty by settling on provisions that seem equitable to all.[43]

[41] For an interesting account stressing circumstances under which parties may not want to articulate the rules of the game in a legally binding form see Charles Lipson, "Why Are Some International Agreements Informal?" *International Organization* 45 (Autumn 1991), 495–538.

[42] On the concept of a constitutional contract see James M. Buchanan, *The Limits of Liberty: Between Anarchy and Leviathan* (Chicago: University of Chicago Press, 1975), esp. chap. 4. The idea of institutional bargaining, as applied to international affairs, is developed in Oran R. Young, "The Politics of International Regime Formation: Managing Natural Resources and the Environment," *International Organization* 43 (Summer 1989), 349–375.

[43] For a seminal account of integrative, in contrast to distributive, bargaining see Richard Walton and Robert B. McKersie, *A Behavioral Theory of Labor Negotiations* (New York: McGraw-Hill, 1965), chaps. 2–5. The idea of a "veil of uncertainty" is discussed in Geoffrey Brennan and James M. Buchanan, *The Reason of Rules: Constitutional Political Economy* (Cambridge, Eng.: Cambridge University Press, 1985), chap. 2.

Why do those engaged in institutional bargaining succeed in establishing governance systems to cope with some environmental problems but fail to do so in connection with other, seemingly similar, problems? Questions of this sort have given rise to a substantial body of theoretical ideas concerning the formation of international governance systems.[44] For the most part, these ideas accentuate single factors such as material conditions (for example, hegemonic stability theory), patterns of interests (for example, many game-theoretic analyses), or ideas (for example, arguments involving epistemic communities). But recent work suggests that single-factor accounts are severely limited in explaining the formation of international governance systems. The challenge before us, then, is to devise a multivariate model of the (re)formation of international institutions.[45] At a minimum, such a model should make it possible to understand substitution effects in the sense of alternative paths to the creation of governance systems and interaction effects in the sense of multiple forces at work in the development of individual governance systems.

Administering Governance Systems

The preceding discussion draws a clear-cut distinction between institutions treated as the rules of the game that define the character of social practices and organizations understood as material entities possessing offices, personnel, equipment, budgets, legal personality, and so forth. But it does not license the conclusion that we should turn the traditional study of international governance on its head by devoting all our attention to institutions and ignoring international organizations altogether. There is a sense, on this account, in which governance systems take priority over organizations. Because it is possible for governance systems to arise and operate in the absence of organizations, students of international organizations need to demonstrate the importance of organizations in achieving international governance. When organizations are needed, moreover, it is important to tailor them to the requirements of governance systems, rather than changing institutions to achieve compatibility with preexisting or pre-

[44] For surveys of the major ideas see Stephan Haggard and Beth A. Simmons, "Theories of International Regimes," *International Organization* 41 (Summer 1987), 491–517; and Oran R. Young and Gail Osherenko, eds., *Polar Politics: Creating International Environmental Regimes* (Ithaca: Cornell University Press, 1993), chap. 1.

[45] Ibid., chap. 7.

conceived organizations. Even so, one of the principal virtues of drawing a distinction between institutions and organizations is that it opens up a major research agenda concerning interactions between the two. Thus organizations not only play roles of some importance in the establishment of many governance systems in international society but they also assume important roles in the day-to-day management or administration of many governance systems.[46]

Some students of international affairs are so concerned with the decentralized character of international society and mesmerized by an idealized conception of the role of markets in exchange systems that they believe there is no need to set up organizations to manage international governance systems. This argument, however, is no more persuasive at the international than at the domestic level. The fact that there is no central government in international society should not blind us to the roles of a wide variety of international organizations in the administration of issue-specific governance systems. Nor should we allow ourselves to be deceived about the conditions necessary for the operation of markets. Even perfectly competitive markets require the services of public authorities to enforce property rights and contracts and to adjudicate the conflicting claims of those who disagree over the content of property rights or the terms of contracts in specific situations.[47] And when market failures occur in actual exchange systems, there are often good reasons to turn to government in the search for solutions. In examining any environmental governance system, then, it makes sense to ask whether there is a need for some organization to administer it and, if so, what administrative tasks are involved (for example, monitoring and information gathering, collective decision making, raising revenue, and operating mechanisms for compliance).

The Effectiveness of Governance Systems

Why are some international governance systems more successful than others at solving the problems that motivate their establishment? More modestly, why are some systems better than others at inducing their members (and other relevant actors) to act in conformity with

---

[46] Young, "International Organizations Perspective."

[47] For a selection of readings on the links between economics and law with particular reference to contracts see Victor P. Goldberg, ed., *Readings in the Economics of Contract Law* (Cambridge, Eng.: Cambridge University Press, 1989).

the rules of the game? To ask these questions is to launch an inquiry into the effectiveness of institutional arrangements in international society.[48] An effective governance system is one that channels behavior in such a way as to eliminate or substantially to ameliorate the problem that led to its creation. A governance system that has little behavioral impact, by contrast, is ineffective. Hence the concept of effectiveness as applied to international governance systems defines a continuous variable. Governance systems can range along a continuum from ineffectual arrangements, which have few behavioral consequences, to highly effective arrangements, which produce quick and clear-cut solutions to the problems at stake. The distinction between effectiveness and the performance of governance systems measured by a variety of normative criteria is also important. A governance system may affect behavior dramatically, for example, without achieving great success in efficiency, equity, or sustainability.

Although students of domestic politics generally take it for granted that institutions matter and set about analyzing the nature of their impact, there is a strong current of thought among students of international affairs that dismisses institutions as epiphenomena. On this realist account, governance systems are surface phenomena that reflect the underlying configuration of power in international society. Such arrangements come and go with shifts in the political fortunes of powerful actors and without affecting outcomes much in their own right.[49] Yet others see institutions, along with material conditions and ideas, as one of the major clusters of factors that determine the course of international affairs. And it is surely inappropriate to dismiss international governance systems as ineffectual just because they are not linked together to form some sort of world government. The analytic challenge in this realm is to devise procedures that allow us to focus on the behavioral effects of international institutions, while holding other factors constant or controlling for their effects. Though this challenge is a tough one, research is now under way that should begin to illuminate this issue in the near future.[50]

[48] For the reflections of a prominent practitioner on these questions see Peter H. Sand, *Lessons Learned in Global Environmental Governance* (Washington, D.C.: World Resources Institute, 1990).

[49] For a particularly well-known expression of this view see Susan Strange, "*Cave! hic dragones:* A Critique of Regime Analysis," in Stephen D. Krasner, ed., *International Regimes* (Ithaca: Cornell University Press, 1983), 337–354.

[50] For some initial results see Young, Demko, and Ramakrishna, eds., *Global Environmental Change*, and Peter M. Haas, Robert O. Keohane, and Marc A. Levy, eds., *Institutions for the Earth: Sources of Effective International Environmental Protection* (Cambridge, Mass.: MIT Press, 1993).

Institutional Stability and Change

Nothing is static in the world of governance systems. Existing arrangements evolve under pressure from a variety of sources. New institutions emerge, and old arrangements pass from the scene. This process suggests questions concerning the dynamics of international governance. Are some governance systems more robust than others? If so, what are the determinants of robustness? Do environmental governance systems vary in their ability to adapt to changing problems and shifting societal conditions? Do some governance systems exhibit a capacity to control the social environment in which they operate as a means of achieving robustness? Are there feedback loops that set up interactive relationships between governance systems and the social environments in which they operate? Does it make sense to think of such systems as passing through institutional life cycles in the sense that they initially gain in robustness, achieve a measure of stability, and eventually run into problems that lead to their decline and even demise?

As in the case of effectiveness, our current understanding of the dynamics of international governance systems is sharply limited.[51] We can, however, draw a distinction between endogenous factors and exogenous factors in thinking about institutional dynamics. A study of endogenous factors leads us to focus on governance systems themselves to determine whether they encompass powerful equilibrating mechanisms, as many proponents believe is the case with competitive markets, or harbor the seeds of their own destruction, as Marxists and other radical thinkers have always maintained is the case with capitalist institutions. This perspective also leads us to ask whether the breakdown of governance systems is likely to be gradual in nature or to involve sudden and sharp nonlinearities of the sort envisioned in chaos theory. Exogenous factors, by contrast, may range across changes in material conditions (for example, the introduction of new technologies or a reconfiguration of power in international society) to shifts in prevailing systems of thought (for example, the rise of the conservation movement in the twentieth century).[52] Of course, these endogenous and exogenous forces are not mutually exclusive. On the contrary, any serious study of stability and change in international

[51] For an initial cut at this set of issues see Keohane and Nye, *Power and Independence.*

[52] In this connection, see Robert W. Cox's account of the roles of material capabilities, institutions, and ideas in "Social Forces, States and World Orders: Beyond International Relations Theory," in Robert O. Keohane, ed., *Neorealism and Its Critics* (New York: Columbia University Press, 1986), 204–254.

environmental governance systems will need to focus on links and interaction effects among these forces to account for the variety of patterns that are empirically observable.

CONCLUSION

The study of governance and governance systems offers an innovative way of organizing our thinking about international affairs. By directing attention to governance in contrast to government and to institutions in contrast to organizations, it allows us to ask new questions and to move away from some conventional concerns arising from the contrast between international society and domestic societies and, more particularly, from the absence of anything resembling a central government in international society. Yet it is also worth emphasizing that the resultant reorientation does not require us to scrap the insights associated with the mainstream concerns of the fields of international law and organization. As I shall endeavor to show in the chapters to follow, in fact, one of the attractive features of the study of international governance is the potential it offers for redirecting and reintegrating the principal streams of analysis that make up the fields of international law, international organization, and international politics.

ILLUSTRATIVE
CASES

CHAPTER TWO

Negotiating a Global Climate Regime

Meeting in a suburb of Washington, D.C., for ten days during February 1991, delegates from 102 countries convened the first session of the United Nations Intergovernmental Negotiating Committee on Climate Change (INC).[1] In so doing, they launched a process of institutional bargaining designed to produce agreement on the terms of an international governance system to regulate human activities that threaten to precipitate major changes in the earth's climate system.[2] To the disappointment of some, the opening session of the INC focused largely on matters of organization and procedure, including the establishment of a working group on commitments or principles and another on institutional mechanisms. But subsequent sessions, held in Geneva, Nairobi, and New York, witnessed intensive negotiations on substantive issues.

By the winter of 1992, a sense of urgency surrounded these negotiations, partly because scientific projections were suggesting that an unchecked buildup of greenhouse gases in the earth's atmosphere could well have far-reaching consequences for human welfare but also in part because pressure was mounting to agree on the text of a convention in time for signature at the United Nations Conference on Environment and Development in Brazil during June 1992. Pro-

---

An earlier version of this chapter appeared as Oran R. Young, "Negotiating an International Climate Regime: Institutional Bargaining for Environmental Governance Systems," in Nazli Choucri, ed., *Global Commons: Environmental Challenges and International Responses* (Cambridge, Mass.: MIT Press, 1993), 431–452.

[1] Representatives of eighteen United Nations and other international bodies as well as seventy-seven nongovernmental organizations also participated in the session.

[2] Keith Schneider, "U.S. to Negotiate Steps in Warming," *New York Times*, 15 February 1991, A7.

pelled by these forces, the INC produced a framework Convention on Climate Change that was opened for signature at UNCED and signed by the heads of state of 153 nations. Reflecting the necessity for compromises on several key issues, this agreement lays out only the rudiments of a climate regime. Although the convention covers all the major greenhouse gases, articulates a commitment to stabilizing concentrations of greenhouse gases in the atmosphere at a level that will not endanger the global climate system, and establishes a procedure for reviewing performance and updating commitments, no agreement was reached on specific targets and timetables for reducing emissions of greenhouse gases in time for inclusion in the 1992 convention. Many observers are optimistic that this convention will emerge as an important milestone in an ongoing process of institutional bargaining leading over time to more substantial governance arrangements for the earth's climate system treated as an international commons. But it is clear that the 1992 convention is not an end in itself; institutional bargaining regarding climate issues will continue for some time to come.

How can we account for these developments, and what are the prospects that continuing negotiations will succeed in moving beyond this framework convention during the near future? A study of previous efforts to create international governance systems through processes of institutional bargaining reveals a mixed record. Some initiatives of this sort succeed; others fail outright or produce framework agreements that do not gather momentum to become effective institutional arrangements with the passage of time. Little by little, students of regime formation are piecing together an account of the principal determinants of success or failure in negotiations of this type.[3] Drawing on the results of prior research, this chapter endeavors to shed light on the case of climate change and to offer some advice to those seeking to maximize the prospects for taking additional steps in this issue area.

POWER, IDEAS, AND INTERESTS

Studies of regime formation to date have concentrated on the role of single factors in the search for explanations of success and failure

---

[3] Volker Rittberger, ed., *International Regimes in East-West Politics* (London: Pinter, 1990); and Oran R. Young and Gail Osherenko, eds., *Polar Politics: Creating International Environmental Regimes* (Ithaca: Cornell University Press, 1993).

in efforts to create governance systems at the international level. This approach leaves much to be desired as the basis for a comprehensive treatment of the creation of international governance systems. But it has yielded insights that can help us to understand the case of global climate change.[4] Three clusters of factors deserve explicit consideration in this context, those dealing with the exercise of power, the impact of ideas, and the interplay of interests.

The Exercise of Power

Empirical research has discredited the proposition derived from hegemonic stability theory that a dominant power (in the sense of a single actor possessing a preponderance of material resources) is necessary to the achievement of success in the process of regime formation. Some years ago, Charles Kindleberger demonstrated that dominant powers sometimes fail to exercise their power in the interest of forming institutional arrangements in international society.[5] More to the point, recent research has shown that regimes can and do form in situations in which no dominant power is present. In the case of climate change, this is just as well because no single participant in the process unfolding under the auspices of the INC qualifies as a dominant power.

Leading participants may also find it difficult to translate power in the material sense into bargaining leverage capable of directing processes of institutional bargaining. The history of regime formation is replete with failed efforts on the part of powerful actors to get their way in bargaining over the content of international regimes. Sometimes this leads to a breakdown of the process, as in the case of the deep seabed mining provisions of the 1982 Convention on the Law of the Sea, or an agreement to settle for a framework convention with little substantive content, as in the case of the 1985 Vienna Convention for the Protection of the Ozone Layer. In other cases, it leads to other participants succeeding in bringing pressure to bear on a powerful actor to accede to their desires, as in the case of the effort to persuade the United States to accept the compensation fund established under the 1990 London Amendments to the 1987 Montreal Protocol on Substances That Deplete the Ozone Layer. This, too, raises doubts about any simple application of the theory of hegemonic

[4] Young and Osherenko, eds., *Polar Politics*, chap. 7.
[5] Charles P. Kindleberger, *The World in Depression, 1929–1939* (Berkeley: University of California Press, 1973).

stability to predict outcomes in the ongoing effort to form a climate regime.

Nonetheless, power is important in institutional bargaining such as that taking place under the auspices of the INC. Given the nature of institutional bargaining, there is a strong case for the proposition that the development of a climate regime is likely to depend on the formation of a small number of bargaining groups or blocs. Such blocs can serve several important functions. They provide a mechanism for articulating the major issues at stake in institutional bargaining and ensuring that these issues are taken into account in any bargain struck. Their existence can reduce substantially the transaction costs that many analysts regard as a major barrier to success in bargaining involving sizable numbers of parties.[6] Because bargaining of this type operates under a consensus rule, interactions among blocs often play a central role in the development of governance systems that meet the basic needs of all major interest groups and are therefore widely accepted as equitable. This is particularly important in cases such as climate change in which some of the products of a regime's operations are likely to exhibit the attributes of public goods and implementation of the regime's provisions is likely to prove costly so that the negotiation of an effective cost-sharing or burden-sharing mechanism is essential.

Although the configuration of blocs in the climate change negotiations remains fluid, several key elements of the bloc politics of these negotiations are already clear.[7] The negotiations on climate change will not be a simple replay of the contest between the advanced industrialized countries and the developing countries that dominated negotiations over a New International Economic Order (NIEO) a decade and more ago. For starters, the industrialized countries have divided into a cautious group led by the United States and a more activist group led by a number of European countries (or the European Community [now Union] acting on behalf of these countries). The developing countries are separating into a group of newly industrialized countries, a group of less developed countries that are influential by virtue of their size (for example, Brazil, China, and India), and a residual group of less important countries.[8]

[6] Miles Kahler, "Multilateralism with Small and Large Numbers," *International Organization* 46 (Summer 1992), 681–708.

[7] Peter M. Morrisette and Andrew J. Plantinga, "The Global Warming Issue: Viewpoints of Different Countries," *Resources* 103 (Spring 1991), 2–6.

[8] Francisco R. Sagasti and Michael E. Colby, "Eco-Development Perspectives in Developing Countries," in Nazli Choucri, ed., *Global Commons: Environmental Challenges and International Responses* (Cambridge, Mass.: MIT Press, 1993), 175–203.

The role of the former socialist states, and the former Soviet Union in particular, in the climate change negotiations is not entirely clear. Yet it seems evident that there will be no socialist bloc in the continuing negotiations over the provisions of a constitutional contract for a climate regime. A newly emerging bloc that has achieved real success within the INC, on the other hand, is the Alliance of Small Island States. This bloc brings together about two dozen island states in the Pacific and Indian oceans and the Caribbean and Mediterranean seas as well as a few others (for example, Bangladesh) likely to be hardest hit by rising sea levels resulting from global warming. Because the concerns of its members are so palpable and because the group has attracted the help of sophisticated advisers from the nongovernmental organizations, the Alliance of Small Island States has proven effective in the climate negotiations, despite the material weakness of its members.

The climate change negotiations also differ profoundly from the negotiations associated with the NIEO because the industrialized countries would find it costly to walk away from the bargaining process, leaving the others to their own devices. There is no way to check global warming without the active participation of the developing countries, and especially large countries such as China, which is exploiting its extensive reserves of coal to fuel its efforts to industrialize, and Brazil, which is critical to the release of carbon resulting from the destruction of moist tropical forests. Nor is it easy for the advanced industrialized countries to persuade developing countries to forgo the benefits they themselves acquired through processes involving a heavy reliance on the use of fossil fuels, unless the industrialized countries are willing to make substantial concessions to the developing countries in return for an agreement on their part to follow some other course. Under the circumstances, efforts to come to terms with climate change at the international level are destined to constitute a major item on the international agenda throughout the 1990s.

The Impact of Ideas

Most observers believe that ideas matter in the sense that their impact on processes of regime formation is independent of the exercise of power or the interplay of interests. But there is no consensus regarding the mechanisms through which ideas exert influence on institutional bargaining. Some have emphasized the role of cognitive convergence encompassing not only ideas about the causes of important problems but also prescriptions concerning appropriate solutions. Richard Cooper's account of the battle between the contagionists and the miasmatists during the nineteenth century and the final victory of the former in effecting the creation of public health regimes at the international level is suggestive in this regard.[9] Others have stressed the role of epistemic communities or, in other words, transnational groups of scientists and public officials who share both causal beliefs and prescriptive preferences and who become influential actors in their own right.[10]

There is, as well, a useful distinction to be drawn between hegemony in the ideational or Gramscian sense and the impact of ideas at the more specific level of day-to-day negotiations. Gramscian hegemony refers to the dominance of an interlocking system of concepts, propositions, and values, in other words, an overarching worldview.[11] Although influence of this type is often associated with the actions of an actor that is dominant in the material sense, ideational hegemony may continue and even intensify as the power of the dominant actor declines.

Yet it is not necessary to focus on such macro-level phenomena, which are inherently difficult to pin down with precision, to observe the impact of ideas on the course of institutional bargaining in an issue area such as climate change. There are at least three distinct ways in which ideas appear to be important in shaping the course of institutional bargaining on this issue. First and arguably foremost, the global environmental change movement has played a role of great importance in highlighting the growing significance of anthropogenic change and providing an intellectual framework within which to think systematically about interactions between physical and biological systems on the one hand and human systems on the other.[12] This movement is still in its infancy; there is much that we do not understand about the systemic interactions in question. Yet the rise of thinking about global environmental change to a position of prominence in the

[9] Richard N. Cooper, "International Cooperation in Public Health as a Prologue to Macroeconomic Cooperation," in Cooper et al., *Can Nations Agree? Issues in International Economic Cooperation* (Washington, D.C.: Brookings Institution, 1989), 178–254.

[10] See the collection of essays on epistemic communities in Peter M. Haas, ed., *Knowledge, Power, and International Policy Coordination*, a special issue of *International Organization* 46 (Winter 1992).

[11] Robert W. Cox, "Gramsci, Hegemony, and International Relations: An Essay in Method," *Millennium: Journal of International Studies* 12 (Summer 1983), 162–175.

[12] Committee on Global Change, *Toward an Understanding of Global Change* (Washington, D.C.: National Academy Press, 1988).

scientific world buttresses the position of those who assert that large-scale environmental issues must be tackled seriously, despite profound uncertainties regarding the mechanisms at work in specific cases. This development also serves to legitimize the views of those who argue that large-scale environmental issues can be solved only through broadly based international cooperation, a perspective that argues forcefully against any effort on the part of advantaged countries to wall themselves off from environmental degradation elsewhere.[13]

More concretely, the force of ideas is apparent in two separate aspects of the work of the INC itself. To begin with, the Intergovernmental Panel on Climate Change (IPCC), organized and administered jointly by the United Nations Environment Programme (UNEP) and the World Meteorological Organization (WMO), played an influential role in setting the stage for negotiations under the auspices of the INC both by catalyzing the growth of scientific consensus regarding the reality of climate change as a phenomenon to be taken seriously and by casting the work of the INC as a process of reaching consensus on the provisions of a global climate regime.[14] The role of ideas has taken on added significance in connection with the work of the INC precisely because there is so much uncertainty both about the overall course of climate change and about the probable impacts of global warming on different parts of the world. The result is a battle between those who tend to resolve uncertainties optimistically in favor of lines of thought that minimize the significance of climate change and those who take the opposite tack, pessimistically projecting worst-case scenarios regarding the trajectory and impacts of climate change.[15] But these are ultimately clashes of ideas.

It seems clear, then, that the course of institutional bargaining over the content of a governance system for climate is being molded by ideas, just as it is being shaped by the efforts of negotiating blocs to translate power in the material sense into bargaining leverage in connection with the work of the INC. This does not ensure, as some of those who focus on the role of epistemic communities seem to suggest, that the course of institutional bargaining can be consciously manipu-

[13] Martin W. Holdgate, "The Environment of Tomorrow," *Environment* 33 (July–August 1991), 14–20, 40–42.
[14] Intergovernmental Panel on Climate Change, "Reports Prepared for IPCC by Working Groups I, II, and III," United Nations Environment Programme and World Meteorological Organization, 1990.
[15] Paul Stern, Oran R. Young, and Dan Drukman, eds., *Global Environmental Change: Understanding the Human Dimensions* (Washington, D.C.: National Academy Press, 1992).

lated. The evolution of ideas such as those that have given rise to the global change movement is a product of the efforts of many actors responding to a wide variety of stimuli.[16] As those who have tried can attest, it is exceedingly difficult to stem the tide of ideas that are flowing against a particular set of interests or to direct such a tide as a means of controlling the outcome of specific processes of institutional bargaining.

The Interplay of Interests

Interactive decision making among parties pursuing their own interests is never a simple or straightforward process. In virtually every case, this process involves an element of competition or conflict which ensures that participants will have incentives to act in such a way as to maximize payoffs to themselves and which gives rise to the complications of strategic interaction.[17] In the case of climate change, other factors add to these generic problems associated with the interplay of interests. Because it is critical to draw a wide array of countries into a climate regime, institutional bargaining in this case necessarily involves southern as well as northern concerns, which makes it imperative to come to terms with the linkages between environment and development in the negotiations taking place under the auspices of the INC. Though it may well be true that changes in life-style can be implemented without excessive aggregate costs to societies, they will inevitably prove costly to some vested interests within countries that wield considerable influence in domestic political processes.[18] And the uncertainties regarding the probable course of climate change—some responsible observers remain unconvinced that global warming is a serious problem at all—enable those who oppose adjustments to combat the greenhouse effect to line up respectable scientific opinion in support of their position.

Small wonder, then, that some commentators speak of "the policy gridlock on global warming."[19] But are efforts to develop an international climate regime really doomed to failure as a consequence of

[16] Peter A. Hall, ed., *The Political Power of Economic Ideas: Keynesianism across Nations* (Princeton: Princeton University Press, 1989).

[17] Norman Frohlich, Joe A. Oppenheimer, and Oran R. Young, *Political Leadership and Collective Goods* (Princeton: Princeton University Press, 1971), chap. 5.

[18] Allan Miller, "Economic Models and Policy on Global Warming," *Environment* 33 (July–August 1991), 3–5, 43–44.

[19] Eugene B. Skolnikoff, "The Policy Gridlock on Global Warming," *Foreign Policy* 79 (Summer 1990), 77–93.

these impediments to bargaining? Studies of the interplay of interests reveal factors that play a role in this context.[20]

First and probably foremost is the question of the degree to which the participants approach the negotiations as a process of integrative in contrast to distributive bargaining. The high degree of uncertainty associated with almost every aspect of climate change allows great scope for interpretation in this context. There is a wide gap between assessments of climate change that stress systemic concerns and treat global warming as a common problem on the one hand and calculations that feature the identification of prospective winners and losers and highlight the conflictual potential of this issue on the other.[21] It is worth emphasizing the extent to which most scientists and many policymakers have joined forces in an effort to focus attention on climate change as a common problem and to avoid becoming bogged down in battles regarding putative winners and losers. The work of the IPCC during 1989 and 1990 certainly helped to set this tone, and the negotiators operating within the INC have carried on, for the most part, in the same vein. This spirit of cooperation does not guarantee that progress will be made on a climate change regime without running afoul of distributive concerns triggered by a growing preoccupation with the identification of probable winners and losers in the wake of global warming. So far, however, in this case uncertainty has served to soften the problems associated with distributive bargaining.

Uncertainty may also play a constructive role in making it difficult for participants in institutional bargaining regarding climate change to make confident predictions about the distributive consequences of alternative institutional arrangements under consideration for inclusion in a climate regime. The resultant veil of uncertainty has the effect of increasing interest in the formation of arrangements that can be justified on the grounds that they are fair in procedural terms, whatever substantive outcomes they produce.[22] Coupled with the operation of the consensus rule characteristic of institutional bargaining, this has led some analysts to argue that "an effective international agreement to limit [greenhouse gas emissions] will not be undertaken unless the

[20] James K. Sebenius, "Negotiating a Regime to Control Global Warming," in Jessica Tuchman Mathews et al., *Greenhouse Warming* (Washington, D.C.: World Resources Institute, 1991), 69–98.
[21] Wallace K. Stevens, "In a Warming World, Who Comes Out Ahead?" *New York Times*, 5 February 1991, C1.
[22] Geoffrey Brennan and James M. Buchanan, *The Reason of Rules: Constitutional Political Economy* (Cambridge, Eng.: Cambridge University Press, 1985), 28–31.

agreement is seen by the participants as fair."[23] Of course, this observation may lead skeptics to conclude that the prospects for the development of a substantial climate regime in the near future are dim. Yet research on regime formation in international society suggests that it would be a mistake to underestimate the potential role of "good" uncertainty in facilitating the efforts of those operating under the auspices of the INC to come to terms on the provisions of a substantial international climate regime.[24]

Other factors associated with the interplay of interests suggest less optimistic conclusions, at least at this stage. It is difficult to identify salient solutions in the sense of focal points around which expectations are likely to converge in the climate change negotiations.[25] There is nothing sacred about any particular percentage cuts in greenhouse gas emissions (is there a salient difference, for example, among 10, 20, or 30 percent?), and common rules regarding what is fair with regard to cost sharing "diverge widely in their prescriptions for an agreement" when applied to the case of climate change.[26] Nor is the problem of compliance easy to solve in this realm. Although advances in technology are undoubtedly enhancing transparency by improving our capacity to monitor compliance with the rules of international regimes in a relatively unintrusive manner, it would be naive to ignore the problems that are likely to arise in achieving compliance with the emission control systems that every member of international society will have to adopt to put a stop to global warming.[27]

Another issue is shocks or crises that are exogenous to the process of institutional bargaining. It seems undeniable, for example, that the public announcement during 1985 of the Antarctic ozone hole played an important role in mobilizing public concern and moving the process of regime formation from the somewhat unimpressive results reflected in the 1985 Vienna Convention to the significant achievements

[23] Dallas Burtraw and Michael A. Toman, "Equity and International Agreements for CO_2 Containment," Discussion Paper ENR91-07 (Washington, D.C.: Resources for the Future, 1991), 1.

[24] Young and Osherenko, eds., *Polar Politics*.

[25] Thomas C. Schelling, *The Strategy of Conflict* (Cambridge, Mass.: Harvard University Press, 1960), chap. 4.

[26] Burtraw and Toman, "Equity and International Agreements," 27.

[27] Abram Chayes and Antonia H. Chayes, "Adjustment and Compliance Processes in International Regulatory Regimes," in Jessica Tuchman Mathews, ed., *Preserving the Global Environment: The Challenge of Shared Leadership* (New York: Norton, 1990), 280–308.

articulated in the 1987 Montreal Protocol.[28] With all due respect to the heat of the summer of 1988, no exogenous shock comparable to the ozone hole has yet surfaced in connection with the effort to develop a global climate regime. Still, given the sensitivity of humans to the weather and the suggestibility arising from the absence of knowledge about the mechanisms of climate change, it would be no cause for surprise if exogenous shocks came to play a significant role in shaping the course of institutional bargaining over climate change during the foreseeable future.

In concluding this discussion of the role of power, ideas, and interests, the importance of leadership on the part of individuals requires attention. Three types of leadership are central in this context: structural leadership, entrepreneurial leadership, and intellectual leadership.[29] Whereas the structural leader works to translate power in the material sense into bargaining leverage focused on the issue at hand, the entrepreneurial leader uses negotiating skills to cast issues in ways that facilitate integrative bargaining and to broker interests so as to build consensus around the choice of a preferred institutional arrangement. Intellectual leaders provide systems of thought that offer a coherent analytic framework within which to think about the formation of regimes to deal with international problems.

Although the evidence from earlier work on regime formation suggests that the role of leadership is crucial to success in institutional bargaining,[30] the role of leaders in the climate change negotiations is unclear at this stage. A credible case can be made for the proposition that we have begun to profit from intellectual leadership in this realm. Thus the nesting of climate change into the broader flow of ideas relating to global environmental change may well prove helpful not only in providing a basis for thinking systematically about this issue but also in influencing negotiators to approach global warming as a common problem rather than a matter to be looked at from a winners-and-losers perspective. The work of the leaders of the IPCC (for example, Bert Bohlin, who chairs the panel) in articulating the intellectual basis for a climate regime seems particularly important.

[28] Sharon L. Roan, *Ozone Crisis: The 15-Year Evolution of a Sudden Global Emergency* (New York: Wiley, 1989), chap. 8.

[29] Oran R. Young, "Political Leadership and Regime Formation: On the Development of Institutions in International Society," *International Organization* 45 (Summer 1991), 281–308.

[30] Young and Osherenko, eds., *Polar Politics*, chap. 7.

45

There is less to report regarding structural and entrepreneurial leadership. No effective structural leaders have yet surfaced in the negotiations taking place under the auspices of the INC, in part because of the failure of the United States to push for agreement on the provisions of a climate convention.[31] It is also in part the result of the inability or unwillingness of others to step forward to fill the vacuum left by the failure of the United States to assume a constructive role. No one has emerged in a publicly visible fashion to assume the entrepreneurial leadership role that Tommy Koh and others played in the law of the sea negotiations or that Mostafa Tolba played in the ozone negotiations. In this connection, the separation of the climate change negotiations from the work of the UNCED Preparatory Committee and from the ongoing efforts of the UNEP and the WMO may well be an obstacle to the emergence of entrepreneurial leaders. Still, this is not to say that capable individuals will not emerge and assume this role as the work of the INC continues.

NORMATIVE CONCERNS

In addition to assessing the prospects for success in institutional bargaining relating to the climate regime during the near future, we are naturally interested in the content that such a regime will acquire over time as the process of institutional evolution unfolds. Part of this interest involves such straightforward matters as the timetable for reducing or phasing out emissions of carbon dioxide and other greenhouse gases and the character of the cost-sharing or burden-sharing mechanisms devised to pay the costs of adjusting to increasingly stringent constraints on these emissions. But there are concerns of a broader, more normative character that a climate regime may address or that may become subjects of social learning in connection with the operation of such a regime.[32] This section explores these concerns by analyzing four intersecting topics: approaches to ecosystems and landscapes, considerations of North-South equity, perspectives on human-environment relations, and ideas of intergenerational equity. These

---

[31] Marlise Simons, "U.S. View Prevails at Climate Parley," *New York Times*, 8 November 1990, A9.

[32] Joseph S. Nye, Jr., "Nuclear Learning and U.S.-Soviet Security Regimes," *International Organization* 41 (Summer 1987), 371–402; and Ernst B. Haas, *When Knowledge Is Power: Three Models of Change in International Organizations* (Berkeley: University of California Press, 1990).

themes are addressed here in declining order of likelihood that they will be taken seriously in the evolution of the climate regime, though there are complexities in each case that make such sweeping judgments hazardous.

Approaches to Ecosystems and Landscapes

The advanced industrialized societies centered in the Northern Hemisphere owe much of their success to patterns of thought that encourage the disaggregation of problems into their component parts and reward efforts to tackle individual issues piecemeal. Such practices have provided the basis for the development and diffusion of technologies that constitute, in many ways, the defining characteristic of modernized systems. Yet the advent of global environmental problems such as ozone depletion, climate change, and the loss of biological diversity has produced growing doubts about the social consequences of these practices, which typically fail to take notice of many of the spillovers or externalities arising from the treatment of problems in a disaggregated fashion.

Today we all appreciate the importance of ecological perspectives, which stress interdependencies and linkages among large clusters of factors, in contrast to technological perspectives. The growing influence of the concept of landscapes adds a concern for processes of change in complex ecosystems and highlights path dependence in the trajectories along which such systems move. The complex, path-dependent systems of ecological thinking are not nearly as malleable as the simpler and more circumscribed systems that populate the world of technological thinking. Because it is unreasonable to expect that we can easily manipulate or control global environmental systems in pursuit of human goals, we must beware of uses of technology that precipitate profoundly disruptive anthropogenic changes in large physical and biological systems.[33]

Ecosystems perspectives have been apparent in agreements establishing international regimes for some time.[34] As early as 1971, the Ramsar Convention on Wetlands of International Importance Especially as Waterfowl Habitat reflected this trend in its concern for preserving habitat to protect wildlife. The 1980 Convention on the Con-

---

[33] Stern, Young, and Drukman, eds., *Global Environmental Change.*
[34] Simon Lyster, *International Wildlife Law* (Cambridge, Eng.: Grotius Publications, 1985).

servation of Antarctic Marine Living Resources is predicated squarely on an ecosystems approach.

Do these agreements mean that we can count on general acceptance of ecosystems thinking in the development of a climate regime and on the adoption of the procedures for environmental accounting needed to translate such thinking into practical measures? Not necessarily. Entrenched modes of thought die slowly, especially when they support the preferences of powerful interest groups. An ecosystems approach will not be welcomed by those (for example, actors who rely on the combustion of fossil fuels to generate electricity or to sustain highly dispersed human settlement patterns) who are likely to find themselves liable for a growing range of unintended or collateral damages as a consequence of the impact of new sensitivities (and new accounting procedures) regarding ecological interdependencies and linkages. What is more, states that remain highly sensitive about matters of sovereignty—including states in many of the developing countries of the Third World—are apt to balk at intrusions into their domestic affairs justified in the name of protecting ecosystems that are essential to the support of human life on earth but that do not conform neatly to the bounds of legal jurisdictions.[35]

Will these obstacles constitute an insuperable barrier to the development of a systems approach in an evolving international climate regime? The answer to this question is almost certainly negative. Systems thinking is an idea whose time has come in our efforts to comprehend global environmental change. Although resistance from some quarters will undoubtedly lead negotiators working on provisions of the emerging climate regime to be somewhat circumspect in the language they use, it is hard to imagine an international climate regime that does not reflect and reinforce systems thinking in dealing with environmental issues.

Considerations of North-South Equity

Efforts to make use of processes of regime (re)formation to deal with basic questions of equity arising from the disparate circumstances of the advanced industrialized countries of the North and the developing

---

[35] Andrew Hurrell, "Brazil and the International Politics of Amazonian Deforestation," in Andrew Hurrell and Benedict Kingsbury, eds., *The International Politics of the Environment: Actors, Interests, and Institutions* (Oxford: Oxford University Press, 1992), 398–429.

countries of the South have not met with great success. The United States (and several other important players in a more circumspect fashion) backed away from key provisions of the 1982 Law of the Sea Convention precisely because they became dissatisfied with provisions in Part XI on deep seabed mining that seemed likely to benefit members of the group of developing countries. The negotiations of the 1970s and early 1980s on various aspects of the NIEO failed because eventually in the bargaining process the advanced industrialized countries chose to walk away and accept no agreement rather than to make substantial concessions. The ozone regime contains modest concessions to the developing countries together with a compensation fund established under the terms of the 1990 London Amendments.[36] But the terms of this regime were worked out with little participation on the part of developing countries, and it remains to be seen whether countries such as China and India will embrace the arrangement in a wholehearted and sustained fashion.

This record is not encouraging. Yet institutional bargaining over climate change may well follow a different course, in part because of the way the problem has been framed. There is no escaping the fact that the increased loading of the earth's atmosphere with greenhouse gases, especially carbon dioxide, is largely attributable to the behavior of modernized societies (even the destruction of moist tropical forests owes much to the actions of investors and consumers located in the North). Nor is it credible to ask Third World leaders to forgo the benefits of industrialization in order to contribute to efforts to save large-scale physical and biological systems that are threatened as a result of the behavior of affluent citizens residing in the North. Thus there is little prospect of reaching substantive agreement at the international level on the issue of climate change unless all parties concerned take the linkage between environment and development seriously and seek to deal with both agendas in an integrated manner.

The South also has substantial bargaining leverage when it comes to the issue of climate change. China, for example, is already the world's third largest emitter of carbon dioxide and fourth largest emitter of all greenhouse gases combined.[37] Both China and India are poised on the brink of rapid growth in demand for refrigerants and an acceleration

[36] Richard Elliot Benedick, *Ozone Diplomacy: New Directions in Safeguarding the Planet* (Cambridge, Mass.: Harvard University Press, 1991).

[37] World Resources Institute, *World Resources, 1990–1991* (New York: Oxford University Press, 1990), chaps. 1 and 2.

of industrial production based on the combustion of fossil fuels. The fate of the world's moist tropical forests lies in the hands of developing countries such as Brazil, Indonesia, Malaysia, and Zaire. To be sure, climate change is likely to affect developing countries as much as— sometimes more than—developed countries so that the bargaining leverage of the South will rest on threats rather than warnings. Some northerners may doubt the credibility of these threats and advocate a bargaining strategy that offers few concessions to the developing countries.[38] But such a strategy is exceedingly risky. Many of those located in developing countries are increasingly angry and desperate. Moreover, it is easy for policymakers in these countries to take decisions based on domestic pressures to increase the production of goods and services with little concern for the impact of their actions on global environmental systems. Faced with this prospect, northerners will ignore the demands of the South regarding climate change at their peril.

The roots of this analysis lie in calculations of bargaining strength. But the result is the emergence of an influential body of opinion that takes the environment/development linkage seriously and accepts the proposition that any planetary bargain regarding climate change must be accepted by all the major parties as fair or equitable. In the short run, the likely result will be the emergence of a climate regime that makes explicit provisions for technology transfers, technical training, and additional financial assistance as means of encouraging the developing countries to participate and of assisting those willing to take part to make the economic changes needed to modernize in a way that produces lower levels of greenhouse gas emissions. In the longer term, these initiatives could set in motion a train of events leading to more constructive approaches to the overarching issues of North-South equity that constitute one of the central concerns in international society today.

Perspectives on Human-Environment Relations

Can the issue of climate change alter the way we think about human-environment relations and precipitate new perspectives on the niche that human beings occupy in the larger scheme of things? We are dealing here with deep-seated and, for the most part, unexamined

[38] As Schelling pointed out many years ago, there is a difference between a warning, which merely indicates an intended course of action, and a threat, which emphasizes a contingent action that one may be loath to take if the threat fails (Schelling, *Strategy of Conflict,*, chap. 2).

attitudes and patterns of thought which are notoriously difficult to change. Nonetheless, the problem of global warming and the international institutions that arise to come to terms with it could well become catalysts for change in this realm.

The key to this development lies in the growing realization that human behavior is a critical driving force behind an array of global environmental changes.[39] Nowhere is the role of anthropogenic change more apparent or more potentially disruptive than in the case of global warming. The traditional Western assumption that nature and natural resources are available to be exploited for human benefit now seems less and less acceptable as a basis for human-environment relations.[40] A result has been increasing interest in alternative perspectives, such as the idea of stewardship under which humans would assume a trust responsibility for the welfare of physical and biological systems[41] or the idea of biotic citizenship under which humans would accept a status of equality with other components of the biosphere rather than thinking of themselves as standing apart from and superior to other components.[42]

Over time, then, it seems probable that we are destined to experience far-reaching changes in the way in which we think about human-environment relations. But how will this process affect and be affected by the formation of an international climate regime during the near future? Emphasis in the terms of the institutional arrangements will almost certainly fall on specific, though by no means trivial, provisions designed to enhance the effectiveness of the regime. It is possible, for example, that efforts will be made to devise new accounting procedures capable of measuring the social as well as private costs and the unintended as well as intended consequences arising from greenhouse gas emissions.[43] It is also possible that a system of liability rules will emerge that make humans responsible for damages to physical and biological systems as well as for injuries inflicted on each other.[44] To the

[39] Stern, Young, and Drukman, eds., *Global Environmental Changes.*

[40] Lynn White, Jr., "The Historical Roots of Our Ecologic Crisis," *Science* 155 (10 March 1967), 1203–1207.

[41] Roderick Frazier Nash, *The Rights of Nature: A History of Environmental Ethics* (Madison: University of Wisconsin Press, 1989).

[42] Aldo Leopold, *A Sand County Almanac, with Essays on Conservation from Round River* (New York: Ballantine Books, 1966), 237–264.

[43] Robert Repetto, "Balance-Sheet Erosion—How to Account for the Loss of Natural Resources," *International Environmental Affairs* 1 (Spring 1989), 103–137.

[44] International Law Commission, *Report of the International Law Commission on the Work of Its Forty-Second Session* (New York: United Nations General Assembly, Forty-Fifth Session Official Records, Supplement No. 10 [A/45/10], 1990).

extent that such features are built into a climate regime, a process might ensue that would lead over time to the evolution of a new system of ethics applicable to human-environment relations.[45]

There is, finally, the prospect that the effort to deal with climate change will stimulate broader institutional changes motivated by a desire to alter our behavior in the area of human-environment relations. A particularly intriguing suggestion in this regard centers on the idea of reconstituting the United Nations Trusteeship Council as a body charged with overseeing the development and implementation of new ways of thinking about human-environment relations, including the problems of controlling anthropogenic impacts on large physical systems and of preserving both biological and cultural diversity. We should not forget that the development of the climate change regime is embedded in a larger flow of events that could well eventuate within the next generation in far-reaching changes in institutional arrangements governing our interactions with the natural environment.

Ideas of Intergenerational Equity

Much has been written in recent years about the importance of building international governance systems to guide human behavior in such a way that future generations do not suffer from environmental degradation caused by the actions of those living today.[46] This concern, first articulated publicly in *World Conservation Strategy*, a document published in 1980 under the auspices of the International Union for the Conservation of Nature and Natural Resources (IUCN), became a central theme of *Our Common Future*, the 1987 report of the World Commission on Environment and Development (widely known as the Brundtland Commission).[47] But what does intergenerational equity require in operational terms, particularly in connection with institutional bargaining over the development of an international climate regime?

It is not easy to determine how to proceed in specific cases, even if we

[45] Nash, *Rights of Nature.*

[46] Edith Brown Weiss, *In Fairness to Future Generations: International Law, Common Patrimony, and Intergenerational Equity* (New York: Transaction Publishers and United Nations University, 1989).

[47] International Union for the Conservation of Nature and Natural Resources, *World Conservation Strategy: Living Resource Conservation for Sustainable Development* (Gland: IUCN, 1980), and World Commission on Environment and Development, *Our Common Future* (New York: Oxford University Press, 1987).

are motivated to fulfill the requirements of intergenerational equity. There is, to begin with, a conceptual problem in specifying the tastes or preferences of members of future generations. These individuals will live in a different world and have preferences that are molded by different, possibly radically different, life experiences. There is also the question of devising a usable criterion or standard of intergenerational equity. As Jerome Rothenberg and others have pointed out, there are numerous ways to incorporate the legitimate claims of members of future generations into current decision making about large-scale environmental issues.[48] These procedures yield different prescriptions, some of which are based on fundamentally different modes of thinking about the problem.

There are, as well, political constraints on the process of incorporating the concerns of future generations into institutional bargaining of the sort unfolding under the auspices of the INC. We encounter here a classic situation in which benefits are likely to accrue to a widely dispersed and, by definition, unorganized group (that is, the members of future generations), whereas the costs of providing these benefits will fall on a specific group (that is, those living today). Nor is it clear who is authorized to speak for the concerns of future generations in these negotiations. Under the circumstances, this matter is likely to be approached as a distributive rather than an integrative issue in a negotiating environment in which most of the potential beneficiaries are poorly placed to defend or promote their own interests.

Can we devise a process of regime formation in a case such as climate change that would reduce the extent to which the deck is stacked against the interests of members of future generations? If we were able to simulate a Rawlsian veil of ignorance in these negotiations, the problem would largely disappear.[49] Because those operating under such a veil do not know which generation they belong to, they have a strong incentive to take the issue of intergenerational equity seriously. But as many commentators have noted, this proviso is highly unrealistic. Can the more realistic notion of negotiating under a veil of uncertainty serve just as well in these terms?[50] Though this notion does not yield the obvious solution to the problem of intergenerational equity

[48] Jerome Rothenberg, "Economic Perspectives on Time Comparisons: Alternative Approaches to Time Comparisons," in Nazli Choucri, ed., *Global Commons: Environmental Challenges and International Responses* (Cambridge, Mass.: MIT Press, 1993), 355–397; and Burtraw and Toman, "Equity and International Agreements."

[49] John Rawls, *A Theory of Justice* (Cambridge, Mass.: Harvard University Press, 1971).

[50] Brennan and Buchanan, *Reason of Rules.*

offered by the concept of a veil of ignorance, it may still prove helpful. Individuals operating under a veil of uncertainty are motivated to establish collective choice procedures that will seem fair, regardless of where they end up in the distribution of payoffs. To the extent that any constitutional contract governing climate change is expected to remain in force indefinitely, its collective choice procedures will apply to the members of future generations as well as to those concerned with the problem today. Hence it appears that the most practical way to safeguard the welfare of members of future generations in the process of creating an international climate regime is to take steps to thicken the veil of uncertainty surrounding the negotiations, rather than running the risk of becoming bogged down in debates of a more substantive nature about criteria or standards of intergenerational equity.

CONCLUSION

The preceding analysis does not license any unqualified predictions regarding the prospects for institutional evolution in the climate regime. To date, the INC process has had in its favor the growing influence of the global environmental change movement, an apparent willingness to resist focusing on winners and losers, and an emerging awareness of the importance of the linkages between environment and development. Yet we cannot reject out of hand the argument of those who expect policy gridlock to slow the process of regime formation in this area. The negotiating strategies of the blocs that will carry much of the weight in the continuing process of institutional bargaining in this issue area are still evolving. It is difficult to identify salient solutions for some of the key issues. Vested interests fearing the consequences of an effective international climate regime remain strong. It is far from clear whether either structural or entrepreneurial leaders will succeed in pushing the process of regime formation beyond the framework convention signed at UNCED in June 1992.

The negotiation of the 1992 Convention on Climate Change is testimony to the results institutional bargaining can produce. Undoubtedly, those who emphasize the failure of the INC to produce more substantial agreement in such areas as the specification of targets and timetables for reductions in the emission of greenhouse gases have a point. Yet international governance systems frequently do evolve, often in ways that their founders can neither predict nor control. If the development of a climate regime is accompanied by increasingly influential shifts from technocratic to systems thinking and from anthropocentric to stewardship or biotic perspectives on human-environment relations, this incipient international governance system could become a force to be reckoned with in the years to come.

CHAPTER THREE

Managing the Arctic's Shared Natural Resources

Shared natural resources—resources and ecosystems extending into the jurisdictional domains of two or more states—abound in international society. Some of the world's richest fisheries comprise migratory or straddling stocks that transcend jurisdictional boundaries. Much the same is true of many marine mammals, such as bowhead whales and northern fur seals, as well as large populations of seabirds, some of whom travel from one polar region to the other in the course of their migratory cycle. Large pools of oil and natural gas extend across jurisdictional boundaries, constituting common pools. Major rivers flow through the territories of as many as eight to ten states. In every case, the essential issue is the same: individual states cannot manage shared natural resources effectively on a unilateral basis. Success in this realm, whether it is measured on the basis of sustainability, efficiency, equity, or any other criterion of evaluation, requires sustained cooperation at the international level.

The recent surge of interest in issues involving global environmental change such as ozone depletion and greenhouse warming has deflected attention from the continuing and, in some cases, growing demand for governance systems tailored to more circumscribed—regional or even subregional—environmental concerns. Yet problems involving shared natural resources are not only numerous, but they also occupy a higher place on the agendas of many stakeholders than

The central themes of this chapter were presented initially at the Arctic Assembly sponsored by the Polar Research Board, the Arctic Research Consortium of the United States, and the United States Arctic Research Commission and held at the National Academy of Sciences in Washington, D.C., 25 March 1992.

do emerging global issues.[1] Efforts to come to terms with these regional and subregional matters offer a rich vein of experience to draw
on in thinking about the determinants of success and failure in the
operation of international governance systems. Although efforts to
deal with the (ab)use of global commons are at best recent and tenta-
tive, there is an extensive record of actual experience with regimes for
shared natural resources. For those in search of insights into the
effectiveness and the robustness of environmental governance systems, therefore, there is much to be said for studying the record of
efforts to manage shared natural resources in some depth.

In this chapter, I examine several regimes for shared natural resources that have made their mark in the Arctic during the twentieth
century. In doing so, I seek not only to draw attention to a body of
evidence little known to students of international relations but also to
provide illustrative materials that will serve to ground theoretical arguments advanced in later chapters of this book. Although it is certainly premature to draw firm conclusions from these Arctic cases,
the final section of the chapter identifies common threads relating to
effectiveness and robustness that run through these cases.

ANALYZING THE ARCTIC CASES

The Arctic has not loomed large in the thinking of most of those
who have contributed to the contemporary literature on sustained
international cooperation. Because this region has often been dis-
missed as little more than a frozen wasteland over which missiles
might fly at high altitudes during a nuclear exchange, it may come as
a surprise to learn that the Circumpolar North has been the locus of
significant and suggestive efforts to devise regimes for shared natural
resources during the twentieth century.[2] The resultant collection of
arrangements is diverse, encompassing both bilateral and multilateral

[1] For a discussion of the concept of shared natural resources that sets forth the
argument for using this terminology and refers explicitly to northern cases see Alex-
andre Timoshenko, "Shared Natural Resources: Conception, Evolution and Perspectives," paper prepared for the International Conference on Shared Living Resources of
the Bering Sea Region, Fairbanks, Alaska, June 1990. For a set of case studies organized
under the rubric of transboundary rather than shared natural resources consult Albert
E. Utton and Ludwik A. Teclaff, eds., *Transboundary Resources Law* (Boulder: Westview
Press, 1987).

[2] For relevant background see Oran R. Young, "The Arctic in World Affairs," The
Donald L. McKernan Lecture in Marine Affairs, 10 May 1989 (Seattle: Washington Sea
Grant Program, 1989); and Oran R. Young and Gail Osherenko, eds., *Polar Politics:
Creating International Environmental Regimes* (Ithaca: Cornell University Press, 1993).

regimes as well as governance systems designed to manage the human use of a variety of resources. The substantial variation in the track records of these arrangements adds to their attraction as grist for this analysis. In the discussion to follow, I consider six cases: Barents Sea fish, marine resources in the Iceland–Jan Mayen area, the Porcupine caribou herd, Beringian birds, northern fur seals, and polar bears. This analysis will set the stage for an effort in the concluding section to draw together the results of the individual case studies in the interests of framing some broader propositions about regimes for shared natural resources.

Barents Sea Fish

Since the 1970s, Norway and the Soviet Union (more recently Russia) have cooperated in developing and maintaining a bilateral regime for the marine fisheries of the Barents Sea. This governance system comprises two components, a coordination arrangement for a disputed area in the central Barents Sea that is nested into a broader collaboration regime covering fish stocks of the entire region that are of interest to fishers from the two participating states.[3] The broader arrangement rests on two bilateral agreements (the 1975 Cooperation in Fisheries Agreement and the 1976 Agreement on Mutual Fisheries), which contain provisions covering the phasing out of third-party fishing in the area in the wake of the extension of coastal state jurisdiction, the determination of allowable catches from the fish stocks covered by the regime, the treatment of Norwegian and Soviet/Russian fishers operating in each other's waters, and the exchange of quotas for fish in waters under the jurisdiction of each of the parties. The agreements also establish a Mixed Norwegian/Soviet Fisheries Commission to administer the major provisions of this bilateral regime.[4]

[3] In coordination regimes, the participants agree on the content of common rules but do not create any supranational organization or administrative mechanism to make collective choices involving the operation of the regime or to play a role in applying its rules to specific situations. In collaboration regimes, by contrast, some authority is granted to a supranational organization or administrative mechanism.

[4] See Olav Schram Stokke and Alf Hakon Hoel, "Splitting the Gains: Political Economy of the Barents Sea Fisheries," *Conflict and Cooperation* 29 (1991), 49–65; and Olav Schram Stokke, Lee Anderson, and Natalia Mirovitskaya, "The Effectiveness of the Barents Sea Fisheries Regime," draft case study prepared for the project on the Effectiveness of International Regimes administered by the Institute of Arctic Studies at Dartmouth College.

The nested component of the regime addresses the special problems of managing fishing activities in an area of 155,000 square kilometers in the middle of the Barents Sea where jurisdictional boundaries are in dispute because of the discrepancy between the claims of Norway, which espouses the equidistance principle, and those of the Soviet Union / Russia, which advocates the sector principle as a means of demarcating the maritime boundary in the area. This arrangement, formalized in the Grey Zone Agreement of 1978, allows fishing vessels from both parties to operate in the disputed area on the understanding that each side will implement common rules for vessels it licenses.

This governance system has been a success in its own terms. It provides a framework for cooperation among coastal state users of the shared living resources of the Barents Sea and for mutually beneficial exchanges of quotas in areas under the jurisdiction of Norway and the Soviet Union / Russia. It has served also to contain latent conflicts arising from simultaneous operations by Norwegian and Soviet/Russian fishers in the grey zone. With regard to the sources of effectiveness, the principal lessons from this case are negative in that they tend to disconfirm some widely held beliefs about the requirements for sustained cooperation in international society. Specifically, the Barents Sea regime has worked well as a two-party system in a situation featuring striking asymmetries in the structural power of the participants as well as sharp differences in their political alignments. It has functioned smoothly in a highly sensitive strategic area—an important deployment zone for nuclear-powered submarines—that is the focus of an unresolved jurisdictional dispute. Overall, this experience suggests that we should not ignore opportunities for devising successful arrangements to manage shared natural resources even when the setting seems politically unpromising.

More broadly, however, the success of the Barents Sea regime leaves a good deal to be desired. The arrangement has not prevented dramatic fluctuations, including severe depletions, of the region's major fish stocks.[5] The knowledge base for making management decisions about allowable harvests of Barents Sea fish is weak, and there is no escaping the politically sensitive issue of introducing effective means

[5] Stokke and Hoel, "Splitting the Gains," 50. There is some uncertainty about the relative significance of anthropogenic and natural forces as causes of these depletions. See Kenneth Sherman, "Large Marine Ecosystems," in *Encyclopedia of Earth System Science* (New York: Academic Press, 1992), 2:653–673.

to limit entry when human demand for such resources exceeds the sustainable yield. Nor are there any provisions in this regime to cope with the contamination of fish caused by marine pollution (for example, the pollution resulting from nuclear wastes that the Soviet Union dumped into the Barents Sea and the Kara Sea over a period of years) or with the disruptions likely to occur when the area's hydrocarbon reserves are developed in the future.[6] Intersectoral linkages connecting various human activities have grown sufficiently that the Barents Sea must be viewed today as a region featuring multiple uses of resources rather than continuing to focus on fishing as a self-contained activity. Yet no simple, much less automatic, process of evolution will bring these larger issues within the purview of the existing Barents Sea regime.

In some ways, this governance system seems remarkably robust. It has remained intact in the face of highly disruptive changes in the former Soviet Union as well as severe economic dislocations in northern Norway. The Grey Zone Agreement has contained latent tensions in the disputed area of the Barents Sea year after year, even though it must be renewed annually. The fisheries commission continues to set allowable catches, although the changes occurring within Russia have taken a toll in terms of the Russian fishers' compliance with the quotas set. All this is surely testimony to the capacity of institutional arrangements to become significant determinants of collective outcomes at the international level. Still, it is hard to see how the Barents Sea regime can go on in its present form indefinitely. It seems likely that its success will eventually be undermined by larger problems that the regime is ill-equipped to handle. Norway and Russia, of course, may devise new and more effective institutional arrangements to manage the Barents Sea as a complex, multidimensional ecosystem. The recent Norwegian initiative aimed at establishing the Barents Euro-Arctic Region as a suitable arena for multilateral cooperation, for example, is a promising step in this regard.[7] It is clear, however, that robustness cannot be ensured by adhering to a strategy of encapsula-

[6] See Olav Schram Stokke, "Western Environmental Interests in the Arctic," *Centrepiece* (a publication of the Centre for Defense Studies of the University of Aberdeen 21 (Winter 1991–1992).

[7] On the initiative of Norway, representatives of Denmark, Finland, Iceland, Norway, Sweden, and Russia met in Kirkenes, Norway, in January 1993 and signed a ministerial declaration titled "Cooperation in the Barents Euro-Arctic Region." For an analysis of the evolving pattern of international relations in the Barents Sea region see Olav Schram Stokke and Rune Castberg, "Regionalization in the Barents Sea Area," in L. Heininen and T. Katermaa, eds., *Regionalism in the North* (Rovaniemi: Arctic Centre, 1993), 19–37.

tion, at least when a variety of human activities increasingly intersect with each other.

Jan Mayen–Iceland Marine Resources

The discovery of commercially significant capelin stocks in an area lying between Iceland and the Norwegian island of Jan Mayen during the autumn of 1978 triggered a process in which a jurisdictional dispute led several years later to a pair of agreements between Iceland and Norway setting up a joint development regime covering the exploitation of both fish and hydrocarbons in the affected area.[8] Though it includes only two members and covers only a limited set of resources, the resultant governance system has often been mentioned as a model for other marine areas.

Under the terms of an agreement signed in 1980, Iceland and Norway settled on the boundaries of fishery conservation zones in the area between Iceland and Jan Mayen and formed a cooperative arrangement to establish and allocate allowable harvests of capelin for the entire area. The agreement also provides for a Joint Icelandic/Norwegian Fisheries Commission to manage fishing operations in the area and a conciliation commission with a mandate to make nonbinding recommendations regarding a solution to the remaining disagreement about the area's outer continental shelf resources. In 1981, Iceland and Norway accepted the recommendations of the commission, agreeing on a regime for the outer continental shelf which extends the demarcation formula of the 1980 agreement to the shelf as well as the water column and sets up a joint development zone for the exploitation of any hydrocarbons that may be discovered in the area.[9] This joint development arrangement, which is the most innovative feature of the regime for the area between Iceland and Jan Mayen, includes detailed provisions covering both the conduct of exploratory activities in the area and the use of joint venture contracts as a means of unitizing any eventual production of hydrocarbons.

The governance system articulated in the 1980 and 1981 agreements has been an undeniable success. It resolved the issue of the maritime boundary in the area between Iceland and Jan Mayen in a

[8] For relevant background see Willy Ostreng, "The Jan Mayen–Iceland Dispute," unpublished essay, n.d.

[9] See Elliot L. Richardson, "Jan Mayen in Perspective," *American Journal of International Law* 82 (July 1998), 443–458, for a thoughtful account by the American who chaired the conciliation commission that recommended creation of a joint development zone.

manner that is fully compatible with the system of exclusive economic zones formalized in the 1982 Convention on the Law of the Sea. The provisions relating to the capelin fishery, a particularly sensitive matter given the political influence of the fishing industries in the two countries, appear to have defused a dispute that could easily have turned nasty. The joint development scheme for outer continental shelf resources remains largely untested because no commercially significant reserves of hydrocarbons have been discovered in the area. But there is no reason to doubt that the regime will operate effectively should such reserves be discovered.

This case yields two significant lessons regarding the determinants of effectiveness. The first concerns the importance of devising arrangements that all participants can accept as equitable and therefore legitimate in situations involving ongoing relationships. Legitimacy may be an unnecessary luxury in the context of single-shot or self-executing agreements, but it is critical to the achievement of compliance or conformance in relationships requiring sustained cooperation. In this case, Norway deserves considerable credit for its sensitivity to Iceland's concerns and its willingness to make concessions to ensure that the regime set forth in the provisions of the 1980 and 1981 agreements meets Iceland's needs. The second lesson underlines the importance of flexibility in arrangements expected to provide a basis for cooperation over extended periods of time. Although the maritime boundaries laid down in the provisions of this regime are not flexible, the arrangement makes up for this lack by granting authority to the Joint Fisheries Commission and establishing an adaptable system for unitizing hydrocarbon production. There is much to be said for this approach, which couples fixed arrangements for the demarcation of maritime boundaries with flexible systems for the management of straddling stocks and common pools.

There is no reason to doubt the robustness of this governance system. Once maritime boundaries are fixed, it is virtually impossible to reopen prior arguments about their location in the absence of wholesale changes in the character of international society. Any other conclusion would introduce uncertainty regarding jurisdictional matters that governments and influential corporations alike would find unacceptable. Although the arrangements for the capelin fishery and hydrocarbons have not yet been severely tested, their staying power— especially the joint development arrangement for hydrocarbons— seems considerable. It is possible to imagine circumstances in which sharp declines in fish stocks coupled with the difficulty of monitoring fishing activities in remote areas might undermine the arrangement for the capelin fishery. But this is not the case for hydrocarbons. Norway is likely to take the lead in exploring for and developing oil or gas in the Iceland–Jan Mayen area.[10] Because any hydrocarbons discovered in the area are unlikely to be of great importance to Norway and there is little prospect of operating covertly in this realm, it is difficult to foresee serious threats to the viability of the joint development system emerging during the near future.

Porcupine Caribou Herd

The Porcupine caribou herd, currently numbering 150,000 to 180,000 animals, migrates annually from its winter range in Canada's Yukon Territory to its summer range on the North Slope of Alaska. The herd is not only prized by environmentalists—some have used phrases like "Serengeti North" in describing the herd and its habitat—but it is also a long-standing source of country food for remote (predominantly indigenous) communities on both sides of the international border. The management task in this case is twofold. There is a need to monitor and manage the consumptive use of animals that make up a herd subject to rapid and poorly understood natural fluctuations. Increasingly, it is important also to protect the herd's habitat from human activities such as hydrocarbon development that might have the unintended effect of eroding the carrying capacity of the range used by the Porcupine caribou herd.

In 1987, Canada and the United States entered into an agreement establishing a management regime for this herd. The arrangement, which seeks simultaneously to conserve the herd, protect its habitat, and accommodate the interests of various user groups, established the International Porcupine Caribou Board as the principal instrument for accomplishing these goals.[11] The board, a supranational body composed of four members from each side, is authorized to make recommendations about a wide range of issues affecting both the harvesting of caribou from the Porcupine herd and the protection of habitat critical to the health of the herd. The board's recommendations are not binding, but the parties undertake to provide written reasons whenever they feel the need to reject its advice or recommen-

[10] Ostreng, "Jan Mayer–Iceland Dispute." Norway is one of the world's major producers of oil, but there is little likelihood of Iceland becoming an important player in this realm.

[11] For the text of the 1987 agreement and an account of the role of the board see International Porcupine Caribou Board, *Second Annual Report,* 1990.

dations. In short, this bilateral governance system is properly regarded as a collaboration regime, even though the grant of authority
to the International Porcupine Caribou Board is highly circumscribed.

In one sense, this regime is untested. Because the size of the herd
has been large and generally stable since the arrangement's inception
in 1987, the regime has not been called upon to allocate resources
among competing users under conditions of scarcity. In other re-
spects, however, the track record of this regime has been disappoint-
ing. Largely because of the composition of the board and a long delay
in establishing a mechanism on the Alaska side (analogous to the
Canadian Porcupine Management Board on the Yukon side) to allocate total allowable harvests among local users, the regime has not
inspired a sense of ownership and legitimacy in the minds of local
people for whom the caribou constitute a critical renewable resource.
This governance system has also failed to live up to the expectations
of many (especially on the Canadian side) regarding issues of habitat
protection. The paramount concern here centers on the debate over
opening the coastal plain of Alaska's Arctic National Wildlife
Refuge—also an important calving ground for the Porcupine caribou
herd—for oil development. This debate has proceeded, largely within the halls of the U.S. Congress, with little reference to the consultative process mandated under the terms of the 1987 agreement. As a
result, the regime has yet to pass the test (increasingly important in
many situations involving shared natural resources) of providing an
effective procedure for bringing the voices of both local users and
international partners into national policy-making regarding the use
of resources (or ecosystems) valued differently by different constituencies.[12]

Although this regime is not likely to collapse in the foreseeable
future, it would be stretching the facts to call it robust at this stage.
The regime has yet to develop a tested method for allocating allowable harvests among local users under conditions of scarcity, and it is
in danger of becoming marginalized with regard to important issues
pertaining to habitat protection. Accordingly, it could end up as a
dead letter even though it continues to function as a nominal presence in the management of the Porcupine caribou herd. A comparison of the determinants of robustness in this case with that of Barents

[12] Robert F. Keith, "Arctic Borderlands: Environment and Development Issues in
Canadian-American Relations," *Northern Notes* 2 (November 1991), 27–51.

Sea fishing is instructive. The Barents Sea regime has produced sustained cooperation between two parties that have been on opposite sides of a major political cleavage in international society. By contrast, the long-standing and generally cordial friendship between Canada and the United States has not helped the bilateral regime for the Porcupine caribou herd to succeed.

Beringian Birds

Beringia, or the greater Bering Sea region, supports some of the world's largest concentrations of birds. The migratory habits of these birds differ considerably. Beringian geese and ducks migrate far to the south during the winter months, whereas many of the area's seabirds remain within the Bering Sea region. Even so, most Beringian bird populations constitute shared living resources in the sense that the birds travel across national boundaries, especially in today's world of extended fishery conservation zones and exclusive economic zones. There is also considerable variation in the extent to which Beringian birds are of interest to human users. Several species of geese, for example, are taken both by subsistence users in the Bering Sea region and by sport hunters far to the south. Gulls and fulmars, however, are of relatively little interest to consumptive users. Even so, all of the region's bird populations are at risk from human activities such as fishing and nonrenewable resource development that pose either direct threats (for example, the danger of entanglement in ghost nets) or indirect threats arising from the degradation of critical habitats.

International efforts to protect and manage these shared living resources have taken an unusual form. The prevailing regime is the de facto product of a series of five bilateral agreements between Canada and the United States (1916), Mexico and the United States (1936), Japan and the United States (1972), Japan and Russia (1973), and Russia and the United States (1976).[13] Each of these agreements sets up a freestanding arrangement that is not limited to Beringia. But taken together, they constitute a web of bilateral agreements that can be thought of as a hybrid arrangement for the Bering Sea region possessing some of the characteristics of a multilateral regime. The resultant governance system is clearly a coordination regime. In every case, the parties agree to follow common rules regarding the taking of

[13] Simon Lyster, *International Wildlife Law* (Cambridge, Eng.: Grotius Publications, 1985), chap. 4.

birds (and their eggs and nests), the protection of critical habitat, the establishment of protected natural areas, and the conduct of scientific research. But the implementation of these rules is the responsibility of each individual party in the areas under its jurisdiction.

It is hard to avoid the conclusion that this hybrid regime has been relatively ineffective in safeguarding the birds of Beringia. Populations of both seabirds, such as kittiwakes and puffins, and highly migratory species, such as geese and brant, have declined significantly in recent years. There has been no sustained effort to protect terrestrial or marine ecosystems from the impacts of human activities (for example, intensified fishing in the Bering Sea) in the interest of conserving the bird populations of Beringia. Nor has the regime been particularly successful in generating a sense of ownership and legitimacy among important constituencies. Though recent efforts to devise co-management arrangements (for example, the Yukon/Kuskokwin Delta Goose Management Plan) have helped in this regard, it would be inaccurate to conclude that harvesters of these resources have become enthusiastic backers of the regime.[14]

Several interacting factors account for the unimpressive track record of this governance system. Particularly in the case of highly migratory species, it is difficult to achieve coordinated management practices covering the entire range of the birds. There is little prospect of systematically monitoring all the human activities (ranging from subsistence harvesting in remote areas to commercial fishing on the high seas) affecting Beringian birds, which makes the absence of a sense of ownership on the part of key constituencies a serious liability. The protection of critical habitat from the unintended effects of contaminants such as agricultural pesticides that show up as non-point-source pollutants is a tall order. Because birds have no straightforward commercial or monetary value, a low priority is attached to their protection in cases of conflict with high-value activities such as commercial fishing or hydrocarbon development.

In purely technical terms, this regime may strike some observers as robust. There is little likelihood that the arrangement will simply collapse in the sense that any of its constitutive agreements will be terminated. There are some indications, moreover, that interest in birds is increasing both as resources of value in their own right and as indicator species that can tell us something about the health of com-

[14] Gail Osherenko, "Can Comanagement Save Arctic Wildlife?" *Environment* 20 (July–August 1988), 6–13, 29–34.

plex ecosystems.[15] Yet the odds on any striking improvement in the effectiveness of this regime during the near future are not good. This is a case that illustrates dramatically not only the need for ecosystems perspectives but also the importance of taking steps simultaneously to strengthen the international agreements underlying the regime and to provide local users with a more meaningful voice in the operation of the regime. The governance system for Beringian birds is not unique in this respect. But it does offer clear evidence of the difficulty of devising management systems capable of meeting these twin demands at the same time.

Northern Fur Seals

By the end of the nineteenth century, extensive and unregulated pelagic harvesting of northern fur seals in the Bering Sea and the North Pacific Ocean had reduced the seal stocks of the region to a small fraction of their original numbers. Unilateral efforts by the United States to protect the large herds breeding on the Pribilof Islands in the central Bering Sea had failed because of the unwillingness of other powerful states—especially Great Britain—to accept the jurisdictional claims that the United States launched in conjunction with these efforts.[16] As evidence mounted that the northern fur seal was rapidly becoming an endangered species, however, the relevant states began to take a serious interest in setting up an international regime to govern the consumptive use of them. The result was a four-party treaty, signed in 1911 by Great Britain (on behalf of Canada), Japan, Russia, and the United States, which established a simple coordination regime for the harvesting of fur seals. When this arrangement was renegotiated in the aftermath of World War II, the parties added an International North Pacific Fur Seal Commission to oversee the implementation of the regime. Though the grant of authority to this commission was highly restricted, it can be interpreted as initiating a significant shift from the original coordination regime toward the emergence of a collaboration regime.

The core of the fur seal regime was an agreement to ban pelagic sealing and to conduct all harvesting of seals on island rookeries

[15] Lyster, *International Wildlife Law,* chap. 4.

[16] On the history of efforts to protect northern fur seals consult James Thomas Gay, *American Fur Seal Diplomacy: The Alaskan Fur Seal Controversy* (New York: Peter Lang, 1987).

under the jurisdiction of Russia and the United States.[17] The two proprietary states agreed to supervise the harvest to ensure the viability of the seal herds and to compensate Canada and Japan for their acceptance of the ban on pelagic sealing by granting them a specified fraction of the sealskins taken in each annual harvest. The regime simply finessed certain jurisdictional complications caused by the limitation of the jurisdiction of coastal states in 1911 to a three-mile band of territorial sea. The four signatories included all those with a demonstrated interest in the fur seals; a united front on the part of these four would certainly deter any others from initiating pelagic sealing on the high seas. The International Fur Seal Commission, added in the 1957 renegotiation of the regime, was given responsibility for carrying out scientific research and recommending (but not imposing) measures to regulate the harvest in the interest of ensuring sustainable yields year after year.

For a long time, this regime was widely cited and admired as an example of the potential of international governance of shared natural resources.[18] Under its auspices, the seal population recovered dramatically, and conflicts over sealing among the parties came to an end. Several factors, taken together, account for this striking success. By compensating Canada and Japan for the termination of pelagic sealing, the regime produced an equitable arrangement that each of the parties could accept as legitimate. The lack of any entrenched tradition of subsistence harvesting or of sport hunting for this species alleviated many of the problems of accommodating the interests of multiple user groups that have plagued other regimes. Above all, this regime became a prominent expression of the scientific management movement and, more specifically, the concern for achieving maximum sustainable yields from consumptive uses of living resources which dominated thinking about resource management in the early twentieth century.

During much of this century, the fur seal regime seemed a model of robustness. Neither the disruptions of World War II nor the antagonisms of the Cold War destroyed its effectiveness. Yet in 1984–1985,

---

[17] For relevant accounts see Oran R. Young, "The Political Economy of the Northern Fur Seal," *Polar Record* 20 (1981), 407–416; and Natalia S. Mirovitskaya, Margaret Clark, and Ronald G. Purver, "North Pacific Fur Seals: Regime Formation as a Means of Resolving Conflict," in Oran R. Young and Gail Osherenko, eds., *Polar Politics: Creating International Environmental Regimes* (Ithaca: Cornell University Press, 1993), chap. 2.

[18] Lyster, *International Wildlife Law*, chap. 3; and U.S. Department of Commerce, *Environmental Impact Statement on the Interim Convention on Conservation of North Pacific Fur Seals*, February 1985.

the United States Senate refused to ratify a protocol extending the life of the fur seal convention, and the regime collapsed.[19] Since then, little effort has been made to replace the old fur seal regime with some alternative form of international governance.[20] This development, attributable to the combined weight of a variety of forces, makes it clear that the robustness of regimes for shared natural resources can never be taken for granted.

The fur seal population began to decline significantly during the late 1970s for no clear-cut reason but probably because of rising interdependencies among the human uses of the Bering Sea region rather than the harvesting of seals per se. The world market for sealskins eroded rapidly in the early 1980s as a result of the antisealing campaign aimed primarily at the harvest of harp seals in eastern Canada but affecting the demand for other sealskins as well. Increasingly, the orientation of the regime toward maximizing sustainable yields became outdated. In the United States, for example, the Marine Mammals Protection Act (enacted initially in 1972) was aimed at limiting consumptive use of marine mammals to traditional subsistence practices. Moreover, the Bering Sea region seemed well-suited to the ecosystems thinking that was coming to supplant the idea of attaining maximum sustainable yields from individual species as an approach to resource management. Taken together, these factors eroded the strength of the fur seal regime and left it vulnerable to attack when the leaders of the animal rights movement chose to train their fire on the regime in a manner that persuaded the Senate not to ratify the 1984 protocol despite a strong endorsement from the Reagan administration.

Polar Bears

Technological advances in the 1950s and 1960s greatly enhanced the ability of hunters to track and kill polar bears in remote Arctic locations.[21] Using snowmobiles and light aircraft, consumptive users—

[19] For an account that clearly reflects the thinking of those opposed to the continuation of the fur seal regime see National Advisory Committee on Oceans and Atmosphere, *North Pacific Fur Seals: Current Problems and Opportunities Concerning Conservation and Management* (Washington, D.C.: U.S. Department of Commerce, 1985).

[20] The creation of Fishery Conservation Zones in the 1970s and Exclusive Economic Zones in the 1980s brought the bulk of the Bering Sea under the management authority of Russia and the United States. But these events, coupled with the increasing influence of whole ecosystems perspectives, have done nothing to reduce the need for sustained international cooperation to manage the shared natural resources of the Bering Sea region.

[21] Ian Stirling, "Research and Management of Polar Bears *Ursus maritimus*," *Polar*

especially sport hunters seeking trophies—increased their take of polar bears rapidly. An alarming feature of this development was the lack
of scientific knowledge about polar bears. Because scientists were unable to provide accurate estimates of the total population of bears in the
Arctic or even to say whether this population comprised a single stock
or several stocks, it was hard to assess the consequences of the rising
harvest of polar bears. This situation provided the impetus for members of the scientific community to initiate a concerted effort to improve their knowledge of polar bears and, in the process, to build a
clear-cut basis for arguments concerning the need for international
cooperation to protect this species.

Though the governance system articulated in the 1973 Agreement
on the Conservation of Polar Bears is properly construed as a simple
coordination regime, this arrangement has several noteworthy features.[22] It is a multilateral regime in which all five range states (Canada,
Denmark/Greenland, Norway, Russia, and the United States) agree to
follow a set of common rules. Although the agreement is explicit in
calling on all parties to devise clear-cut systems to regulate the taking of
polar bears, it leaves each party substantial leeway in deciding how to
effectuate this commitment within its own jurisdiction. The regime is
notable also as an early effort to move beyond the regulation of consumptive use by introducing rules dealing with the protection of habitats essential to the well-being of living resources.

What is more, the polar bear regime rests on an ingenious solution to
a set of jurisdictional problems that could easily have hindered cooperation in managing bear stocks. Polar bears are highly mobile marine
mammals that often move beyond the bounds of coastal state jurisdiction (this was particularly true in 1973, when exclusive economic zones
had not yet been established). Yet the parties to the polar bear regime
could not make rules that would be legally binding on others. To solve
this problem, the regime simply finesses the issue of jurisdiction on the
(reasonable) presumption that nationals of other states will not risk
defying a united front on the part of the range states by taking polar
bears on the high seas.

Record 23 (1986), 167–176. For a more general account of what is known about polar
bears and their management consult Stirling, *Polar Bears* (Ann Arbor: University of
Michigan Press, 1988).

[22] For an account of the formation of the polar bear regime see Anne Fikkan, Gail
Osherenko, and Alexander Arikainen, "Polar Bears: The Importance of Simplicity," in
Young and Osherenko, eds., *Polar Politics,* chap. 4.

Some commentators have expressed the view that the 1973 agreement merely ratified a series of management practices that had evolved within the individual range states during the preceding years. Whatever the merits of this view, it seems undeniable that the polar bear regime has achieved an impressive track record in organizing and sustaining cooperation in the management of polar bear stocks over the ensuing decades. Today, the stocks are healthy; significant steps have been taken to protect critical bear habitats, and scientific knowledge of this species has improved dramatically.[23] Several factors operating together appear to account for this success. The simplicity (even elegance) of this regime has given it a clarity and salience that ensures that any failure to sustain healthy polar bear stocks will not go unnoticed. The regime has achieved a high level of legitimacy in the minds of important user groups. The willingness of local user groups to nest specialized arrangements for specific polar bear stocks, such as the rules for southern Beaufort Sea bears articulated in the 1988 agreement between the North Slope Borough and the Inuvialuit Game Council, within the overarching regime set forth in the 1973 agreement is a sign of considerable success in this regard.[24] Additionally, all the parties have made good faith efforts to implement their commitment to protect polar bear habitat. Although far from perfect, the regime has performed well relative to other arrangements for shared living resources.

Yet none of this success offers any guarantee that the polar bear regime will remain robust over the foreseeable future. Two sets of threats require serious consideration. First, there are growing pressures to reintroduce sport hunting for polar bears in some areas, particularly in Russia, where the urgent need for new sources of hard currency may make the idea of organizing a trophy hunt for wealthy Europeans and North Americans seem increasingly attractive. There are also subtle threats arising from the complex linkages among the elements of large marine and coastal ecosystems. Despite the emphasis on habitat protection in the polar bear regime, the capacity of any single-species arrangement to deal with threats arising from unrelated activities, such as offshore hydrocarbon development, the long-range

[23] Stirling, *Polar Bears.*
[24] This is an agreement between organizations representing Alaskan and Canadian users to provide special protection to the shared population of polar bears in the southern Beaufort Sea and to harmonize divergent management systems in place in the two jurisdictions.

transport of airborne and seaborne pollutants, or even greenhouse warming, is severely limited. The polar bear case is, in short, one more illustration of the importance of adopting whole ecosystems perspectives in devising management systems for shared natural resources under contemporary conditions.

IDENTIFYING COMMON THEMES

What conclusions can we draw from this account that will prove useful not only to those responsible for managing shared natural resources in the Arctic but also to those charged with creating and administering governance systems for such resources in other parts of the world? Needless to say, a clear note of caution is in order. Though by no means trivial, six cases do not constitute a large sample, and these cases may not be representative of the entire class of regimes for shared natural resources. The Arctic may have attributes that make it different from other international regions in managing natural resources. Even so, the preceding analysis does support some preliminary inferences that should be of interest to all those concerned with creating and operating governance systems for shared natural resources. The discussion to follow seeks to extract some of the central themes regarding the effectiveness and the robustness of governance systems that run through the Arctic cases and to express them in a manner that will provide insights for practitioners concerned with these matters as well as ideas to be tested and refined by analysts working on similar issues in other regions of the world.

Effectiveness

Some of the most striking lessons about the effectiveness of resource regimes to be drawn from this analysis are negative in that they tend to disconfirm propositions often voiced in casual discussions. The evidence from the Arctic cases does not support the view that bilateral regimes are likely to be more effective than multilateral arrangements. A political setting characterized by generally friendly relations among the parties is neither necessary nor sufficient to ensure success in creating effective regimes for shared natural resources. Nor is there any indication in these cases that some rough balance or symmetry among the participants with regard to the possession of structural power is essential to success in devising effective management systems. Contrary to the views of many, moreover, this analysis does not suggest that creating effective regimes for shared natural resources will be unusually difficult or impossible in areas of great strategic sensitivity; few areas have been more sensitive in these terms during the recent past than the Barents Sea. The existence of unresolved jurisdictional issues need not become an insuperable impediment to success in the management of shared natural resources. Although resolution of the jurisdictional issues is a prominent feature of the joint development arrangements for the Iceland–Jan Mayen area, the Barents Sea regime seeks to manage rather than to solve the jurisdictional differences there. Several of the successful regimes in this set owe at least part of their success to a strategy of finessing critical jurisdictional issues.

Successful governance systems for shared natural resources are typically limited in geographical scope. This does not mean that they can be framed in such a way as to truncate complex ecosystems; far from it. But more often than not, they involve arrangements that are subregional rather than region-wide. In the Arctic, for instance, they can be expected to focus on the Barents Sea or the Bering Sea as complex marine systems or on the Alaska-Yukon borderlands as a complex terrestrial system in contrast to the Circumpolar North as a whole because most effective governance systems are highly sensitive to the concerns of local user groups and other directly affected constituencies. Although it is possible to persuade members of these groups to accept the logic of constructing a regime that encompasses a range of activities occurring in the same general area, it is difficult to convince them that institutions geared to the concerns of a whole region are suitable vehicles for managing shared natural resources. That arrangements extending across an entire region and beyond would be necessary to achieve effective management for highly migratory birds undoubtedly helps to explain the difficulties that have arisen in managing these shared resources.

Yet another determinant of effectiveness in regimes for shared natural resources involves a cluster of factors that may be labeled equity/ownership/voice. Though it may seem counterintuitive to those schooled in realist perspectives on international affairs, effective governance systems in international society generally show signs of genuine sensitivity toward the equity claims of key parties, as in the case of the compensation system for Canadian and Japanese interests in the fur seal regime and the Norwegian acknowledgment of the intensity of

Icelandic interests in the Iceland/Jan Mayen area.[25] They also tend to set up procedural devices that offer regular opportunities for various constituencies to articulate their concerns, as in the nesting of specialized local rules for the southern Beaufort Sea into the overarching polar bear regime and the (not yet fully realized) potential of the International Porcupine Caribou Board to serve as a mechanism for expressing local concerns. The need for such mechanisms to generate and sustain feelings of ownership on all sides arises from the twin facts that governance systems for shared natural resources are meant to have an indefinite life span and that arrangements featuring enforcement as a means of eliciting compliance are not of much use in international society (whatever their attractions in other social settings).

We come next to the role of ideas and, more specifically, to the question of the extent to which specific regimes for shared natural resources are consistent with prevailing perspectives on resource management or, for that matter, broader streams of thought regarding human-environment relations. It is hard to escape the conclusion that governance systems work best when they reflect and build on larger sets of ideas. The fur seal regime did well for some decades as an expression of the ideals of scientific conservation; it foundered in the 1980s when this vision had been eclipsed, partly as a result of changes in material conditions that made it increasingly outmoded and partly as a consequence of the emergence of new management principles. The polar bear regime, by contrast, constitutes an early expression of the ecosystems perspectives that have increasingly supplanted the old ideal of achieving maximum sustainable yield from consumptive use. There can be little doubt that the growing influence of this perspective during the years since 1973 has buttressed efforts to go beyond the regulation of takings in favor of efforts to protect habitats of critical importance to polar bears. Certainly, compatibility with larger systems of thought is not sufficient to ensure effectiveness in regimes for shared natural resources. We are all familiar with the repeated failures of fisheries regimes based on the conservationist principles of maximum sustainable yield, and ecosystems thinking may offer little protection to some shared natural resources in an era of global environmental changes including greenhouse warming. Nevertheless, it is difficult to achieve success with arrangements that run counter to prevailing ideas about human-environment relations.

[25] For an analysis of the role of equity considerations in the establishment of international regimes see Young and Osherenko, eds., *Polar Politics,* chap. 7.

On a more pragmatic note, the evidence from the Arctic cases lends support to the proposition that transparency is a major determinant of the success of international governance systems.[26] The relative ease of determining whether sealskins originated with authorized harvests on the Pribilof or Commander islands surely contributed to the effectiveness of the ban on pelagic sealing. Conversely, limitations on the ability of officials to monitor rules pertaining to the harvesting of birds and their eggs, especially when combined with the low level of legitimacy of some of these rules, have undoubtedly contributed to the lack of success of management practices relating to Beringian birds. This suggests that regimes that seek to protect critical habitats from the impacts of non-point-source pollution will encounter serious problems. It is one thing to regulate pollutants stemming from the production of crude oil, where the wellheads are easily located, and quite another to protect wetlands of great importance to birds from agricultural runoffs that emanate from a wide variety of sources. Hence those responsible for defining and operationalizing the core rules of regimes for shared natural resources would be well advised to work hard at formulating standards that are difficult to violate in a covert or undetected fashion.

Robustness

One key to creating robust regimes for shared natural resources appears to be an ability to strike a proper balance between inclusiveness and workability. In an era of rising interdependencies among differentiable human activities, institutional arrangements should be created with a broad enough scope to encompass activities that impinge on each other. Thus the days of single-species management systems are essentially over. Yet expanding the scope of governance systems introduces problems of workability. Partly, this is a matter of coping with complexities that enter into the management process as more activities and actors come within a regime's purview. In part, however, it arises from the fact that problems of maintaining legitimacy in the eyes of user groups mount rapidly as management processes become more distant and less connected to the day-to-day concerns of local users and

[26] For theoretically informed accounts that stress the role of transparency see Jesse H. Ausubel and David G. Victor, "Verification of International Environmental Agreements," *Annual Review of Energy and Environment* 17 (1992), 1–43, and Abram Chayes and Antonia Handler Chayes, "On Compliance," *International Organization* 47 (Spring 1993), 175–205.

related constituencies. There is no simple formula that will enable the designers of regimes for shared natural resources to strike a balance between inclusiveness and workability. But the evidence from the Arctic cases suggests that it is appropriate under current conditions to focus on complex ecosystems that are subregional in scope. It makes sense, in other words, to think of the Barents Sea or the Bering Sea or the Alaska-Yukon borderlands as suitable units for purposes of management rather than endeavoring to create resource regimes for the Arctic region as a whole.

The evidence from the Arctic cases also suggests that shifts in intellectual underpinnings can easily erode the viability of regimes for shared natural resources. Perhaps the most dramatic illustration is the collapse of the fur seal regime. This arrangement rested on maximizing harvests from a single species year after year and relying on government agencies to conduct the harvests to ensure compliance with key rules. But just as the 1970s witnessed the growth of ecosystems perspectives emphasizing optimal sustainable populations in contrast to maximum sustainable yields, the 1980s brought a rising tide of interest in privatization as a means of eliminating previously accepted roles for governments.[27] This is not to deny the role of preservationist groups in organizing opposition to the ratification of the protocol to the fur seal convention when the issue reached the U.S. Senate in 1984–1985. But it seems unlikely that this opposition could have precipitated such a sudden and decisive collapse of the fur seal regime if the regime's intellectual underpinnings were still intact.

A reasonable inference to be drawn from this discussion is that flexibility, or the capacity of a governance system to adapt to changing circumstances without losing its identity, is an important determinant of robustness. Thus a strong case can be made for building regimes that have the capacity to modify important rules or practices without the need to renegotiate the provisions of the constitutional contracts on which they rest. Collaboration regimes enjoy some advantages over coordination regimes in this regard because they normally set up institutionalized mechanisms that allow the parties to make authoritative collective choices on a routine basis. Even so, the Arctic cases offer some grounds for skepticism. The International North Pacific Fur Seal Commission lacked sufficient authority to make significant alterations in the regime it served, and the changing circumstances confronting

---

[27] For an expression of this point of view in the context of the fur seal case see National Advisory Committee on Oceans and Atmosphere, *North Pacific Fur Seals.*

this regime might have overwhelmed an organization with considerably greater authority in any case. It has not proven easy to establish the International Porcupine Caribou Board in such a way as to ensure that those affected by its decisions will accept them as authoritative and feel some obligation to comply with them. The Arctic cases suggest, then, that although collaboration regimes have potential for building flexibility into resource regimes, this potential is not always easy to realize in practice.

Finally, contextual factors play a role as determinants of robustness. Regimes for shared natural resources are sensitive to occurrences in the broader political and socioeconomic settings in which they operate. The fur seal regime was suspended for the duration of World War II. The economic imperatives experienced by the government of Russia during the current period of transformation could generate intense pressure to reintroduce sport hunting of polar bears. It is possible to foresee circumstances in which the quest for secure reserves of oil or gas could prove disruptive to the regimes for the Barents Sea, the Iceland–Jan Mayen area, or the Porcupine caribou herd. Nonetheless, it is easy to overdo the importance of context as a determinant of robustness. The fur seal regime survived two world wars and the onset of the Cold War. The polar bear regime has remained robust in the face of far-reaching economic and juridical changes in the Arctic. The Barents Sea regime may well survive the current turmoil in Russia; its tasks could even expand as a result of these changes. Under the circumstances, it is important not to fall into a casual realism that exaggerates the fragility of regimes for shared natural resources as a function of changes in the economic and political settings in which they operate.

THEORETICAL
CONCERNS

CHAPTER FOUR

Institutional Bargaining: Creating International Governance Systems

Why do actors in international society succeed in forming governance systems or regimes to deal with some transboundary problems but fail to achieve success in connection with other, equally important, problems? Why is the process of forming governance systems so much more protracted and arduous in some cases than others? Or, to consider some specific cases, why did the effort to deal with ozone depletion yield weak and seemingly unpromising results in 1985 but evolve so quickly into the robust regime articulated in the 1987 Montreal Protocol on Substances That Deplete the Ozone Layer and the London Amendments of 1990? Why did the terms of the environmental regime for Antarctica come together so rapidly in 1991, whereas the laboriously negotiated 1988 Convention on the Regulation of Antarctic Mineral Resource Activities collapsed without ever coming into force? Why do we have a robust international regime for polar bears but not for other marine mammals such as walruses, sea lions, or sea otters?

In this chapter, I address these questions first by drawing a distinction among three stages of the regime formation process and then identifying and critiquing the principal streams of analysis embedded in mainstream thinking about regime formation, an endeavor that demonstrates the limits of our current understanding of the creation

An earlier version of this chapter appeared as Oran R. Young, "The Politics of International Regime Formation: Managing Natural Resources and the Environment," *International Organization* 43 (Summer 1989), 349–375.

of international institutions. An alternative model of the process is introduced, which I describe as institutional bargaining. The hallmark of this model is an emphasis on regime formation as an interactive process involving the interplay of distinguishable forces. The final substantive section of the chapter employs this model to derive some initial hypotheses about the determinants of success in institutional bargaining and makes use of these hypotheses, in a preliminary way, to illuminate the process of forming governance systems for natural resources and the environment in international society.

STAGES OF REGIME FORMATION

With few exceptions, international regime formation aims at reaching agreement on the terms of mutually acceptable provisions suitable for expresson in the form of documents that are treated as constitutional contracts.[1] Although they do not always take the form of binding agreements having the force of law, such documents are important benchmarks in the sense that they constitute evidence of the defining characteristics of regimes or governance systems as understood by their creators.[2] In some cases, the process of reaching agreement is long and drawn out. It took eight years, for instance, to negotiate the 1982 United Nations Convention on the Law of the Sea, and ensuing problems prevented the convention from coming into force until 1994.[3] In other cases, the full process of regime formation involves a series of incremental steps over a period of years. This is especially true when the process begins with the negotiation of a framework convention, such as the 1979 Convention on Long-Range Transboundary Air Pollution, and encompasses a series of efforts to flesh out the regime through the addition of substantive protocols, such as the 1985 protocol on sulfur dioxide, the 1988 protocol on nitrogen oxide, and the 1991 protocol on volatile organic compounds.[4] But in virtually every case, the process of regime formation

---

[1] Oran R. Young and Gail Osherenko, eds., *Polar Politics: Creating International Environmental Regimes* (Ithaca: Cornell University Press, 1993), chap. 7.

[2] For a discussion of informal agreements see Charles Lipson, "Why Are Some International Agreements Informal?" *International Organization* 45 (Autumn 1991), 495–538.

[3] James K. Sebenius, *Negotiating the Law of the Sea: Lessons in the Art and Science of Reaching Agreement* (Cambridge, Mass.: Harvard University Press, 1984); and Robert L. Friedheim, *Negotiating the New Ocean Regime* (Columbia: University of South Carolina Press, 1993).

[4] Marvin S. Soroos, "Arctic Haze and Transboundary Air Pollution: Conditions Governing Success and Failure," in Young and Osherenko, eds., *Polar Politics,* chap. 6. .

in international society centers on the establishment of sets of rules intended to guide the behavior of those involved in the relevant issue areas.

To understand the forces at work in this process, it is helpful to divide the overall sequence into at least three stages: prenegotiation, negotiation, and postnegotiation. The central stage, which I treat in this chapter as a bargaining process, begins with the initiation of direct and focused negotiations and ends with the signing of an agreement. The negotiation stage in the case of the law of the sea, for instance, began with the opening session of the Third United Nations Conference on the Law of the Sea in 1974 and closed with the signing of the convention in 1982. Similarly, the negotiation stage in the case of climate change started with the first session of the Intergovernmental Negotiating Committee in February 1991 and came to an end with the signing of the Convention on Climate Change at Rio de Janeiro in June 1992.

The prenegotiation stage encompasses the process through which an issue initially finds its way onto the international agenda, gets defined or framed as a topic for international consideration, and reaches a sufficiently prominent place on the agenda to justify expending the time and effort involved in explicit negotiations.[5] The postnegotiation stage covers all those steps needed to transform an international agreement signed by the parties who have agreed on its terms into an actual institutional arrangement in place.[6] Among other things, this entails ratification by the signatories and implementation within the domestic jurisdiction of the individual members. As the case of the failed Antarctic minerals convention makes clear, this part of the process can pose problems that may prove insoluble.

These distinctions among the stages are not always easy to maintain in practice. The three stages can and often do overlap so that they cannot be separated in a neat chronological fashion in specific instances. The prenegotiation stage, for example, sometimes involves hard bargaining over such matters as the identity of the parties to be included in a regime or the functional scope of an institutional arrangement. Those negotiating the terms of a governance system may seek to redefine the nature of the underlying problem, even while

---

[5] Janice Gross Stein, ed., *Getting to the Table: The Processes of International Prenegotiation* (Baltimore: Johns Hopkins University Press, 1989).
[6] Bertram I. Spector and Anna Korula, "The Post-Agreement Negotiation Process: The Problems of Ratifying International Environmental Agreements," IIASA Working Paper, WP-92-90, 1992.

they are negotiating the terms of a constitutional contract. These matters become even more complex when regimes are created piecemeal as in the current practice of starting with a framework agreement and fleshing it out over time with a series of substantive protocols. Under these circumstances, the negotiation of specific protocols may commence while the parties are still ratifying and implementing the terms of the initial framework agreement. And the parties may seize the opportunity afforded by the negotiation of additional protocols to redefine the nature of the problem the arrangement addresses. In areas such as ozone depletion, where our understanding of the problem is evolving rapidly, substantive restatements of the problem commonly occur.

Nonetheless, the division of the process of regime formation into three stages is helpful for purposes of analysis. That the nature of the process differs considerably from one stage to another is highly significant in trying to sort out and come to terms with the differing interpretations of regime formation embedded in the rapidly growing literature on international institutions. The negotiation stage is fundamentally a process of hard bargaining—tacit as well as explicit—in which the parties seek to hammer out the terms of mutually acceptable agreements,[7] whereas the prenegotiation stage is a more open-ended process that affords greater scope for the impact of ideas. Distinguishing among stages of regime formation has the additional virtue of making it possible to pinpoint the central concerns of this chapter. Thus the analysis to follow emphasizes the bargaining process through which parties either succeed or fail in the effort to reach agreement on the provisions of regimes to be articulated in conventions, treaties, executive agreements, or other explicit statements. Important as the prenegotiation and postnegotiation stages undoubtedly are, a systematic examination of the issues arising in connection with these stages will have to await another occasion.

EXISTING MODELS: A CRITIQUE

Three separate streams of analysis, each pointing to a distinct set of driving forces, dominate the study of regime formation in interna-

---

[7] On the distinction between explicit and tacit bargaining see Thomas C. Schelling, *The Strategy of Conflict* (Cambridge, Mass.: Harvard University Press, 1960), chap. 3; and George W. Downs and David M. Rocke, *Tacit Bargaining, Arms Races, and Arms Control* (Ann Arbor: University of Michigan Press, 1990).

tional society. Those trained to look at the world through the lens of mainstream utilitarian models emphasize the interplay of interests and typically assume that utility-maximizing actors will reach agreement on the content of mutually beneficial institutional arrangements, including international regimes, whenever a distinct contract zone or zone of agreement exists.[8] Working with models rooted in game theory or microeconomics, the utilitarians seek to predict or, more often, to prescribe the locus of final settlements as well as the trajectories formed by sequences of offers and counteroffers leading to these settlements.[9] Because they generally regard the process of institution building as unproductive, these analysts expect rational actors to find ways to realize feasible joint gains while simultaneously devising procedures to minimize the attendant transaction costs.[10]

Political scientists and others trained to look to material conditions as the key to understanding collective outcomes, by contrast, emphasize the exercise of power and regularly assume that institutional arrangements, such as international governance systems, reflect the configuration of power in the relevant social system; specific arrangements come into existence when those possessing sufficient power take the necessary steps to create them.[11] Many of these realists or neorealists stress the role of dominant actors or, in the current vocabulary of international relations, hegemons in the process of regime formation. Some even assert that the presence of a dominant actor is a necessary condition for the emergence of institutional arrangements at the international level.[12]

A third (somewhat more diffuse) group of analysts attuned to the role of cognitive factors in interactive decision making direct attention to the impact of ideas in the development of social institutions,

---

[8] For a sophisticated exposition of the concept of a contract zone or zone of agreement, see Howard Raiffa, *The Art and Science of Negotiation* (Cambridge, Mass.: Harvard University Press, 1982).

[9] For a survey of the principal models, see Oran R. Young, ed., *Bargaining: Formal Theories of Negotiation* (Urbana: University of Illinois Press, 1975).

[10] For a forceful expression of this point of view, see Gordon Tullock, *Private Wants, Public Means: An Economic Analysis of the Desirable Scope of Government* (New York: Basic Books, 1970), chap. 3.

[11] See Susan Strange, "*Cave! hic dragones*: A Critique of Regime Analysis," in Stephen D. Krasner, ed., *International Regimes* (Ithaca: Cornell University Press, 1983), 337–354; Stephen D. Krasner, *Structural Conflict: The Third World against Global Liberalism* (Berkeley: University of California Press, 1985); and Robert Gilpin, *The Political Economy of International Relations* (Princeton: Princeton University Press, 1987).

[12] See Robert O. Keohane, "The Theory of Hegemonic Stability and Changes in International Economic Systems, 1967–1977," ACIS working paper 22, Center for International and Strategic Affairs, University of California, Los Angeles, 1980.

including international regimes or governance systems. Those who have developed this perspective generally begin by rejecting the unitary actor assumptions embedded in most of the work of the utilitarians and the realists/neorealists. They emphasize the prospects of social learning leading to the redefinition of actors' interests; they also point to the importance of internal processes affecting the actions of individual parties to the institutional bargaining that constitutes the central focus of the process of regime formation in international society.[13]

Not only do these streams of analysis license disparate explanations of regime formation in international society, but advocates of each perspective also tend to treat the very factors singled out by the others as impediments to the promotion of social welfare. The utilitarians ordinarily react negatively to extreme concentrations of power on the grounds that such conditions result in monopoly (or monopsony), which in turn leads to misallocations of resources and reduces social welfare.[14] Conversely, the power theorists typically view the dispersal of power or the presence of numerous parties possessing roughly equal bargaining strength as a problem because such conditions raise transaction costs, sometimes to the point of preventing agreement on institutional arrangements.[15] The cognitivists view the fixed preference structures commonly assumed by both the utilitarians and the power theorists as part of the problem on the grounds that success in regime formation usually entails a process of social learning through which the parties are able to find mutually agreeable solutions to their common problems. The three groups differ in their prescriptions for achieving success in efforts to form international regimes as well as in the predictions they offer regarding probable outcomes in the realm of regime formation. Whereas the realists recommend concentration of power in the hands of a dominant actor, the utilitarians prescribe the dispersal of power among a sizable number of rational utility maximizers, and the cognitivists advocate a shift away from thinking

[13] Christer Jonsson, "Cognitive Factors in Explaining Regime Dynamics," in Volker Rittberger, ed., *Regime Theory and International Relations* (Oxford: Oxford University Press, 1993), chap. 9.

[14] For a standard exposition of the importance of competition in systems of social exchange, see Robert H. Haveman and Kenyon A. Knopf, *The Market System*, 3d ed. (New York: John Wiley, 1979).

[15] For an account stressing the role of transaction costs in connection with international institutions, see Todd Sandler and Jon Cauley, "The Design of Supranational Structures: An Economic Perspective," *International Studies Quarterly* 21 (June 1977), 251–276.

about power to a greater concern for the techniques of problem solving.

How can we come to terms with these conflicting perspectives on institution building and formulate a satisfactory account of regime formation in international society? In this section, I argue that the models associated with all three streams of analysis are seriously flawed as accounts of the process of regime formation capable of explaining the actual record of successes and failures in efforts to form international governance systems. They are, I seek to demonstrate, particularly deficient when it comes to understanding the process of convergence on the provisions of constitutional contracts that is the principal feature of the negotiation stage of regime formation. Although each stream of analysis has something to contribute, then, I conclude that we need to develop a more realistic model of the interactions involved in regime formation, a challenge I address in the following section of the chapter.

Realist or neorealist models

Many students of international relations, impressed by the role of Great Britain in creating regimes for international commerce and the oceans during the nineteenth century and the role of the United States in establishing monetary and trade regimes in the aftermath of World War II, are currently preoccupied with the place of dominant actors or hegemons in international society.[16] There is much talk, for instance, about the sources of hegemonic power and the reasons for the rise and fall of dominant states;[17] a lively debate has sprung up concerning the viability of existing international institutions in the wake of the presumed decline of American dominance in international affairs.[18] Because of this intellectual climate, it is not hard to understand why students of international relations are attracted to the view

[16] Although he may have come to regret it, it seems clear that Charles Kindleberger's analysis of international economic relations in the 1930s played an important part in the development of this set of intellectual concerns (*The World in Depression, 1929–1939* [Berkeley: University of California Press, 1973]).

[17] For an account that has received much popular acclaim, see Paul Kennedy, *The Rise and Fall of the Great Powers* (New York: Random House, 1987).

[18] See Robert O. Keohane, *After Hegemony: Cooperation and Discord in the World Political Economy* (Princeton: Princeton University Press, 1984). For a forceful presentation of the view that the dominance of the United States in international affairs persists, see Susan Strange, "The Persistent Myth of Lost Hegemony," *International Organization* 41 (Autumn 1987), 551–574.

that the presence of a hegemon constitutes a critical, perhaps necessary, condition for regime formation at the international level.

Yet it is easy to demonstrate that arguments relying so heavily on the role of dominant actors in the formation of international regimes cannot withstand the test of empirical application. A few significant examples will suffice. The regime for northern fur seals, established initially in 1911 and long regarded as a model for international conservation efforts, involved a mutually beneficial deal among four major powers: the United States, Japan, Russia, and Great Britain (acting on behalf of Canada).[19] The more recent complex of arrangements for Antarctica and the Southern Ocean encompasses not only the United States and the former Soviet Union but also other important powers working together as members of the Antarctic club.[20] The pollution-control regime for the Mediterranean Basin encompasses important states that span the Arab-Israeli conflict and the Greek-Turkish conflict.[21]

What is more, the drive to form several important environmental governance systems has been spearheaded by intergovernmental organizations or by international nongovernmental organizations so that states have not taken the lead in the relevant processes of regime formation. There is general agreement, for example, that the International Union for the Conservation of Nature and Natural Resources was a motivating force in establishing the regime regulating trade in endangered species of fauna and flora spelled out in the provisions of the Convention on International Trade in Endangered Species.[22] And there is no escaping the central role the United Nations Environment Programme played in the negotiating process that resulted in the 1985 convention and the 1987 protocol on ozone depletion.[23]

From the perspective of those desiring to promote international

[19] See Simon Lyster, *International Wildlife Law* (Cambridge, Eng.: Grotius Publications, 1985), chap. 3; and Oran R. Young, *Natural Resources and the State: The Political Economy of Resource Management* (Berkeley: University of California Press, 1981), chap. 3.

[20] Gillian D. Triggs, ed., *The Antarctic Treaty Regime: Law, Environment and Resources* (Cambridge, Eng.: Cambridge University Press, 1987).

[21] Peter M. Haas, "Do Regimes Matter? Epistemic Communities and Mediterranean Pollution Control," *International Organization* 43 (Summer 1989), 377–403.

[22] See Lyster, *International Wildlife Law*, chap. 12; and Laura H. Kosloff and Mark C. Trexler, "The Convention on International Trade in Endangered Species; No Carrot, But Where's the Stick?" *Environmental Law Reporter* 17 (July 1987), 10222–10236.

[23] Philip Shabecoff, "Ozone Agreement Is Hailed as a First Step in Cooperation," *New York Times*, 5 May 1987, C1 and C7.

cooperation through regime formation, this is just as well because—as many observers are coming to realize—hegemony is an extreme case in international society. This is not to deny, of course, the existence of striking asymmetries among parties interested in a given issue area with respect both to the intensity of their interest in the problem and to the usable bargaining strength at their disposal. Nonetheless, there are several interlocking reasons why true hegemony is the exception rather than the rule in international society.[24] There is, to begin with, the well-known fact that power in the sense of control over material resources or tangible assets—what the neorealists call structural power—is often difficult to translate into power in the sense of the ability to determine collective outcomes.[25] Situations in which other states coalesce in opposition to a state that appears to have hegemonic pretensions are routine in international society.[26] It will come as no surprise, therefore, that even acknowledged great powers are likely to find the opportunity costs of exercising power high in specific situations. Because great powers always strive to participate actively in a number of policy arenas simultaneously, moreover, the prospect of high opportunity costs is sufficient to induce such powers to negotiate rather than impose the terms of international regimes relating to most specific activities.[27]

Additionally, contemporary international society features many situations in which states possess blocking power or the capacity to veto institutional arrangements they dislike, even if they cannot impose their own preferences on others.[28] Cases in point are the control of radioactive fallout crossing national boundaries or the regulation of the emission of greenhouse gases.[29] In such cases, it is hard to see how

[24] See also Duncan Snidal, "The Limits of Hegemonic Stability Theory," *International Organization* 39 (Autumn 1985), 579–614.

[25] Jeffrey Hart, "Three Approaches to the Measurement of Power in International Relations," *International Organization* 30 (Spring 1976), 299–305.

[26] Zeev Maoz and Dan S. Felsenthal, "Self-Binding Commitments, the Inducement of Trust, Social Choice, and the Theory of International Cooperation," *International Studies Quarterly* 31 (June 1987), 177–200.

[27] The growth of international interdependencies in the modern era reinforces this argument because this growth drives up the opportunity costs associated with all efforts to exercise power. See Oran R. Young, "Interdependencies in World Politics," *International Journal* 24 (Autumn 1969), 726–50.

[28] For an extensive analysis of blocking as well as winning coalitions, see William H. Riker, *A Theory of Political Coalitions* (New Haven: Yale University Press, 1962).

[29] James G. Titus, ed., *Effects of Changes in Stratospheric Ozone and Global Climate 1* (Washington, D.C.: U.S. Environmental Protection Agency and U.N. Environmental Programme, 1986).

any international regime could be effective if it failed to satisfy the concerns of both the industrialized and the industrializing members of international society. For all practical purposes, then, the great powers today routinely find themselves in situations in which they must negotiate the terms of international regimes covering specific issue areas, whether they like it or not.

None of this makes power irrelevant to the process of negotiating the terms of international regimes; far from it. But it does put a premium on a form of leadership that differs from the unilateralism or imposition we ordinarily associate with the actions of a hegemon. Contrary to Charles Kindleberger's argument that "a hegemon presumably wants to do it in his own behalf" and that "a leader, one who is responsible or responds to need, who is answerable or answers to the demands of others, is forced to 'do it' by ethical training and by the circumstances of position,"[30] leadership is not simply a matter of motivation. Nor is leadership merely a form of benevolent behavior exhibited by the principal members of privileged groups who act in such a way as to supply public goods to others even if they are unwilling to contribute themselves.[31] Rather, leadership (or, to be more precise, what I have described elsewhere as structural leadership) is a matter of deploying material resources strategically to induce others to sign onto the central deals that make constitutional contracts go; it is apt to involve the use of rewards or side payments to persuade recalcitrant parties at least as much as the use of threats aimed at coercing these parties to acquiesce in the terms of constitutional contracts.[32]

A leader in this context is a representative of one of the parties to the process of regime formation who, desiring to see a regime emerge and realizing that imposition is not feasible, undertakes to use structural resources to craft attractive institutional arrangements and to persuade others to join forces in support of such arrangements. There is a good case to be made, for instance, that Leonid Brezhnev played such a role in the case of long-range transboundary air pollution, as did the chief American negotiator, Richard Benedick, in gain-

---

[30] Charles P. Kindleberger, "Hierarchy versus Inertial Cooperation," *International Organization* 40 (Autumn 1986), 845–46.

[31] On privileged groups, see Mancur Olson, Jr., *The Logic of Collective Action* (Cambridge, Mass.: Harvard University Press, 1965), chap. 1.

[32] For a general discussion of the role of political leadership in connection with regime formation see Oran R. Young, "Political Leadership and Regime Formation: On the Development of Institutions in International Society," *International Organization* 45 (Summer 1991), 281–308.

ing agreement on the central terms of the 1987 Montreal protocol to the convention on ozone depletion.

Utilitarian Models

The mainstream utilitarians exhibit an unjustified faith in the ability of rational utility mazimizers to realize feasible joint gains. As all well-trained students of international affairs now realize, even rational actors regularly experience difficulties in cooperating, with the result that suboptimal (sometimes drastically suboptimal) outcomes are a common occurrence.[33] More than anything else, this realization has provided the impetus for the remarkable rise of the field of public choice in recent years and made a growth industry of the analysis of institutional arrangements designed to overcome or alleviate collective-action problems.[34]

Even when there is general agreement on the existence and the basic contours of a zone of agreement, those negotiating the terms of institutional arrangements often encounter severe obstacles in their efforts to work out the details of mutually acceptable regimes. Difficulties frequently ensue from a widespread resort to strategic behavior or committal tactics on the part of those wanting the outcomes to favor their interests to the maximum degree possible.[35] The behavior of the American negotiators that resulted in the refusal of the United States to accept the regime for deep seabed mining set forth in Part XI of the 1982 Convention on the Law of the Sea is a case in point.[36] Intraparty bargaining that pits powerful forces against each other in the negotiation of the provisions of an international governance system can also make it difficult to reach agreement at the international level.[37] Such internal problems undoubtedly played a role in the decision of the United States to abandon the fur seal regime in the 1980s, and they have afflicted the negotiating posture of some of the partici-

[33] See Russell Hardin, *Collective Action* (Baltimore: Johns Hopkins University Press, 1982); and Kenneth A. Oye, ed., *Cooperation under Anarchy* (Princeton: Princeton University Press, 1986).

[34] For a seminal example, see James M. Buchanan and Gordon Tullock, *The Calculus of Consent* (Ann Arbor: University of Michigan Press, 1962). For a variety of perspectives on the use of public choice theory to examine institutional arrangements, see Clifford S. Russell, ed., *Collective Decision Making: Applications from Public Choice Theory* (Baltimore: Johns Hopkins University Press, 1979).

[35] Schelling, *Strategy of Conflict.*

[36] James L. Malone, "Who Needs the Sea Treaty?" *Foreign Policy* 54 (Spring 1984), 27–43.

[37] Robert D. Putnam, "Diplomacy and Domestic Politics: The Logic of Two-Level Games," *International Organization* 42 (Summer 1988), 427–460.

pants in the ongoing effort to build a regime to regulate global climate change.

There are also common problems attributable to linkages among issue areas in international society. Thus parties are frequently loath to make concessions regarding specific issues more out of a concern for how doing so might affect their negotiating postures in other issue areas than out of any commitment to the particular issue at hand.[38] Certainly the reluctance of the United States and some other industrialized states to go far toward meeting the "common heritage of mankind" arguments of the developing states in the context of the law of the sea negotiations was based in considerable measure on a concern that this would simply reinforce the demands of the developing states in negotiations regarding satellite broadcasting, Antarctica, and, ultimately, an array of issues grouped under the heading of the New International Economic Order.[39] Negotiators also regularly encounter difficulties in settling on the terms of international regimes because some of the participants do not trust others to comply with the terms of the resultant arrangements rather than because they are unhappy with the substantive provisions of the arrangements themselves.[40] In some cases, this is essentially a problem of verification, as in pollution-control measures relating to non-point-source pollutants or in efforts to control the illegal trade in endangered species.[41] In other cases, it is more a matter of devising appropriate incentives or sanctions, as in arrangements aimed at avoiding the destruction of habitat necessary for the maintenance of biological diversity. But in either situation, it is not hard to understand the reluctance of states to subscribe to international regimes that seem likely to end up as dead letters as a consequence of widespread noncompliance with their substantive provisions.

More profoundly, mainstream utilitarian accounts of international regime formation rest on an inappropriate, albeit well-specified and analytically appealing, model of bargaining. All this work takes as its

---

[38] For a more general account, see James K. Sebenius, "Negotiation Arithmetic: Adding and Subtracting Issues and Parties," *International Organization* 37 (Spring 1983), 281–316.

[39] For a straightforward introduction to the components of the NIEO, see Marvin S. Soroos, *Beyond Sovereignty: The Challenge of Global Policy* (Columbia: University of South Carolina Press, 1986), chap. 6.

[40] For a broader analysis of compliance problems, see Roger Fisher, *Improving Compliance with International Law* (Charlottesville: University Press of Virginia, 1981).

[41] On the illegal trade in endangered species, see Kosloff and Trexler, "Convention on International Trade in Endangered Species."

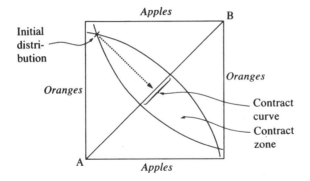

Figure 1. Edgeworth box diagram

point of departure either an Edgeworth box with its depiction of a well-defined contract curve (see Figure 1) or a game-theoretic formulation with its identification of a well-defined negotiation set (see Figure 2).[42] Both of these analytic devices abstract away a great many considerations that are major preoccupations of negotiators under real-world circumstances.[43] They assume, for instance, that (1) the identity of the participants is known at the outset and fixed during the course of negotiations, (2) the alternatives or strategies available to the parties are fully specified, (3) the outcome associated with every feasible combination of choices on the part of the participants is known, and (4) the preference orderings of the parties over the outcomes are identifiable (at least in ordinal terms) and not subject to change. The introduction of these assumptions makes it possible to specify the parameters of the utility possibility set in an Edgeworth box or the payoff space in game-theoretic analysis. And it is a short step from this point to the preoccupation with defining solution concepts that characterizes game-theoretic analyses of bargaining and the concern with "the process of concession" that dominates economic models of bargaining.[44]

As appealing as the resultant constructs may be in analytic terms,

[42] See Young, *Bargaining*. Part I of this book deals with game-theoretic models of bargaining based on the concept of the negotiation set. Part II turns to economic models of bargaining stemming from the Edgeworth box construct.

[43] Ibid., 391–408.

[44] See R. Duncan Luce and Howard Raiffa, *Games and Decisions* (New York: Wiley, 1957); and John G. Cross, *The Economics of Bargaining* (New York: Basic Books, 1969). The quotation is from Cross, p. 8.

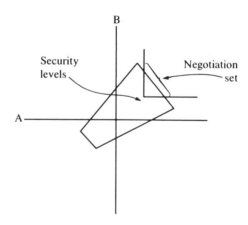

Figure 2. Negotiation set

they are of limited value in helping us comprehend the politics of international regime formation. The identity of the relevant participants in these negotiations is seldom cast in concrete. As recent experience in both the Arctic and the Antarctic suggests, the scope of the membership in international governance systems can become an important focus of bargaining in its own right. It will come as no surprise, then, that efforts to spell out menus of alternatives or strategy sets in advance of these negotiations are generally doomed to failure. No doubt, there is some heuristic value in thinking about problem structure through an assessment of the extent to which specific collective-action problems in international society resemble prisoner's dilemma, chicken, stag hunt, or other analytic models.[45] But mapping the contours of real-world collective-action problems in terms of such analytic constructs is seldom feasible,[46] and our ability to foresee the consequences, unfolding over time, that result from the choice of specific options is particularly limited in connection with ongoing arrangements such as international governance systems. Those who approach these matters in contractarian terms have pointed out that

[45] See Duncan Snidal, "Coordination versus Prisoner's Dilemma: Implications for International Cooperation and Regimes," *American Political Science Review* 79 (December 1985), 923–942; and Kenneth A. Oye, "Explaining Cooperation under Anarchy," in Oye, ed., *Cooperation under Anarchy*, 1–24. For a discussion of regime formation that highlights the significance of problem structure see Volker Rittberger, ed., *International Regimes in East-West Politics* (London: Pinter, 1990).

[46] Anatol Rapoport, *Two-Person Game Theory: The Essential Ideas* (Ann Arbor: University of Michigan Press, 1966), chap. 2.

this may well be a good thing because it serves to dilute the relevance of particularistic interests in the responses of individual parties to proposed institutional arrangements at the international level.[47] Even so, this fact typically rules out the specification of a well-defined contract curve or negotiation set in connection with negotiations focusing on the formation of international governance systems.

Cognitivist Models

The cognitivists generally stake their claims in the form of critiques of important building blocks of both the realist or neorealist and the utilitarian models. They do not accept the characterization of the parties to regime formation as unitary actors weighing the costs and benefits of alternative institutional options in a synoptic manner. They reject the idea that the participants in the process of regime formation possess well-defined preference structures that are not subject to change during the course of the process. What is more, they see forces at work in efforts to form international regimes or governance systems that cannot be captured in the calculations of the power theorists or the utilitarians. These forces include belief systems, decision cultures or styles, and attitudes toward risk and uncertainty.[48] With the shift to this stream of analysis, therefore, we encounter complexities that are familiar to all those who have faced difficult choices under a variety of conditions but that inevitably pose complications absent from the simple, analytically tractable models of the other streams.

Two sets of ideas have emerged with particular clarity from the work of those associated with this perspective on regime formation. One prominent theme is the role of a form of social learning that can give rise to consensual knowledge—ordinarily of the scientific variety—both about the nature of the problem to be solved and about the relative merits of alternative solutions.[49] On this account, a convergence of views among the principal participants is a prerequisite

[47] For a general discussion of this point, see Geoffrey Brennan and James M. Buchanan, *The Reason of Rules: Constitutional Political Economy* (Cambridge, Eng.: Cambridge University Press, 1985), chap. 2.

[48] Jonsson, "Cognitive Factors," For a discussion focusing explicitly on decision cultures or styles see Raymond Vernon, "Behind the Scenes: How Policymaking in the European Community, Japan, and the United States Affects Global Negotiations," *Environment* 35 (August 1993), 12–20, 35–43.

[49] Ernst B. Haas, *When Knowledge Is Power: Three Models of Change in International Organizations* (Berkeley: University of California Press, 1990), esp. chap. 1.

for success in the process of regime formation. In the eyes of some, such a convergence may be sufficient to produce success in the effort to form a regime as well. Richard Cooper's account of the role of the victory of the contagionists over the miasmatists in the emergence of an international public health regime illustrates this line of thinking.[50] Similar arguments have been advanced by some analysts regarding the emergence of the regime for the protection of stratospheric ozone in recent years.

Yet there is something disembodied about this line of thought; it seems to rely on a spontaneous process that has no engine to drive it. Concern with this problem has given rise to a growing literature on the role that epistemic communities play in the process of regime formation.[51] On this account, epistemic communities are coalitions of scientists and policymakers—usually transnational in scope—who share a common understanding of the nature of the problem and the appropriate solution and who make a concerted effort to inject their point of view into the process of regime formation. Most of those who emphasize the role of such communities have made relatively modest claims. For instance, they have generally avoided assertions to the effect that an active epistemic community is either necessary or sufficient to the achievement of regime formation. Rather, they are normally content to assert that such communities regularly constitute an important presence in cases of success.

What are we to make of these arguments? Although they clearly direct our attention to the independent role of ideas, they have shortcomings that limit their value to those endeavoring to account for successes and failures in the process of regime formation. There are, to begin with, problems in testing both the idea of consensual knowledge and the concept of epistemic communities. It is hard to determine when knowledge becomes consensual and whether an epistemic community is present in some fashion that is independent of the outcome of the process itself. There is thus a constant danger of falling into the trap of post hoc reasoning, finding evidence of consensual knowledge in cases of success in regime formation and failing to locate epistemic communities in cases of failure. Studies in which a

---

[50] Richard N. Cooper, "International Cooperation in Public Health as a Prologue to Macroeconomic Cooperation," in Cooper et al., *Can Nations Agree? Issues in International Economic Cooperation* (Washington, D.C.: Brookings Institutions, 1989), 178–254.

[51] Peter M. Haas, ed., *Knowledge, Power, and International Policy Coordination,* a special issue of *International Organization* 46 (Winter 1992).

concerted effort has been made to overcome these problems of operationalization, moreover, have not produced convincing evidence of the importance of these cognitive factors. Thus it is easy to identify cases in which regimes have formed without the benefit of consensual knowledge or the presence of an epistemic community.[52]

This observation suggests several additional concerns regarding this stream of analysis. Many of the cognitivists pay scant attention to the politics of knowledge. Although it may be true, as Ernst Haas has argued forcefully, that knowledge is power under some conditions, it is equally true that those in possession of power in the material sense can and often do exercise great influence over decisions about what scientists and other scholars study and what conclusions they draw from their work.[53] Those who have examined actual cases of regime formation have been impressed also by the efforts of the parties to manipulate information and knowledge to advance their cause in the context of institutional bargaining.[54] None of this is to suggest that ideas do not have an independent role to play in the creation of international regimes or governance systems. But it would be naive to think of this as a one-way relationship. In the typical case, the important task is to understand the interactions between the efforts of those with knowledge to define the problem at issue and, therefore, the contours of the bargaining process and the efforts of parties to the bargaining process to exploit ideas to advance their own interests.

As these comments suggest, another drawback of this stream of analysis is that it lacks a clear picture of the bargaining process through which the provisions of international regimes are ultimately hammered out among the participants.[55] Without denying that ideas matter, there is no escaping the fact that the process through which parties converge toward a mutually agreeable constitutional contract is dominated by hard bargaining among those who have a clear sense of both the nature of the problem and their own interests. There is a sense, on this account, in which the independent role of ideas tapers off as the process of regime formation moves into the negotiation

[52] Young and Osherenko, eds., *Polar Politics.*

[53] Haas, *When Knowledge Is Power.*

[54] For a discussion of the sociology of scientific knowledge see S. Jasanoff, "Pluralism and Convergence in International Science Policy," in International Institute of Applied Systems Analysis, *Science and Sustainability: Selected Papers on IIASA's 20th Anniversary* (Laxenburg: IIASA, 1992), chap. 5.

[55] James K. Sebenius, "Challenging Conventional Explanations of International Cooperation: Negotiation Analysis and the Case of Epistemic Communities," *International Organization* 46 (Winter 1992), 323–365.

stage. In the case of climate change, for instance, it seems clear that
the Intergovernmental Panel on Climate Change has been influential
in bringing ideas to bear as a means of defining the scope and nature
of the problem. But it is equally clear that the IPCC has not been a
major force in the bargaining process unfolding under the auspices of
the Intergovernmental Negotiating Committee from February 1991
onward.

These observations license two additional inferences that may offer
leads for those interested in moving ahead with cognitivist analyses of
regime formation. It may well be that the independent force of ideas
is greater during the prenegotiation stage than it is during the negotiation stage of regime formation. Whether a problem is construed as
achieving maximum sustainable yield from the harvest of a single
species or of managing whole ecosystems in a balanced fashion, for
example, is largely determined by the conceptual lenses through
which the problem is seen. In hard bargaining over the specific provisions of a convention or treaty, however, ideas are more likely to be
exploited for political advantage than to play an independent role in
guiding the process. A case can also be made for the proposition that
ideas are more important as a determinant of the process of regime
formation in some issue areas than in others. In areas such as climate
change in which our scientific understanding of the problem is
changing rapidly, for example, the role of ideas may loom larger than
in areas in which the nature of the problem is well-known. Curiously,
this proposition is hard to square with the argument about consensual
knowledge presented earlier. But this merely reinforces the conclusion that we have a long way to go in developing useful cognitive
models of the regime formation process.

AN ALTERNATIVE MODEL: INSTITUTIONAL BARGAINING

There is no denying that each of these streams of analysis directs
our attention to important features of the process of regime formation. But the principal conclusion I draw from the preceding discussion is that we need an alternative model to arrive at satisfactory
answers to the questions posed at the beginning of this chapter, especially those pertaining to the negotiation stage of the process. In my
judgment, this model should retain an emphasis on bargaining
among self-interested parties seeking to reap joint gains by devising

institutional arrangements to avoid or overcome collective-action problems. But it should, at the same time, depart in several fundamental ways from the mainstream utilitarian accounts of the bargaining process. In this section, I spell out the defining characteristics of such a model of institutional bargaining and draw on environmental cases to illustrate how it applies to real-world conditions.

Multiple Actors and Consensus Rules

Although there may be disagreement (and sometimes even hard bargaining) regarding the identity of the actors that participate in specific cases, efforts to devise international regimes generally involve several autonomous parties. There may be only a handful, such as the four states that negotiated the fur seal regime, or a modest number, such as the sixteen parties to the regime for Antarctic marine living resources or the twenty-seven parties to the 1987 protocol to the ozone depletion convention. In extreme cases, more than 150 states may be involved, as in the efforts to work out a deep seabed mining regime in the context of the law of the sea negotiations. Though it would certainly be helpful in analytic terms, it is seldom feasible to collapse the resultant negotiations into two-sided bargaining processes by grouping the players into two coalitions or blocs. Hence analytic constructs closely tied to a two-party view of the world, like the Edgeworth box, cannot carry us far in coming to terms with the politics of international regime formation.[56]

Equally important, the multilateral interactions involved in regime formation do not lend themselves well to analysis in terms of the usual game-theoretic treatments of n-party situations which center on the identification of winning coalitions coupled with efforts to single out those coalitions that are most likely to form.[57] Unlike the situation prevailing in most municipal legislatures, efforts to form international regimes generally focus on the formulation of arrangements acceptable to as many of those engaged in the negotiations as possible. This is tantamount to saying that institutional bargaining in international society operates on the basis of a consensus rule in contrast to a majoritarian rule or some other decision rule justifying a focus on the

[56] In principle, we can think of an Edgeworth box in n-space. But such a construct would not be analytically tractable.

[57] For a classic account of the principal constructs of n-person game theory, see Luce and Raiffa, *Games and Decisions*.

development of winning coalitions.[58] Those negotiating the terms of international regimes may seek to exclude parties deemed likely to object to any reasonable institutional arrangements or threaten to go forward with particular arrangements regardless of the opposition of one or more parties. Such concerns may account, for example, for the resistance that members of the Antarctic club have displayed toward proposals to shift negotiations regarding Antarctica into the arena of the United Nations, and they may well underlie some of the problems that have arisen in efforts to devise workable regimes for deep seabed mining or the use of the electromagnetic spectrum.[59] Yet once the membership of the relevant group is set, negotiations regarding international governance systems generally revolve around efforts to come up with arrangements that all participants can accept.

Mixed-Motive Bargaining

The resultant negotiations are saved from certain failure because regime formation in international society typically provides considerable scope for integrative (or productive) bargaining in contrast to distributive (or positional) bargaining.[60] As Richard Walton and Robert McKersie observed in their early and influential discussion of bargaining, the key to this distinction lies in the presence or absence of a fixed, unchanging, and generally acknowledged contract curve or negotiation set.[61] Negotiators who know the locus of a contract curve or the shape of a welfare frontier to begin with will be motivated primarily by a desire to achieve an outcome on this curve or frontier that is as favorable to their own interests as possible. They will, therefore, turn to calculations regarding strategic behaviors or committal tactics that may help them achieve their distributive goals.[62]

Negotiators who do not start with a common understanding of the

---

[58] Of course, this does not rule out an array of devices, including threats, promises, and side payments, that are aimed at inducing parties to accept particular institutional arrangements. For an account that emphasizes the attractions of unanimity or consensus rules, see Buchanan and Tullock, *Calculus of Consent*.

[59] On the case of Antarctica, see Lee Kimball, "Antarctica: Testing the Great Experiment," *Environment* 27 (September 1985), 14–17, 26–30.

[60] The term *productive bargaining* is from Cross, *Economics of Bargaining*. The term *positional bargaining* is from Roger Fisher and William Ury, *Getting to Yes* (Harmondsworth, Eng.: Penguin, 1981).

[61] Richard Walton and Robert B. McKersie, *A Behavioral Theory of Labor Negotiations* (New York; McGraw-Hill, 1965), chaps. 2–5.

[62] For a classic account of such tactics, see Schelling, *Strategy of Conflict*.

contours of the contract curve or the locus of the negotiation set, by contrast, have strong incentives to engage in exploratory interactions to identify opportunities for devising mutually beneficial deals. Such negotiators may never discover the actual shape of the contract curve or locus of the negotiation set, and they may consequently end up with arrangements that are Pareto-inferior in the sense that they leave feasible joint gains on the table.[63] At the same time, however, they are less likely to engage in negotiations that bog down into protracted stalemates brought about by efforts to improve the outcome for one party or another through initiatives involving strategic behavior and committal tactics. Needless to say, this does not eliminate the distributive aspects of bargaining in connection with efforts to form regimes or the role of power in efforts to achieve distributive advantages.[64] But it does provide an important counterweight to the arguments of those, like Thomas Schelling, who have concentrated almost exclusively on distributive issues.[65]

The Veil of Uncertainty

Another factor serving to mitigate the threat of stalemate in interactions governed by consensus rules is what James Buchanan has described as the veil of uncertainty. It is not that those negotiating the terms of international regimes ordinarily lack information about their own identity or roles in society, as John Rawls supposes in explicating his concept of the veil of ignorance as a constraint on the behavior of those negotiating social contracts under conditions approximating what he calls the original position.[66] The point is, rather, that institutional arrangements, unlike specific or self-contained deals, typically apply across a wide range of contexts and over a more or less extended period of time. And, to use the formulation of James Buchanan and his colleague Geoffrey Brennan, "As both the generality and the permanence of rules are increased, the individual who

[63] The result is a collective analogue to Simon's notion of "satisficing" with regard to individual decision making. See James G. March and Herbert A. Simon, *Organizations* (New York: Wiley, 1958), esp. chap. 3.3.

[64] Stephen D. Krasner, "Global Communications and National Power: Life on the Pareto Frontier," *World Politics* 43 (April 1991), 336–366.

[65] Consider the comment in Schelling, *Strategy of Conflict*, 21, to the effect that "we shall be concerned with what might be called the 'distributional' aspect of bargaining: the situations in which a better bargain for one means less for the other."

[66] John Rawls, *A Theory of Justice* (Cambridge, Mass.: Harvard University Press, 1971), esp. 136–142.

faces choice alternatives becomes more uncertain about the effects of alternatives on his own position."[67] This "good" uncertainty actually facilitates efforts to reach agreement on the substantive provisions of institutional arrangements. As Brennan and Buchanan observe, in a discussion directed toward municipal institutions, "to the extent that a person faced with constitutional choice remains uncertain as to what his position will be under separate choice options, he will tend to agree on arrangements that might be called 'fair' in the sense that patterns of outcomes generated under such arrangements will be broadly acceptable, regardless of where the participant might be located in such outcomes."[68]

Surely this observation applies with equal force to the behavior of collective entities such as nation-states that dominates negotiations regarding the content of international governance systems. This line of analysis undoubtedly helps to explain why collections of actors have reached agreement regarding the provisions of arrangements governing such matters as whaling, the pollution of the Mediterranean Basin, and some of the problems associated with the transboundary flow of radioactive fallout. It also helps us understand the obstacles that must be overcome by those working to devise mutually acceptable arrangements dealing with acid precipitation, biological diversity, or climate change. Put simply, the key players are likely to find it easier to see through the veil of uncertainty in these cases than in some of the other areas referred to in this discussion.

Problems and Approaches

Faced with the prospect of mixed-motive bargaining under a veil of uncertainty, the parties endeavoring to form international regimes seldom, if ever, make a sustained effort to perfect their information regarding the full range of outcomes or the exact dimensions of contract zones before getting down to serious bargaining. Instead, they typically zero in on a few key problems, articulate several approaches to the treatment of these problems, and seek to reconcile differences among these approaches in the course of their negotiations. In the case of deep seabed mining, for instance, the problems included matters such as the role of the Enterprise in the conduct of mining operations, production controls in the hands of the International Seabed

---

[67] Brennan and Buchanan, *Reason of Rules*, 29–30.
[68] Ibid., 30.

Authority, and technology transfer.[69] Those negotiating the regime for Antarctic marine living resources focused on the problem of whether to adopt a whole ecosystems approach, as advocated by the United States, or some approach emphasizing the pursuit of maximum sustainable yields on a species-by-species basis, as advocated by some other participants.[70] Similarly, the negotiations that eventually led to the 1987 protocol on the protection of the ozone layer centered, for a time, on the relative merits of emphasizing a comprehensive ban on aerosols or of mandating an across-the-board cut in the production of chlorofluorocarbons.[71]

There is no guarantee, of course, that the parties can reconcile divergent approaches to such problems, although it helps to be dealing with several differentiable concerns so that trades can be devised among those who feel more or less intensely about individual problems and approaches. But when progress is made in reconciling divergent approaches to relatively well-defined problems, the parties typically begin to formulate a negotiating text and to use this device to structure their ongoing efforts to develop the deals required to reach agreement on the terms of a regime.[72] Such a text can serve both to organize the negotiations involved in regime formation, as in the case of the various negotiating texts used in the law of the sea negotiations, and to provide a basis to guide the expansion or extension of a regime over time, as in the cases of the negotiation of several subsequent protocols to the 1976 convention on pollution control in the Mediterranean Basin and of the 1987 protocol and the 1990 amendments to the 1985 convention on ozone depletion.[73]

Transnational Alliances

As many observers have pointed out, negotiations pertaining to the formation of international governance systems commonly involve extensive intraparty bargaining, which often occurs simultaneously with the relevant interparty bargaining.[74] There is nothing surprising

[69] For a straightforward descriptive account, see Soroos, *Beyond Sovereignty*, chap. 8.

[70] Lyster, *International Wildlife Law*, chap. 9.

[71] For helpful background on this case, see Allan S. Miller and Irving M. Mintzer, "The Sky Is the Limit: Strategies for Protecting the Ozone Layer," *Research Report*, no. 3 (Washington, D.C.: World Resources Institute, 1986).

[72] For an account rooted in an analysis of the law of the sea negotiations, see Friedheim, *Negotiating the New Ocean Regime*.

[73] For additional comments on the role of negotiating texts, see Raiffa, *Art and Science of Negotiation*.

[74] Putnam, "Diplomacy and Domestic Politics."

about this situation when we consider that states are complex collective entities encompassing numerous groups whose interests often differ widely with respect to any given issue area. The about-face of the United States regarding the law of the sea convention, for example, is surely attributable more to the advent of an administration more attuned to the concerns of big business than its predecessor than to any objective change in the national interests of the United States. Internal splits between industrialists and environmentalists are common in connection with most pollution-control arrangements. And members of the European Community experienced relatively sharp internal conflicts in negotiating the regime to protect stratospheric ozone.

What is interesting in connection with this discussion of institutional bargaining, however, is the potential that situations of this kind generate for the development of transnational alliances among interest groups supporting the formation of specific international regimes. An extensive network of scientific supporters located in all the Mediterranean Basin states played an important role in bringing pressure to bear on hesitant governments to support the pollution-control regime for the Mediterranean.[75] The transnational environmental community played a central, perhaps dominant, role in pushing through the regime governing international trade in endangered species. And the transnational scientific and environmental communities have often joined forces in efforts to develop and defend effective regimes for Antarctica.[76] In some cases, these efforts are facilitated by organizations that serve to aggregate and articulate the concerns of transnational interest groups regarding international regimes. For example, the IUCN clearly played a critical role in devising the regime governing trade in endangered species[77] The Scientific Committee on Antarctic Research (SCAR), together with its parent organization, the International Council of Scientific Unions, has been instrumental in the development of the governance system for Antarctica.[78] And it is intriguing to consider the remarkable role of

[75] Peter M. Haas, *Saving the Mediterranean: The Politics of International Environmental Protection* (New York: Columbia University Press, 1990).

[76] This cooperation has resulted, among other things, in the development of the Antarctic and Southern Ocean Coalition, a nongovernmental organization that has exercised considerable influence on negotiations relating to Antarctica.

[77] Kosloff and Trexler, "Convention on International Trade in Endangered Species."

[78] Polar Research Board, *Antarctic Treaty System: An Assessment* (Washington, D.C.: National Academy Press, 1986).

UNEP in the negotiations leading to the 1985 convention and the 1987 protocol regarding the protection of stratospheric ozone. I am not suggesting that states no longer dominate bargaining in international society, but it would be a serious mistake to overlook the role of transnational alliances among influential interest groups in developing and maintaining governance systems at the international level.[79]

Shifting Involvements

Whereas the vision of negotiation incorporated in the mainstream utilitarian models emphasizes self-contained interactions, institutional bargaining in the formation of international governance systems almost always features a rich array of linkages to other events occurring in the socioeconomic or political environment.[80] Sometimes these linkages pose more or less serious problems for those seeking to establish institutional arrangements at the international level.[81] Parties may deliberately drag their feet in hopes that their bargaining strength will increase with the passage of time. Individual participants may knowingly complicate the negotiations by linking several issues in such a way as to necessitate the development of complex bargains over an array of problems. Players may become so preoccupied with domestic matters, such as protracted election campaigns or serious civil strife, that they are not in a position to pursue institutional bargaining at the international level vigorously. Or they may simply choose to emphasize other issue areas for the time being in recognition of their limited capacity to engage in international negotiations. The history of efforts to form regimes governing deep seabed mining, satellite broadcasting, and the trade in endangered species offers a rich array of examples of such problems.

In some cases, however, linkages work in favor of efforts to form international regimes. Those concerned about possible erosions of bargaining strength in the future may be willing to make significant concessions to reach agreement quickly on the terms of specific regimes. Linking together disparate issues sometimes opens up possibilities for mutually acceptable arrangements by creating oppor-

[79] The recent work of Peter Haas and his colleagues on the role of epistemic communities in regime formation is suggestive in this context.
[80] See also Fred Charles Iklé, *How Nations Negotiate* (New York: Harper & Row, 1964).
[81] For an accessible account of these problems as well as techniques for coping with them, see I. William Zartman and Maureen R. Berman, *The Practical Negotiator* (New Haven: Yale University Press, 1982).

tunities for the international equivalent of logrolling and the formulation of package deals.[82] Those possessing insufficient capacity to handle numerous issues simultaneously may be willing to leave much of the negotiating about the terms of certain regimes to nongovernmental actors who are part of a transnational network and who have developed a considerable ability to work together in the course of prior interactions. The package deals incorporated in the 1982 law of the sea convention and the role of nongovernmental experts in devising the regimes covering polar bears and trade in endangered species certainly illustrate these possibilities. The conclusion to be drawn from this discussion, therefore, is not that these linkages necessarily make it difficult to form international regimes but, rather, that those involved in processes of regime formation must remain alert at all times to connections of this sort. The natural tendency to become preoccupied with the technical aspects of the specific subject at hand can easily lead to failure in negotiations involving regime formation, which are highly sensitive to occurrences in the broader socio-economic or political environment.

DETERMINANTS OF SUCCESS:
HYPOTHESES ABOUT INSTITUTIONAL BARGAINING

The record clearly shows that institutional bargaining does result in the formation of new international governance systems under some conditions. Some recent examples are the development of institutional arrangements pertaining to the protection of stratospheric ozone, Antarctic environmental matters, and the transboundary movement of hazardous wastes. Yet success in such endeavors is far from ensured. Like self-interested actors in all social arenas, those attempting to work out the terms of international regimes are often stymied by impediments to bargaining that prolong negotiations over institutional arrangements and that can easily end in deadlock. It is not surprising, for instance, that the negotiations over a regime for deep seabed mining took so long and yielded such an ambiguous outcome. Nor is it hard to understand why interested parties have found it difficult to agree on substantive arrangements to protect the biological diversity

[82] Sebenius, "Negotiation Arithmetic."

of the earth's ecosphere or to cope with the global climate change expected to result from the emission of greenhouse gases.[83]

The next task, then, is to make use of the model of institutional bargaining to pinpoint the determinants of success and failure in efforts to form institutional arrangements in international society. In this section, I initiate this process by deriving some hypotheses about factors governing the likelihood of success in efforts to form international regimes and applying these hypotheses, in a preliminary way, to regimes for natural resources and the environment. Needless to say, this initial analysis is not sufficient to constitute a test of any of the hypotheses. Even so, it should trigger a line of analysis that could well result in the formulation of more satisfactory answers to the questions with which this chapter began.

Institutional bargaining can succeed only when the issues at stake lend themselves to treatment in a contractarian mode. Those engaged in efforts to form international governance systems will be motivated to approach the process as a problem-solving exercise aimed at reaching agreement on the terms of a social contract to the extent that the absence of a fully specified zone of agreement encourages integrative bargaining and the presence of imperfect information ensures that a veil of uncertainty prevails. In situations governed by consensus rules, a contractarian environment of this sort is necessary to avoid the positional deadlocks that commonly arise in connection with distributive bargaining. It is therefore critical to observe that collective-action problems in international society of the sort engendering an interest in devising arrangements to institutionalize cooperation vary in the degree to which they lend themselves to treatment in contractarian terms. In addition, those involved in efforts to form international governance systems often differ markedly in the skill they display in presenting problems of regime formation in contractarian terms.

To see the relevance of this factor to the success of institutional bargaining, consider, to begin with, some extreme cases. It is exceedingly difficult, for instance, to portray the problem of controlling acid precipitation in North America in contractarian terms both because

---

[83] For a variety of perspectives on global climate change, see the essays in Titus, ed., *Effects of Changes in Stratospheric Ozone;* and Irving M. Mintzer, "A Matter of Degrees: The Potential for Controlling the Greenhouse Effect," *Research Report*, no. 5 (Washington, D.C.: World Resources Institute, 1987).

the producers of the relevant emissions and the victims of acid deposition are so clearly identified and because there is not much overlap in the membership of the two groups.[84] The problem of controlling transboundary radioactive fallout resulting from nuclear accidents, by contrast, is comparatively easy to treat in contractarian terms.[85] Although a good deal is known about the dangers of radioactive fallout, individual members of international society ordinarily cannot know in advance whether they will occupy the role of site of an accident, victim state, or unharmed bystander with respect to specific accidents. This is exactly the sort of situation that gives rise to incentives to consider the common good in devising institutional arrangements.

Although they are less extreme, other cases add to our understanding of the importance of this proposition about the significance of contractarianism. There are substantial differences, for example, between the problems of ozone depletion and global climate change that affect the extent to which they lend themselves to formulation in contractarian terms. Although the impact may vary somewhat on the basis of latitude, human populations in every part of the world would be harmed if the depletion of stratospheric ozone were to continue at its present rate.[86] In the case of global warming, by contrast, there will almost certainly be winners and losers who are comparatively easy to differentiate.[87] Significant increases in sea level will cause severe damage to certain low-lying coastal areas (for example, one-half to two-thirds of Bangladesh could be submerged) while bestowing benefits on other regions. Global warming is expected to make some areas increasingly hospitable to large-scale agriculture, even as other areas lose their current role in agricultural production. And the impact of these differences on processes of regime formation is heightened because the sources of greenhouse gas emissions are numerous and widely dispersed, whereas the producers of CFCs are few in number and located in a relatively small number of states. Hence it is no cause

[84] The fact that some countries, such as the Federal Republic of Germany, are both major producers of acid precipitation and important victims of this form of pollution makes the problem of devising a regime to control acid precipitation more tractable in Europe than it is in North America.

[85] Oran R. Young, *International Cooperation: Building Regimes for Natural Resources and the Environment* (Ithaca: Cornell University Press, 1989), chap. 6.

[86] See also the projections in Miller and Mintzer, "Sky Is the Limit."

[87] For some interesting projections regarding this point, see E. F. Roots, "The Cost of Inaction: An Example from Climate Change Studies," unpublished paper, 1988.

for surprise that a substantial international regime designed to protect the ozone layer is now in place, whereas a regime to deal with global climate change is still in the initial phase of development.

The availability of arrangements that all participants can accept as equitable is necessary for institutional bargaining to succeed. Economists and others who approach the issue of regime formation in utilitarian terms generally place primary emphasis on the achievement of allocative efficiency in discussing the formation of new institutions as well as in evaluating the performance of existing arrangements.[88] Such analysts are apt to be highly critical of arrangements that encourage misallocations of scarce resources or that seem likely to produce outcomes lying inside the relevant welfare frontier. To be more concrete, they find much to criticize in arrangements allocating some of the choicest deep seabed mining sites to the Enterprise, imposing across-the-board percentage cuts on the production of CFCs by current producers, or reserving at least one orbital slot for each state that may become interested in satellite broadcasting.[89]

Yet those who negotiate the terms of international regimes seldom focus on these questions of allocative efficiency. In a negotiating environment featuring a consensus rule, they must occupy themselves, for the most part, with considerations of equity on the understanding that institutional bargaining in international society can succeed only when all the major parties and interest groups come away with a sense that their primary concerns have been treated fairly. Allocative efficiency is an abstract concept; no one can determine whether the outcomes flowing from a given regime are in fact efficient until much later. And even then, economists often disagree vigorously in their assessments of the efficiency of observable outcomes. Equity, by contrast, is an immediate concern that evokes strong feelings on all sides. To return to the previous examples, no reasonable observer could have expected the less developed countries participating in the law of

[88] For a helpful introduction to the principal approaches to the concept of efficiency, see Robert Dorfman and Nancy S. Dorfman, eds., *The Economics of the Environment*, 2d ed. (New York: Norton, 1977), 1–37. For an explicit assertion regarding the appropriateness of emphasizing efficiency in this context, see Ross D. Eckert, "Exploitation of Deep Ocean Minerals: Regulatory Mechanisms and United States Policy," *Journal of Law and Economics* 17 (April 1974), 143–177.

[89] See Daniel J. Dudek, "Chlorofluorocarbon Policy: Choice and Consequences," paper distributed by the Environmental Defense Fund, April 1987; and Gregory C. Staple, "The New World Satellite Order: A Report from Geneva," *American Journal of International Law* 80 (July 1986), 699–720.

the sea negotiations to accept an arrangement that explicitly excluded the Enterprise from mining operations, thereby ensuring that a few highly industrialized states would dominate this commercial activity. There is a sense of fairness that everyone can relate to in across-the-board percentage cuts, which is hard to match in more complex arrangements featuring charges or transferable emissions permits.[90] And it is surely easy to understand why the less developed countries regard as unjust any system that would allocate orbital slots on a first-come, first-served basis. Although it is important to recognize that there are no objective standards of equity which can be applied to human affairs, identifiable community standards regarding equity do exist in specific social settings. There is much to be said for the proposition that satisfying these standards is a necessary condition for international regime formation, whatever outside observers may think of the long-term consequences of the resultant arrangements with respect to allocative efficiency.

The identification of salient solutions (or focal points) describable in simple terms increases the probability of success in institutional bargaining. Those endeavoring to craft statutes in municipal legislatures sometimes construct, for tactical reasons, formulas that are so complex or obscure that interest groups actually or potentially opposed to the relevant provisions have difficulty comprehending what is being put to a vote. No doubt, such tactics can prove useful in the efforts to form winning coalitions that dominate legislative bargaining. For the most part, by contrast, salience based on simplicity and clarity contributes to success in institutional bargaining involving numerous parties operating under consensus rules.[91] The idea of a simple ban or prohibition on pelagic sealing, for example, was a key factor in the success of the negotiations that produced the original regime for the conservation of northern fur seals in 1911. In a more contemporary setting, the salience of the formula of across-the-board percentage cuts in the production and consumption of CFCs certainly played a role in the successful effort to reach agreement on the 1987 protocol regarding ozone depletion. The fact that early warning procedures are markedly simpler to administer than provisions covering compensa-

[90] On the distinctions among these policy instruments, see Dudek, "Chlorofluorocarbon Policy."
[91] For a seminal account of salience in facilitating the convergence of expectations in such settings, see Schelling, *Strategy of Conflict*, chap. 4.

tion for damages surely has much to do with the ease of achieving agreement on the early notification convention of 1986 as well as with the failure to incorporate compensation provisions into the two 1986 conventions relating to nuclear accidents.[92]

Conversely, it is hard to avoid the conclusion that the complexity of arrangements encompassing permits or licenses, production controls, technology transfers, the role of the Enterprise, and so forth bedeviled the effort to negotiate a regime for the deep seabed (known as the Area) in the law of the sea negotiations and played a significant role in accounting for the ambiguity of the final outcome. Similar problems plague ongoing efforts to reach agreement on the provisions of the emerging regime relating to global climate change. The power of salience can become a serious constraint on efforts to devise appropriate institutional arrangements; it constitutes a barrier to the introduction of some clever and attractive devices that students of institutional design have proposed to handle collective-action problems.[93] But this in no way detracts from the role of salience as a determinant of success in the formation of governance systems in international society.

The probability of success in institutional bargaining rises when clear-cut and reliable compliance mechanisms are available. It is common knowledge among those who study collective-action problems that negotiators can fail to reach agreement on arrangements that would yield benefits for all parties concerned because they do not trust each other to comply with the terms of the arrangements once they are established.[94] This situation places a premium on the development of rules that are transparent in the sense that compliance with their requirements is easy to verify, as in the case of cuts in the production of CFCs by a small number of easily identified producers.[95] It also accounts for the attraction of arrangements that are comparatively easy to police, such as the licensing system for deep seabed mining contem-

[92] For an excellent account of the prior legal developments leading to these conventions, see Phillipe J. Sands, *Chernobyl: Law and Communication* (Cambridge, Eng.: Grotius Publications, 1988).

[93] For a discussion of some of these devices in connection with the problem of ozone depletion, see Dudek, "Chlorofluorocarbon Policy."

[94] See also Schelling, *Strategy of Conflict;* and Robert Axelrod, *The Evolution of Cooperation* (New York: Basic Books, 1984).

[95] Konrad von Moltke, "Memorandum on International Chlorofluorocarbon Controls and Free Trade," paper distributed by the Institute for European Environmental Policy, 1987.

plated under the regime for the Area. Presumably, some such reasoning played a role, as well, in the decision to orient the regime for endangered species toward the regulation of international trade in contrast to the control of habitat destruction within individual nations. Although trade restrictions are hard enough to verify and police, it is not easy even to imagine how to implement a regime requiring that individual members take effective steps to control the forces causing habitat destruction within their jurisdictions. Similar problems will undoubtedly afflict the ongoing effort to develop a workable regime to protect biological diversity.

At the same time, the lack of well-entrenched and properly financed supranational organizations in international society ensures that international governance systems must rely heavily on the ability and willingness of individual members to elicit compliance with key provisions within their own jurisdictions.[96] A problem that has dogged the regime for endangered species, for example, is the sheer lack of capacity or inability of many states to control the activities of poachers and others involved in the illegal trade in furs, skins, and animal parts within their jurisdictions.[97] By contrast, under the fur seal regime, any harvest of seals was either closely regulated or actually carried out by state agencies, thereby enabling municipal governments to exercise effective control over the relevant activities whenever they chose to do so.[98] It is thus easy to understand why regime formation in international society is most likely to succeed when the participants can rely on relatively simple, nonintrusive compliance mechanisms that municipal governments can operate without undue effort or the need to expend scarce political capital. The 1987 protocol on ozone depletion, which has a remarkably straightforward formula coupled with an explicit delegation of implementation authority to individual participants, offers a clear illustration of this proposition.

Exogenous shocks or crises increase the probability of success in efforts to negotiate the terms of governance systems. Even in negotiations that allow considerable scope for integrative bargaining under a veil of uncer-

---

[96] For a more general discussion of compliance in decentralized social settings, see Oran R. Young, *Compliance and Public Authority: A Theory with International Applications* (Baltimore: Johns Hopkins University Press, 1979).

[97] Kosloff and Trexler, "Convention on International Trade in Endangered Species."

[98] Young, *Natural Resources and the State,* chap. 3.

tainty, institutional bargaining exhibits a natural tendency to bog down into a sparring match in which participants jockey for positional advantages and lose track of their common interest in solving the relevant collective-action problems. All too often, the net result is failure to reach agreement regarding feasible arrangements that would prove mutually beneficial. Therefore, it will come as no surprise that shocks or crises exogenous to the bargaining process frequently play a significant role in breaking these logjams and propelling the parties toward agreement on the terms of institutional arrangements. The precipitous decline in the northern fur seal population in the early years of this century and the extraordinary drop in blue whale stocks in the 1930s clearly played major roles in inducing the relevant parties to drop their bargaining ploys so as to reach agreement on the provisions of regulatory regimes before it was too late.[99] It is hard to overstate the shock value of the 1986 Chernobyl accident in motivating the parties to come to terms on at least some of the provisions of a regime for nuclear accidents within six months of this dramatic event.[100] And the 1985 discovery and subsequent publicization of an ozone hole over Antarctica became a driving force behind the efforts that produced the 1987 protocol on stratospheric ozone and subsequent amendments, even though ozone depletion over Antarctica is not an immediate threat to major centers of human population.[101]

When these cases are compared with the problem of global climate change, a good case can be made for the proposition that the disruptive impacts of nuclear accidents and ozone depletion are likely to pale by comparison with the consequences of the global warming trend over the next century.[102] To date, however, we have not experienced an exogenous shock or crisis in this realm that can compare with the Chernobyl accident or the ozone hole in capturing and galvanizing the attention of policymakers and broader publics alike. Talk of a creeping crisis with regard to global warming simply cannot produce the impact of the exogenous shocks mentioned previously as

[99] On the case of the blue whale, see George L. Small, *The Blue Whale* (New York: Columbia University Press, 1971).

[100] Stuart Diamond, "Chernobyl Causing Big Revisions in Global Nuclear Power Policies," *New York Times*, 27 October 1986, A1 and A10.

[101] Shabecoff, "Ozone Agreement."

[102] In November 1988, for example, a broad coalition of American environmental groups designated the global warming trend as the most serious environmental threat of the foreseeable future.

a force in breaking the logjams that commonly arise in institutional bargaining. This is no doubt frustrating to those working on many important collective-action problems. It is hard to contrive credible crises, and there is no reason to suppose that the occurrence of exogenous shocks will correlate well with the ultimate importance of the problems at hand. Nevertheless, exogenous shocks or crises play a powerful role in determining success in efforts to build governance systems in international society.[103]

Institutional bargaining cannot succeed in the absence of effective entrepreneurial leadership on the part of individuals. I come back, in the end, to the role of leadership in determining outcomes arising from institutional bargaining in international society. It is no exaggeration to say that efforts to negotiate the terms of international regimes are apt to succeed when one or more individuals emerge as effective leaders and that in the absence of such leadership, they will fail. Those engaged in institutional bargaining must strive to invent options capable of solving major problems in a straightforward fashion and to fashion deals that are acceptable to all. To the extent that the participants have incentives to engage in integrative bargaining, a veil of uncertainty prevails, and linkages among problems allow for logrolling, the task of those negotiating the terms of international regimes will be made easier. But such considerations cannot eliminate the crucial role of entrepreneurship at the international level.

Entrepreneurial leaders in institutional bargaining are neither representatives of hegemons who can impose their will on others nor ethically motivated actors who seek to fashion workable institutional arrangements as contributions to the common good or the supply of public goods in international society. Rather, international entrepreneurs are participants who are skilled in inventing new institutional arrangements and brokering the overlapping interests of parties concerned with a particular issue area.[104] Such leaders are surely self-interested in the sense that they seek gains for themselves in the form

---

[103] The effects of exogenous shocks or crises on the maintenance of existing regimes may differ from their effects on the formation of regimes. It is widely believed, for example, that the refusal of the United States to ratify a 1984 protocol extending the life of the fur seal regime was the result of a sharp decline in the northern fur seal population during the 1980s and the belief of many American advocates of animal rights that the regime was inadequate to cope with this problem.

[104] For a theoretical discussion of political entrepreneurship see Norman Frohlich, Joe A. Oppenheimer, and Oran R. Young, *Political Leadership and Collective Goods* (Princeton: Princeton University Press, 1971).

of material rewards or enhanced reputations, but this in no way detracts from the role they play. There is, in fact, much that is reassuring in the observation that leaders are motivated to engage in entrepreneurial activities out of a durable sense of self-interest rather than more fleeting considerations of ethical behavior or altruism.[105]

The preceding discussion suggests also that representatives of intergovernmental and nongovernmental organizations can become leaders in efforts to form international regimes. The role of those associated with the Comité Spécial de l'Année Geophysique Internationale in establishing SCAR in 1958 and, through SCAR, in forming the regime for Antarctica in 1959 is comparatively well-known. The parts played by those representing IUCN in promoting the regimes governing trade in endangered species and conservation of polar bears are also impressive examples of success in entrepreneurial leadership. A particularly striking case is the remarkable achievement of Mostafa Tolba, UNEP's executive director, in shepherding the negotiations regarding the protection of stratospheric ozone to a successful conclusion.[106] Of course, this does not mean that representatives of states cannot assume leadership roles in negotiating international regimes. The activities of American negotiators in connection with the 1987 protocol on ozone, of French negotiators in the case of Mediterranean pollution control, and of representatives of several developing countries in the context of deep seabed mining deserve mention in this connection, to name just a few examples.

CONCLUSION

The analytic perspectives currently dominating the study of regime formation in international society not only clash with one another but are also incapable of capturing some of the essential features of the process involved in the formation of international governance systems. The mainstream utilitarians fail to attach sufficient weight to an array of factors that can block the efforts of utility-maximizing actors to realize feasible joint gains. Moreover, they base their accounts of regime formation on models of bargaining that are fundamentally inappropriate, even though their analytic tractability is appealing.

[105] For a somewhat similar account, see Anthony Downs, *An Economy Theory of Democracy* (New York: Harper & Row, 1957), chap. 15.

[106] Similar comments are probably in order regarding the role of Hans Blix, the executive director of the International Atomic Energy Agency, in promoting the 1986 conventions relating to nuclear accidents.

The power theorists overemphasize the role of dominant actors or hegemons in the formation of institutional arrangements at the international level. This is just as well, however, because true hegemons are the exception rather than the rule in international society. For their part, the cognitivists have not developed a model of the process through which social learning leads to convergence around mutually agreeable provisions of international regimes. They are often insensitive to the manipulation of knowledge by politically motivated actors as well.

What is needed now to provide a satisfactory account of the process of regime formation and, especially, of the negotiation stage of this process is a model of institutional bargaining that takes into account the essential features of international society, including those that distinguish this social setting from the situation prevailing in domestic societies. The central section of this chapter, which sketches the defining characteristics of such a model of institutional bargaining, emphasizes the significance of multiple actors, consensus rules, integrative bargaining, the veil of uncertainty, problem-solving activities, transnational alliances, and shifting involvements.

Institutional bargaining does yield successful outcomes in some efforts to reach agreement on the terms of international governance systems. But it certainly offers no guarantee of success in this realm. On the contrary, ventures in institutional bargaining that fail to result in the formation of new international regimes are just as common as those that succeed. Accordingly, the final substantive section of the chapter initiates the process of deriving hypotheses about the determinants of success and failure in institutional bargaining in international society. It points both to the role of structural considerations, such as the extent to which collective-action problems lend themselves to contractarian formulations, and to process considerations, such as the degree to which the participants can devise arrangements that meet the principal equity demands of all parties concerned. Because the separate perspectives of the power theorists, the mainstream utilitarians, and the cognitivists have dominated prior thinking in this realm, our understanding of institutional bargaining in international society currently leaves much to be desired. To the extent that the argument set forth in this chapter in convincing, then, it should be apparent that we need to devote much more attention in the future to exploring the nature of institutional bargaining.

CHAPTER FIVE

Bargaining Leverage versus Structural Power in the Formation of Governance Systems

A parsimonious, intuitively appealing, and deeply entrenched line of thought among students of international relations has it that the course of institutional bargaining in international society is shaped in large measure by the distribution of power among the participants in the bargaining process. On this account, those in possession of superior power can and generally do call the shots in hammering out the terms of constitutional contracts establishing governance systems or regimes intended to guide the interactions of states in specific issue areas. By extension, the restructuring of existing institutions occurs in response to shifts in the distribution of power at the international level.

Is this line of analysis compelling? If so, how can we explain cases such as the bargaining over the deep seabed mining provisions of the 1982 Convention on the Law of the Sea or the interactive process eventuating in the collapse of the 1988 Convention on the Regulation of Antarctic Mineral Resource Activities, in which acknowledged great powers—the United States in the law of the sea case and the United States and Great Britain in the Antarctic minerals case—are unable to prevail on others to accept their preferred arrangements? And what are we to make of cases such as the negotiations that produced the 1990 London Amendments to the 1987 Montreal Protocol on Substances That Deplete the Ozone Layer or the 1991 Environment Protocol to the Antarctic Treaty, in which others are able to pressure a great power—the United States again—into accepting provisions it initially opposes?

In this chapter, I endeavor to answer these questions by focusing on what has come to be known as structural power and exploring the distinction between power understood in these material terms and bargaining leverage. The picture of international negotiations that emerges from this analysis certainly does not exclude a role for structural power. But it does show that structural power is only one determinant of the outcomes of institutional bargaining in international society, a conclusion implying that simple efforts to equate outcomes with the prevailing distribution of structural power can never yield more than partial explanations of observable events and that such efforts are apt to prove dangerously misleading when treated as guides for policymakers and diplomats.

CIRCULAR REASONING IN THE ANALYSIS OF POWER

It is remarkably easy to fall prey to circular reasoning in thinking about the role of power in institutional bargaining. To put it bluntly, analysts—including many who should know better—frequently begin by asking whose preferences fare best in the outcomes emerging from the bargaining process and then infer that those who do well must be the most powerful participants in the process. Unfortunately, this line of thinking is faulty. So long as outcomes serve as indicators of the distribution of power among parties engaged in bargaining processes, power cannot explain or predict the outcomes that occur. Any effort to construct arguments about the role of power in determining the outcomes of bargaining processes must begin with an independent definition of power and then proceed to formulate testable propositions concerning the links between power so defined and observable outcomes.

Kenneth Waltz, together with a group of analysts who call themselves neorealists and who focus on the concept of structural power,[1] define structural power as the possession of or control over material resources, thereby making power a function of the distribution of empirically measurable capabilities. As Robert Keohane puts it in his widely read discussion of hegemony, power is associated with "control over raw materials, control over sources of capital, control over mar-

[1] See Kenneth Waltz, *Theory of World Politics* (Reading, Mass.: Addison-Wesley, 1979; and Robert O. Keohane, ed., *Neorealism and Its Critics* (New York: Columbia University Press, 1986).

kets, and competitive advantages in the production of highly valued goods."[2] In an equally well-known rendering, Susan Strange broadens this list by asserting that the sources of structural power include "control over security; control over production; control over credit; and control over knowledge, beliefs and ideas."[3]

Welcome as these efforts to escape the trap of circular reasoning are, they are not without problems. First, there is an absence of intersubjective agreement among those who have contributed to the development of the idea of structural power. The disparity between the lists of elements proposed by Keohane and Strange, both prominent contributors to this line of thought, illustrates this point. Second, there is a lack of clarity about the form of the relationship among the elements of structural power. Is the weight of each element the same? Are we expected to resort to a simple process of addition in aggregating them to gain some understanding of the overall configuration of power in international society? Is there room for substitutability in the sense that an actor with little control over security, for example, can make up for this lack by achieving exceptional control over productive processes, capital flows, or markets? These problems are further compounded by the emphasis of those who analyze structural power on the idea of exercising *control* over raw materials, capital flows, markets, modes of production, and so forth. Who really controls the hydrocarbons of the Middle East? To what extent are national governments able to exercise effective control over international capital flows? To put it mildly, these are contentious issues.

Two additional concerns add to the difficulties confronting those endeavoring to use the concept of structural power to avoid the trap of circular reasoning in thinking about institutional bargaining: the problem of relativity and the problem of fungibility. In most structuralist arguments, it is the amount of power an actor possesses relative to the power of others (in contrast to its absolute level of power) that counts. But this means we must confront the difficult task of constructing an index or indices of power that work for all actors involved in institutional bargaining in order to be able to deploy structuralist arguments to good effect. The problem of fungibility, by contrast, has to do with the extent to which power, like money, can be

[2] Robert O. Keohane, *After Hegemony: Cooperation and Discord in the World Political Economy* (Princeton: Princeton University Press, 1984), 32.
[3] Susan Strange, *States and Markets: An Introduction to International Political Economy* (New York: Basil Blackwell, 1988), 26.

used in dealing with any issue area or, alternatively, is confined to specific issues. As David Baldwin argued some years ago, power and money may well be quite different in these terms.[4] More recently, scholars have talked about issue-specific hegemony, a term that suggests the power of states may vary substantially from one issue area to another. Yet the realist and neorealist formulations offered by leading scholars like Strange and Keohane do not suggest how structural power can be treated in this way. It may make sense to think of a capacity to control some markets but not others. But it is not readily apparent what this segmentation would mean with regard to control over capital flows or security.

These problems are severe enough without considering the difficulties that would confront anyone seeking to operationalize the concept of structural power for purposes of empirical analysis. Still, this way of thinking does offer a way to circumvent the circularity trap. Even if we are able to measure structural power only in a rough-and-ready fashion, it should be possible to use this approach to begin evaluating the argument that those in possession of power call the shots in bargaining over the terms of constitutional contracts. We can, for instance, ask how the United States fared in institutional bargaining during the last four or five decades and whether the record of its actual achievements conforms to the expectations engendered by those who frame their analyses in terms of structural power. The remainder of this chapter tackles this task in a preliminary fashion; the contributions of many others will be needed before we can arrive at fully satisfactory answers to the questions posed at the outset.

SOURCES OF BARGAINING LEVERAGE

The processes that dominate institutional bargaining in international society differ in several ways from those envisioned in mainstream models of bargaining. Most important, multilateral negotiations aimed at hammering out or revising the terms of constitutional contracts ordinarily proceed on the basis of a consensus rule (in contrast to a majoritarian rule) and unfold in an environment in which information regarding the content of the contract zone (or the locus of the welfare frontier) is limited.[5] This means that actors participat-

---

[4] David A. Baldwin, *Paradoxes of Power* (New York: Basil Blackwell, 1989), chap. 2.

[5] In the theory of games and related theoretical work, the contours of the payoff space are generally taken as given at the outset, and analyses of n-person interactions

ing in institutional bargaining experience strong incentives both to forge coalitions of the whole around generally agreeable negotiating texts and to value the integrative as opposed to the distributive aspects of bargaining.

Success in these interactive processes depends on a range of factors other than the distribution of material resources among the participants. In this section, I identify some of these factors and illustrate their operation through references to contemporary international negotiations. The concluding section then returns to the idea of structural power and explores the interplay between power of this type and what I call bargaining leverage in accounting for the results arising from specific instances of institutional bargaining in international society.

Constitutive Principles

Though subject to continuous social change that may eventually alter its defining characteristics, international society consists of states organized around a distinctive set of constitutive principles that define the nature of that society and guide interactions among its members.[6] The member states are territorially based units that are juridically equal; each of them can appeal to the principle of sovereignty as a barrier to intervention in its domestic affairs in the name of collective goals or values. The rules that lend character to specific international governance systems or regimes do not become binding on individual states unless and until these actors accept them as binding through some process of ratification or through participation in a well-defined pattern of usage.[7] Yet once these rules are accepted as binding, the doctrine of *pacta sunt servanda* enjoins participants to

---

center on the identification of winning coalitions. For an early but still seminal account see R. Duncan Luce and Howard Raiffa, *Games and Decisions* (New York: Wiley, 1957).

[6] For an interesting effort to trace the evolution of these constitutive principles over the last several centuries see Dorothy V. Jones, *Code of Peace: Ethics and Security in the World of Warlord States* (Chicago: University of Chicago Press, 1991). On the idea that these rules are important determinants of the identity and interests of the members of international society see Alexander Wendt, "Anarchy is What States Make of It: The Social Construction of Power Politics," *International Organization* 46 (Spring 1992), 391–425.

[7] For sophisticated accounts of the operation of rules in international society consult Friedrich V. Kratochwil, *Rules, Norms, and Decisions: On the Preconditions of Practical and Legal Reasoning in International Relations and Domestic Affairs* (Cambridge, Eng.: Cambridge University Press, 1989); and Nicholas Greenwood Onuf, *World of Our Making: Rules and Rule in Social Theory and International Relations* (Columbia: University of South Carolina Press, 1989).

honor commitments and comply with the requirements of the rules in their dealings with one another. Although it is accurate to describe international society as anarchical in the sense that it lacks a central government, therefore, it is certainly not the case that this society is anarchical in the sense that it lacks an extensive and widely acknowledged system of rules guiding relations among its members.[8]

These constitutive principles leave ample room for efforts to bring structural power to bear in institutional bargaining, but they limit what even the most powerful actors can achieve in such settings. Institutional arrangements that explicitly grant some members more weight in decision-making processes than others, for example, are the exception rather than the rule in international society. Even in cases in which such arrangements have been established (for example, the voting rules of the International Monetary Fund [IMF] and the World Bank), disadvantaged members are seldom content to accept such provisions indefinitely; they can be counted on to fight hard against proposals envisioning any extension of these arrangements to new activities or issue areas. The resistance of the developing countries to the idea of relying on the Global Environment Facility—an entity sponsored by the United Nations Environment Programme, the United Nations Development Programme (UNDP), and the World Bank but administered largely by the bank—as the principal funding mechanism for a climate regime and other governance systems pertaining to large-scale environmental issues illustrates this proposition. Similarly, the members of international society invariably put up stout resistance to any institutional arrangements that might curtail their authority over matters unfolding within their own jurisdiction. This "sovereignty sensitivity" is particularly pronounced at the present time among developing states such as Brazil and Malaysia that oppose efforts to interfere in their domestic affairs in the name of preserving biological diversity.[9] Though these constraints are not always insurmountable, any great power that tried to ignore them in the context of institutional bargaining would be asking for trouble.

[8] Hedley Bull, *The Anarchical Society: A Study of Order in World Politics* (New York: Columbia University Press, 1977); and James N. Rosenau and Ernst-Otto Czempiel, eds., *Governance without Government: Order and Change in World Politics* (Cambridge, Eng.: Cambridge University Press, 1992).

[9] Ken Conca, "Environmental Protection, International Norms, and National Sovereignty: The Case of the Brazilian Amazon," paper prepared for the conference on International Intervention, State Sovereignty, and the Future of International Society, Dartmouth College, Hanover, N.H., May 1992.

Negotiation Arithmetic

Institutional bargaining does not occur in a vacuum; it is a stage in a process whose earlier phases, often extending over a period of years, involve issue definition and agenda formation.[10] There is nothing predetermined about the way most issues are framed for purposes of institutional bargaining, the extent to which individual issues are joined together in the negotiating process, and the identity of the actors involved in the process.[11] Negotiations dealing with the Antarctic Treaty System, for example, have been treated as a self-contained process involving (at least initially) a small number of participants, whereas negotiations dealing with deep seabed mining have been far more inclusive both in the issues covered and in the actors involved. Though the effort to protect great whales as endangered species is the business of the international whaling regime, similar measures covering a host of other species (including a number of cetaceans) are handled under the terms of the more comprehensive regime for endangered species set forth in the provisions of the Convention on International Trade in Endangered Species of Fauna and Flora (CITES). And most attempts to protect endangered species at the international level have separated the problems of regulating consumptive use and preserving critical habitats, which has led to unfortunate consequences that have become increasingly apparent with the passage of time.

Agenda formation and the choice of actors to participate are seldom neutral matters in institutional bargaining. It is no accident, for instance, that the Antarctic Treaty Consultative Parties vigorously oppose United Nations involvement in Antarctic affairs or that the former Soviet Union long sought to limit the participation of outsiders in negotiations pertaining to international cooperation in the Arctic. But I want to stress here that even those in possession of abundant sources of structural power often have difficulty controlling the formation of the agenda and the identification of participants in the formation of international regimes. Sometimes this is a consequence of the impact of recent experiences on the thinking of key

[10] For a discussion of these earlier phases characterized as prenegotiation see Janice Gross Stein, ed., *Getting to the Table: The Processes of International Prenegotiation* (Baltimore: Johns Hopkins University Press, 1989).
[11] For an account that introduces the concept of negotiation arithmetic in analyzing these issues see James K. Sebenius, "Negotiation Arithmetic: Adding and Subtracting Issues and Parties," *International Organization* 37 (Spring 1983), 281–316.

decision makers, as in the disenchantment with comprehensive approaches in the aftermath of the latest round of law of the sea negotiations and the pervasive assumption that the development of a climate regime should follow the framework convention/protocol model exemplified by the widely admired effort to form a regime to protect the ozone layer.[12] In some cases, great powers find themselves stuck with procedures that enable the United Nations General Assembly to assert the authority to make decisions about issues and actors in the context of institutional bargaining; the 1990 decision to create the Intergovernmental Negotiating Committee on Climate Change rather than allowing the negotiations to proceed under the auspices of the United Nations Environment Programme is a recent case in point.[13] In still other cases, the real problem is for influential actors to find ways to persuade reluctant states to join in processes of regime formation; the efforts of leading powers to devise incentives for developing countries such as Brazil, China, and India to participate actively in the ozone regime illustrate this phenomenon.

The Force of Ideas

Ideas and power are closely related. As realists have long observed, those in possession of material resources (especially wealth) are often able to exert a profound influence over the way people think about public affairs. Conversely, as Ernst Haas has reminded us in a recent effort to counter the thrust of the realist argument, in many instances knowledge becomes a source of power.[14] But the main point in this discussion is that ideas regularly acquire a life of their own which actors cannot control, regardless of the sources of structural power at their disposal. Sometimes ideas exert pressure to accept a comprehensive system of thought, even when there are good reasons to believe that such a move will have adverse consequences for the interests of influential groups in society. Something of this sort appears to be happening today with regard to the vision of human-environment relations embedded in rapidly evolving ideas about global environ-

[12] James K. Sebenius, "Designing Negotiations toward a New Regime: The Case of Global Warming," *International Security* 15 (Spring 1991), 110–148.

[13] Oran R. Young, "Negotiating an International Climate Regime: Institutional Bargaining for Environmental Governance Systems," in Nazli Choucri, ed., *Global Commons: Environmental Challenges and International Responses* (Cambridge, Mass.: MIT Press, 1993), 431–452.

[14] Ernst B. Haas, *When Knowledge Is Power: Three Models of Change in International Organizations* (Berkeley: University of California Press, 1990).

mental change, despite the arguments of economists and others to the effect that the case for action in this realm is far from overwhelming.[15] Perhaps we are witnessing, in this context, the emergence of a new form of Gramscian hegemony.[16]

More modestly, a compelling case can be made for the proposition that specific sets of ideas influence processes of regime formation, quite apart from any calculations of their consequences for the interests of individual participants. The rise of the scientific management movement in the early part of this century, with its emphasis on the achievement of maximum sustainable yields from the consumptive use of living resources, for instance, played a formative role in the development of international regimes for fur seals and whales as well as a wide range of international fisheries. And there is an equally persuasive case for the proposition that the ecosystems thinking which has supplanted the concern for achieving maximum sustainable yields from individual species over the last several decades has begun to exert a powerful influence on the outcomes of institutional bargaining. There is no other way to explain cases such as the recently adopted Protocol on Environmental Protection to the Antarctic Treaty in which great powers have to be pressured into accepting the terms of environmental governance systems. Equally interesting in this context are clashes that take the form of confrontations between divergent systems of thought, like the battle over the future of the whaling regime, which pits supporters of sustainable yields as a guide to consumptive use, against opponents of all consumptive use, who present arguments based on ecosystems thinking.

Internal Dissensus

It will come as no surprise that actors possessing great structural power are sometimes unable to exercise much influence on the course of institutional bargaining because they are crippled by a lack of consensus among their own policymakers regarding the issues at stake. As Charles Kindleberger has argued persuasively in his influential work on the Great Depression, great powers—the United States in this instance—may fail to provide structural leadership on specific

---

[15] For an articulate expression of the economist's perspective see Thomas C. Schelling, "Some Economics of Global Warming," *American Economic Review* 82 (March 1992), 1–14.

[16] Robert W. Cox, "Gramsci, Hegemony and International Relations: An Essay in Method," *Millennium, Journal of International Studies* 12 (Summer 1983), 162–175.

institutional issues because of sharp disagreements in domestic forums about the proper way to approach these issues.[17] A striking
contemporary case involves the failure of American leadership in the
ongoing climate negotiations. Although the United States possesses
great structural power in this realm, it became the odd man out in
efforts to hammer out the terms of the 1992 Convention on Climate
Change because an internal debate over this issue limited the ability of
American negotiators to play a constructive role in shaping the
emerging consensus about the actions required to deal with climate
change (for example, an agreement to reduce carbon dioxide emissions on an accepted timetable).

In other cases, the ability of great powers to influence the course of
institutional bargaining is limited because those negotiating on their
behalf cannot promise that the deals they work out in international
negotiations will survive domestic battles over the ratification of conventions or treaties setting forth the terms of constitutional contracts
and over implementing legislation once the agreements are ratified.
Again, the United States is a prime example.[18] The U.S. Senate refused to ratify the Covenant of the League of Nations in 1920, the
Charter of the International Trade Organization in 1949–1950, and
the protocol extending the international regime for fur seals in 1984
even though incumbent administrations strongly recommended that
all three of these arrangements be ratified. In some cases (for instance, the SALT II agreement of 1979), the administration has re-
frained from submitting an agreement to the Senate because it realized that a costly political defeat might well ensue. American
negotiators are occasionally able to turn such problems into a source
of bargaining leverage in international negotiations, arguing that others must make important concessions to avoid defeat of an agreement
by the Senate. Nonetheless, it is hard to escape the conclusion that
internal dissensus often limits the capacity of an actor to bring structural power to bear in the processes of institutional bargaining.

Integrative Bargaining

There is a deeply ingrained tendency to assume, as Stephen
Krasner has aptly put it, that international negotiations are generally

[17] Charles P. Kindleberger, *The World in Depression, 1929–1939* (Berkeley: University
of California Press, 1973).
[18] See Louis Henkin, *Constitutionalism, Democracy, and Foreign Affairs* (New York: Columbia University Press, 1990), chap. 3.

about "life on the Pareto frontier," that is, the distribution of fixed payoffs as opposed to the production of expanded benefits.[19] Partly, this belief is testimony to the impact of realist thinking about international relations on the perspectives of those whose careers spanned World War II and the ensuing Cold War. In part, it is a consequence of the intellectual attractions of the ideas about bargaining tactics articulated by Thomas Schelling and others during the 1950s and 1960s.[20] Although Schelling has carefully noted that his analysis is limited to the distributive aspects of bargaining, this nuance seems to have escaped many of his readers.[21] Thus it is not surprising that many students of international relations simply assume that structural power is a key determinant of the outcomes of institutional bargaining.

Yet a study of actual cases of regime (re)formation does not lend much support to this way of thinking. It is seldom possible to identify the locus of the Pareto (or welfare) frontier in situations involving institutional bargaining because so many factors are operating, including the complexity of the issues at stake, the role of what James Buchanan calls the veil of uncertainty, and the skill of leaders in inventing new options that influence the thinking of those engaged in bargaining.[22] In fact, those endeavoring to work out the terms of new institutions, such as the ozone regime or the transboundary air pollution regime, seldom devote much attention to efforts to pinpoint the Pareto frontier. None of this disposes of the problem of distributive bargaining in the formation of international regimes. As the ongoing efforts to develop a climate regime clearly indicate, real conflicts of interest are common in such processes. Nonetheless, institutional bargaining almost always involves a major element of integrative bargaining in contrast to distributive bargaining.[23] Structural power is not irrelevant to integrative bargaining; it can, for example, provide great powers with the wherewithal to offer lesser powers attractive side payments in return for their participation in emerging governance

[19] Stephen D. Krasner, "Global Communications and National Power: Life on the Pareto Frontier," *World Politics* 43 (April 1991), 336–366.

[20] The seminal account is Thomas C. Schelling, *The Strategy of Conflict* (Cambridge, Mass.: Harvard University Press, 1960).

[21] See ibid., 21.

[22] On the veil of uncertainty see Geoffrey Brennan and James M. Buchanan, *The Reason of Rules: Constitutional Political Economy* (Cambridge, Eng.: Cambridge University Press, 1984), chap. 2.

[23] For an early account of integrative bargaining that remains a classic see Richard E. Walton and Robert B. McKersie, *A Behavioral Theory of Labor Negotiations: An Analysis of a Social Interaction System* (New York: McGraw-Hill, 1965), chaps. 4–5.

systems. Even so, there can be no doubt that structural power is less critical as a source of bargaining leverage in negotiations featuring a sizable element of integrative as opposed to distributive bargaining.

Strategic Position

Even when distributive bargaining is the order of the day, those possessing abundant supplies of structural power are not always able to impose their will on others in the formation of institutional arrangements. One important reason for this failure involves the bargaining leverage that stems from what we may characterize as strategic position. Several familiar examples from the world of domestic politics illustrate this phenomenon. Thus, electoral systems featuring proportional representation frequently accord disproportionate leverage to small swing parties whose support is needed by larger parties to form a parliamentary majority. Similarly, systems of private property rights often allow owners of small parcels of land or real property to drive hard bargains when their parcels are needed for a major development to go forward. Of course, players possessing sufficient structural power may be able to overcome such problems by offering attractive side payments and, if all else fails, by altering the rules of the game. But the existence of these options does not diminish the importance of strategic position in a wide range of bargaining situations.

Strategic position can also play a role in offsetting structural power in institutional bargaining at the international level. For example, upstream parties, such as the Sudan in the case of the Nile River Basin, are often able to drive hard bargains with downstream parties—Egypt in this case—in devising cooperative management systems for transnational river basins because they can threaten to divert or withhold water.[24] Actors possessing jurisdiction over critical habitat for migratory species, such as a number of African states in the case of migratory waterfowl, are frequently able to exert considerable influence even when others (in this case, a variety of European

---

[24] For accounts that deal with efforts to develop cooperative management systems for a number of international river basins see Genady N. Golubev, "Availability and Quality of Fresh-Water Resources: Perspective from the North," paper prepared for a conference on Global Environmental Change and International Governance held at Dartmouth College in June 1991; and Robert Mandel, "Sources of International River Basin Disputes," paper prepared for presentation at the 1991 annual meeting of the International Studies Association.

states) possess far more structural power. A state that occupies a key position with respect to a particularly important natural resource, such as Saudi Arabia in the case of oil, may be able to exercise an effective veto over international institutions affecting that resource, even though it has little structural power in any other realm. These cases do not make structural power irrelevant to institutional bargaining, yet they do underline the dangers of simply assuming that those in possession of structural power can call the shots when negotiating the terms of constitutional contracts in international society.

Bargaining Skill

As students of distributive bargaining from Thomas Schelling onward have regularly pointed out, bargaining skill can be just as important as the possession of structural power in achieving preferred outcomes in interactions of a competitive/cooperative or mixed-motive character.[25] In essence, this is because all participants in such interactions would rather strike a bargain than settle for no agreement, and they all know this. We are all familiar with the role of committal tactics and the uses of brinkmanship in situations of this sort. Even an actor that is relatively weak in structural power, such as Australia in the case of the Antarctic minerals convention, can achieve striking success when it is able to stake out a clear-cut position and convince others that it is willing to go to any lengths in defense of that position. And the role of bargaining skill is even more striking when it involves efforts to convince others to accept an individual actor's characterization of the issue at stake. The role of small but affluent countries such as Norway and the other Nordic states in joining together an array of economic and environmental issues to form a broadly based agenda centered on the idea of sustainable development constitutes a tour de force in these terms.[26]

If anything, the role of bargaining skill, in contrast to the deployment of structural power, becomes even more prominent in situations involving a substantial element of integrative bargaining. Without doubt, the possession of structural power can be useful to those en-

[25] Schelling, *Strategy of Conflict*, esp. chap. 2.

[26] These efforts are clearly reflected in the work of the World Commission on Environment and Development (known also as the Brundtland Commission). For an extended discussion of sustainable development see the report of the Commission, *Our Common Future* (New York: Oxford University Press, 1987).

gaged in integrative activities. It can allow powerful actors such as the United States to put together effective deals by offering sizable side payments in such forms as the fund set up under the 1990 London Amendments to the Montreal Protocol to help developing countries avoid becoming dependent on the use of ozone-depleting chemicals. Yet integrative bargaining places a premium on the inventiveness required to devise creative institutional arrangements and the entrepreneurial skills needed to sell others on the virtues of such arrangements. These qualities do not correlate well with the possession of structural power. In fact, they often involve the talents of individuals who become leaders in processes of regime formation in contrast to the resources available to states. The remarkable achievements of individuals such as Tommy Koh in guiding the law of the sea negotiations, Janos Stanovnik in forming the regime, for long-range transboundary air pollution, and Mostafa Tolba in developing the ozone regime provide evidence of the dangers of placing too much weight on the role of structural power in processes of regime formation at the international level.[27]

The Dangers of Becoming a Bully

An examination of actual cases of institutional bargaining makes it clear that it is dangerous to flaunt structural power, if not to use it subtly, in negotiations over the provisions of constitutional contracts. As every successful negotiator knows, there is nothing worse than being perceived by others as a bully or a bull in a china shop in dealings with those negotiating on behalf of actors possessing less structural power. The United States has often been accused of being an international bully, especially in its dealings with developing countries over proposals for the restructuring of institutional arrangements such as the various elements of the New International Economic Order. But there have also been cases in which American negotiators have avoided this danger in the pursuit of international regimes. Curtis Bohlen, as chief American negotiator, adroitly side-

[27] For a general account of the role of leadership in the formation of international regimes see Oran R. Young, "Political Leadership and Regime Formation: On the Development of Institutions in International Society," *International Organization* 45 (Summer 1991), 280–308. A detailed account of Tommy Koh's role in the law of the sea negotiations appears in Lance N. Antrim and James K. Sebenius, "Formal Individual Mediation and the Negotiators' Dilemma: Tommy Koh at the Law of the Sea Conference," forthcoming.

stepped this problem in the final stages of the negotiations that produced the 1973 Agreement on the Conservation of Polar Bears.[28] And Richard Benedick, who served as chief American negotiator during the negotiations leading to the 1987 Montreal Protocol on ozone-depletion and who has written a thoughtful account of these negotiations, was careful to emphasize his own commitment to amicable problem solving, even when the U.S. Congress was threatening the Europeans with import restrictions on ozone-depleting chemicals as a means of pressuring them to accede to the American position.[29]

Negotiators for great powers use a variety of procedural devices to avoid the appearance of acting as a bully without giving up influence over the course of institutional bargaining. Representatives of lesser powers are often selected to chair negotiations aimed at forming international regimes. Tommy Koh of Singapore in the extended law of the sea negotiations and Winfried Lang of Austria in the negotiations leading to the Vienna Convention and the Montreal Protocol on ozone depletion are prominent cases in point.[30] Similarly, negotiating sessions are often held on neutral territory (for example, Geneva in the case of the climate change negotiations) or on the territory of lesser powers that are particularly important to the issues at stake for one reason or another (for example, Oslo in the polar bear case, Wellington in the case of Antarctic minerals, and Nairobi in the case of climate change). Somewhat more subtle is the tactic of persuading one or more of the lesser powers to carry substantive proposals in order to avoid the sense that they are being crammed down the throats of others by one or another of the great powers. It appears that some such logic was involved in the prominent roles of several smaller states in the negotiations conducted during the course of the Third United Nations Conference on the Law of the Sea and of the Seychelles in efforts to reform the whaling regime during the 1980s.[31]

---

[28] See Anne Fikkan, Gail Osherenko, and Alexander Arikainen, "Polar Bears: The Importance of Simplicity," in Oran R. Young and Gail Osherenko, eds., *Polar Politics: Creating International Environmental Regimes* (Ithaca: Cornell University Press, 1993), chap. 4.

[29] Richard Elliot Benedick, *Ozone Diplomacy: New Directions in Safeguarding the Planet* (Cambridge, Mass.: Harvard University Press, 1991).

[30] For Lang's own reflections on these negotiations see Winfried Lang, "Negotiations on the Environment," in Victor A. Kremenyuk, ed., *International Negotiation: Analysis, Approaches, Issues* (San Francisco: Jossey-Bass, 1991), 343–356.

[31] For a sophisticated account of the bargaining process in the law of the sea negotiations consult Robert L. Friedheim, *Negotiating the New Ocean Regime* (Columbia: Univer-

The Strength of Weakness

Many observers have noted that structural weakness can actually become a source of bargaining leverage in international negotiations.[32] In extreme cases, a weak actor can use the threat to collapse as a functioning entity as a means of demanding favorable treatment at the hands of other states. A recent example is the successful efforts of Russian negotiators to gain admission for their country to international economic regimes such as the International Monetary Fund and to garner financial aid from the Organization for Economic Cooperation and Development (OECD) countries and the World Bank. Even more common are arguments centered on the capacity of individual states to implement the provisions of constitutional contracts within their own jurisdictions. The developing countries, for example, have made good use of such arguments in negotiations dealing with their participation in international arrangements intended to protect the ozone layer. Some of them, like China and India, have succeeded in extracting concessions regarding implementation schedules as well as provisions for additional financial aid and technological assistance in return for agreeing to forgo major increases in their production and consumption of ozone-depleting chemicals.

To be effective, efforts to exploit the strength of weakness must be coupled with a favorable strategic position; it helps as well if weak actors can occupy high moral ground. Those in possession of material resources may simply walk away from negotiations without making any real concessions so long as they can ignore the demands of weak states without serious consequences for themselves, as happened in the negotiations over the NIEO.[33] As the demands of the developing countries became more strident, the advanced industrial states began to realize that they could dismiss these demands without serious consequences, and the negotiations trailed off without achieving any significant agreements regarding new or revised institutions.

This failure contrasts with cases such as the ongoing efforts to develop international regimes to limit climate change and to protect

---

sity of South Carolina Press, 1993). And on the current confrontation arising from efforts to reform the whaling regime see Friedheim, "Crisis in the International Whaling Commission: Can It Be Resolved?" discussion paper prepared for the 1992 annual meeting of the Western Regional Science Association.

[32] For an early but clear expression of this insight see Schelling, *Strategy of Conflict*.

[33] For an account that focuses on international trade in commodities see Jock A. Finlayson and Mark W. Zacher, *Managing International Markets: Developing Countries and the Commodity Trade Regime* (New York: Columbia University Press, 1988).

biological diversity. On these issues, some of the weak states occupy strategic positions that give them real bargaining leverage. An agreement to curtail emissions of greenhouse gases that does not include China and India cannot succeed; an arrangement to protect biological diversity that does not evoke positive responses in Brazil, Indonesia, and Malaysia would be a hollow shell. In the case of climate change, moreover, there is no escaping the moral implications of the fact that the advanced industrial states are the primary sources of the problem and therefore the chief culprits. Despite their structural weakness, Brazil, China, and India are well aware of their bargaining leverage; they can be expected to make the most of it in continuing institutional bargaining pertaining to climate change and biological diversity.

Equity and Ownership

Those who emphasize the role of power in international affairs are apt to dismiss considerations of equity as normative concerns that have little bearing on the course of events. In institutional bargaining, however, there are good reasons for participants to take a genuine interest in matters of equity, even if they possess abundant sources of structural power. Partly, this is became institutional bargaining at the international level—unlike legislative bargaining in most domestic arenas—proceeds under a consensus rule. Such bargaining can succeed only when it yields contractual formulas acceptable to all the relevant parties or coalitions of parties. Of course, those with structural power may be able to buy acquiescence from others by providing them with compensation. This is exactly what happened in the case of ozone and what must happen if the continuing climate change negotiations are to produce an effective governance system. But such arrangements already constitute a move in the direction of equity in the sense that they involve a departure from the image of great powers simply calling the shots without any concern for the interests of others.

Even more important in this connection, most of the provisions of international regimes require implementation on an ongoing basis within the domestic jurisdictions of the member states. Actors can and do accept international obligations to curb transboundary air pollution, reduce the consumption of ozone-depleting chemicals, or control emissions of carbon dioxide, but they must take individual steps to apply the resultant rules within their territories or to their nationals operating abroad. The crucial point is that it is virtually impossible to achieve high levels of implementation and compliance over time through coercion. Those who believe that they have been treated fairly and that their core demands have been addressed will voluntarily endeavor to make regimes work. Those who lack any sense of ownership regarding the arrangements because they have been pressured into pro forma participation, on the other hand, can be counted on to drag their feet in fulfilling the requirements of governance systems. It follows that even great powers have a stake in the development of international institutions that meet reasonable standards of equity. In this context, a striking virtue of the evolving regime for the protection of the ozone layer is that it reflects a real effort to accommodate the needs of a variety of constituencies. The bitterness surrounding ongoing efforts to reform the whaling regime, by contrast, surely is owing in part to the belief of important constituencies that they are being shortchanged or treated unfairly.

THE INTERPLAY OF BARGAINING LEVERAGE AND STRUCTURAL POWER

I have gone to considerable lengths to demonstrate that structural power does not translate automatically into bargaining leverage in interactions centered on the development of constitutional contracts laying out the rules of the game for issue-specific international regimes. Actors with little structural power sometimes turn in striking performances in such negotiations. By the same token, those in possession of considerable structural power are sometimes miserable failures as participants in processes of institutional bargaining. There are even cases in which the possession of structural power is counterproductive because it leads others to react to the powerful actor as a bully.

Certainly it would be a mistake to carry this line of reasoning too far. There is an important link between the possession of structural power and the achievement of bargaining leverage in a wide range of situations; any effort to deny this truth would lead to serious distortions in our understanding of regime (re)formation in international society. Even so, this link is not nearly as straightforward or direct as it is commonly made out to be by the realists and those neorealists who seek to explain collective outcomes as reflecting the configuration of structural power among the participants. Some concrete examples will illustrate this observation along with the proposition that structural power and other sources of bargaining leverage regularly interact with each other in complex ways in actual negotiations over the terms of constitutional contracts establishing international governance systems.

In the typical case, the ability of actors to bring structural power to bear effectively on processes of institutional bargaining is critically dependent on strategic position. During the negotiations leading to the 1987 Montreal Protocol, for instance, the United States was able to exploit structural power by threatening to restrict imports of ozone-depleting chemicals from European states but only because American producers, which were not significant exporters of the chemicals at the time, were not vulnerable to retaliation. Similarly, the United States was able to bring effective pressure to bear on Japan in the process of reaching the recent agreement to ban mid-ocean drift-nets because it could exploit asymmetries in the fishing and fish products industries of the two countries allowing American policymakers to make credible threats to restrict both imports of Japanese fish products and Japanese access to fisheries under American jurisdiction under the terms of the Pelly and Packwood Amendments. But similar threats have not proven successful in efforts to gain the acquiescence of Iceland, a country with little structural power, to changes in the international whaling regime designed to limit and in some cases to eliminate the consumptive use of whales. Not only is Iceland largely invulnerable to the threats envisioned under the terms of the Pelly and Packwood Amendments, but the United States has long been concerned to avoid fanning the flames of domestic opposition within Iceland to the arrangements governing American use of the air base at Keflavik.[34]

These comments suggest two additional observations about the interplay of structural power and bargaining leverage in the (re)formation of international institutions. Because governance systems involve ongoing relationships, those in possession of structural power will often find that they can achieve more by using their power to make promises and offer rewards than they can by relying on threats and punishments. Although it may be possible to coerce structurally weak actors into accepting the terms of a constitutional contract in some

[34] It will be of interest to see whether this situation changes with the ending of the Cold War and the declining military significance of the base at Keflavik.

superficial sense, these actors will lack a sense of ownership of or loyalty to the resultant governance system. In the absence of continuing pressure that is costly to maintain, then, the participation of such actors is likely to be halfhearted and their levels of compliance are apt to leave much to be desired. Faced with such problems, those in possession of great structural power will often find that they are well-advised to seek to influence the behavior of others through promises of rewards rather than threats of punishments. That was the reason why the advanced industrial countries agreed to establish a compensation fund under the terms of the ozone regime. And it is precisely the point at issue in the discussions centering on capacity building, additionality, and technology transfers in the context of the continuing negotiations dealing with the development of a climate regime.

This is an appropriate juncture at which to revisit the issue of the transferability or substitutability of the various elements of structural power. To what extent is it possible to substitute one form of structural power for another in the context of institutional bargaining? The answer to this question is far from straightforward. There is little reason to believe that military power has much relevance in the negotiation of the environmental regimes referred to for illustrative purposes in this chapter. It would be implausible for the United States, for example, to make threats involving matters of military security to pressure others into accepting American preferences regarding environmental protection in Antarctica or the loss of biological diversity in Amazonia. Much the same can be said about the control of world trade. The United States was able to make credible threats in efforts to reduce the production of ozone-depleting chemicals and to ban the international trade in elephant ivory because it was a key importer of the relevant products. But there is no basis for assuming that an actor can make headway in specific cases just because it is an important player in world trade in some more general sense. On the other hand, structural power in the form of control over the flow of capital, technologies, and ideas may well prove more transferable from one issue area to another. At a minimum, an actor in possession of these sources of structural power will be able to make side payments that can influence the behavior of others in a variety of situations.

One of the most efficient ways to achieve results with structural power is to use it to gain a reputation for being an effective player in processes of institutional bargaining. Those negotiating on behalf of weaker players often act in anticipation of the moves of a party thought to possess great structural power; they are deferential to the presumed preferences of the great power, even when that actor does little overtly to exercise its structural power in the situation at hand. This phenomenon is observable again and again in the way others have treated the United States in the context of institutional bargaining during the postwar era. Many actors clearly looked to the United States to take the lead in formulating the terms of the whaling regime in the 1940s, the regime for Antarctica in the 1950s, and the regime governing trade in endangered species in the 1970s. Perhaps this pattern helps to explain why many were disturbed when the United States allowed the fur seal regime to lapse in the 1980s. And the apparent failure of American leadership during recent negotiations on climate change constitutes a stunning abandonment of this leadership role in the minds of many. A reputation for being influential can carry an actor far in turning structural power into bargaining leverage, but such a reputation requires careful tending to remain effective.

It is also relevant at this point to draw a distinction between structural power and willpower. Whereas structural power refers to the possession of or control over material resources, willpower is associated with the intensity of an actor's preferences regarding a given issue or issue area. As students of domestic politics have long observed, willpower can be as important a determinant of collective outcomes as structural power. A hegemon can impose outcomes even in areas in which its interests are little affected and its preferences weak. But in more normal circumstances, where the possession of material resources is circumscribed, actors must pick their issues with care and concentrate their efforts on top priorities so that middle or even small powers with overwhelming concerns about particular issues can achieve their goals despite their limited resources. Canada's successful insistence on the inclusion of Article 234 dealing with ice-covered areas in the 1982 Convention on the Law of the Sea constitutes a striking illustration of this phenomenon.[35] The efforts of the Alliance of Small Island States in the climate negotiations constitute even more striking evidence of the importance of willpower in institutional bargaining.

One important inference to be drawn from this discussion is that

[35] See D. M. McRae, "The Negotiation of Article 234," in Franklyn Griffiths, ed., *Politics of the Northwest Passage* (Kingston: McGill-Queen's University Press, 1987), 98–114.

the interplay between structural power and bargaining leverage generates important roles for what I have described elsewhere as structural leaders.[36] The structural leader is one who develops and deploys expertise in translating the structural power of individual actors into influence over negotiations dealing with the terms of constitutional contracts. Curtis Bohlen in the polar bear case and Richard Benedick in the ozone depletion case both played this leadership role with considerable skill. But the important point is that there is nothing automatic about the emergence of the leadership needed to translate structural power into bargaining leverage. There are many cases in which those acting on behalf of actors possessing great structural power have failed to seize opportunities presented to them or bungled their efforts to bring structural power to bear on specific negotiations. Examples include American efforts to restructure the bargain on deep seabed mining during the final phase of the law of the sea negotiations and to gain acceptance of the abortive Antarctic minerals convention. Of course, this realization detracts from the parsimony that is such an attractive feature of the arguments of those who see a simple relationship between power and the outcomes of institutional bargaining. Yet it also opens up a rich vein of analysis for those interested in explaining or predicting the (re)formation of international institutions.

CONCLUSION

Not surprisingly, there is little prospect of arriving at simple answers to the questions posed at the beginning of this chapter. The realists and the neorealists are not entirely off base in their emphasis on the role of structural power. Nonetheless, the inferences to be drawn from this line of thought are incomplete at best and can be downright misleading in many cases. When we define power in a manner that avoids the trap of circular reasoning, it soon becomes apparent that a variety of other factors interact with structural power as determinants of bargaining leverage in negotiations concerning the provisions of constitutional contracts. Even the most powerful actors are constrained by the rules of the game, the force of ideas, the impact of strategic position, and a host of other factors. Like that of

---

[36] Young, "Political Leadership and Regime Formation."

others, their performance will be affected by their ability to achieve internal consensus regarding the issues at stake, to grasp the integrative potential of institutional bargaining, and, above all, to comprehend the interplay of structural power and bargaining leverage in negotiations of this type. Admittedly, future analyses of such processes will be less parsimonious than the arguments the structuralists have advanced; some may find them less intuitively appealing as well. Even so, such analyses offer students of international governance systems not only the prospect of being able to mine a rich vein of insights into the workings of international society but also the means of arriving at results of real value to practitioners engaged in efforts to (re)form institutional arrangements at the international level.

CHAPTER SIX

The Effectiveness of
International Governance Systems

Critical threats to the earth's habitability demand that humankind rise to the challenge of creating new and more effective systems of international environmental governance. These threats are largely anthropogenic in origin and manifest themselves in such forms as desertification, deforestation, ozone depletion, climate change, the loss of biological diversity, disruptions of the global hydrological cycle, and, ultimately, perturbations in coupled atmosphere/ocean/land systems capable of triggering worldwide ecological crises. They have stimulated an unprecedented growth in the demand for governance at the international level. Protecting the stratospheric ozone layer requires sustained cooperation among affluent residents of North America, Europe, and Japan, who must find substitutes for chlorofluorocarbons, and aspiring residents of Brazil, China, India, and other developing countries, who must resist the temptation to increase dramatically their consumption of refrigerants containing these chemicals. Avoiding global warming calls for the development of effective and coordinated emission-control systems to limit the release of greenhouse gases—carbon dioxide, methane, CFCs, nitrous oxide—from a wide range of sources in every corner of the globe. Stemming the loss of biological diversity entails harnessing socioeconomic forces such as international trade and monetary sys-

A somewhat different version of this chapter is slated to appear as Oran R. Young, "Introduction: The Effectiveness of International Governance Systems," in Oran R. Young and George J. Demko, eds., *Global Environmental Change and International Governance*, forthcoming.

tems that transcend national borders, even though the actual losses may be region-specific and closely linked to the destruction of moist tropical forests.

What does it take to develop and maintain effective governance systems to deal with these problems? When we turn from generalities to the specifics of such complex environmental problems as climate change or the loss of biological diversity, the barriers to sustained cooperation seem more substantial than they may appear to be in the simple scenarios often used to illustrate the concepts of interactive decision making and collective action. More often than not, these environmental matters present sharp challenges to those in search of appropriate ways to conceptualize the problem to be solved and of satisfactory methods to address issues of sustainability, social welfare, and equity embedded in them. It is not easy, for example, to devise international regimes that satisfy, at one and the same time, the concerns of those whose aim is to spread the benefits of economic growth—and the material wealth that sometimes goes with it—to the developing world and those who are convinced that sustainable development requires profound changes in the materialistic life-styles of people in both the developed and the developing worlds. Much the same can be said of the difficulties confronting those endeavoring to reconcile emerging northern concerns for relieving pressure on the earth's life support systems and the increasingly insistent southern demands for a restructuring of persistent economic imbalances to meet reasonable standards of equity.

The record shows considerable variation in the effectiveness of environmental governance systems operative at the international level. Some regimes (for example, the Antarctic Treaty System or the evolving ozone regime) have been notable successes, while others (for example, many of the international fisheries regimes) have proven relatively ineffective. Despite the unprecedented scope of some of today's environmental problems, much can be learned about the factors that determine the effectiveness of international governance systems from an examination of actual experience with a variety of environmental regimes. This chapter sets the stage for a systematic study of these determinants of effectiveness by addressing conceptual issues in this realm and exploring the range of variables that require consideration in thinking about effectiveness. A growing number of students of international governance are preparing to take up the challenge of improving our knowledge of this subject.

The Meaning of Effectiveness

What do we mean when we speak of the effectiveness of international regimes or governance systems? Can we devise some simple way to describe and, ideally, to measure variations in levels of institutional effectiveness? What are the prospects for pinpointing factors that, singly or in combination, determine the success or failure of institutional arrangements in international society? Are some of these factors so central that they constitute important, perhaps even necessary, conditions for the achievement of effectiveness across a wide range of places and times? Posed in these general terms, the issue of effectiveness seems straightforward enough. Simply put, we want to find out why some regimes work well, while others have little impact or even become dead letters. Quite apart from the value of such knowledge to those seeking to understand the workings of international society, persuasive answers to this question would be of obvious interest to those responsible for designing and managing governance systems dealing with specific issues.

Effectiveness, it is clear, figures in this line of inquiry mainly as the dependent variable, that is, the phenomenon we seek to account for or to explain. Accordingly, our goal is to observe and measure variations in levels of effectiveness (or in some index of effectiveness) and then to construct a set of propositions to explain or predict these variations. Yet the more we bear down on the specification of effectiveness as a dependent variable, the clearer it becomes that we are dealing with a suite of related variables or, at best, a multidimensional variable whose separate dimensions need not and frequently do not co-vary in any simple way.[1] In the course of my work on international

[1] For other recent accounts touching on the concept of effectiveness see Peter M. Haas, "Do Regimes Matter? Epistemic Communities and Mediterranean Pollution Control," *International Organization* 43 (Summer 1989), 377–405; Volker Rittberger, ed., *International Regimes in East-West Politics* (London: Pinter, 1990); Arild Underdal, "Negotiating Effective Solutions: The Art and Science of 'Political Engineering,'" unpublished essay, University of Oslo, 1990; Robert O. Keohane, "Multilateralism: An Agenda for Research," *International Journal* 45 (Autumn 1990), 731–764; Jorgen Wettestad and Steinar Andresen, "The 'Effectiveness' of International Resource Cooperation: Some Preliminary Findings," paper presented at the annual convention of the International Studies Association, March 1991; Oran R. Young, "The Effectiveness of International Institutions: Hard Cases and Critical Variables," in James N. Rosenau and Ernst-Otto Czempiel, eds., *Governance without Government: Change and Order in World Politics* (New York: Cambridge University Press, 1992), 160–194; and Peter M. Haas, Robert O. Keohane, and Marc A. Levy, eds., *Institutions for the Earth: Sources of Effective International Environmental Protection* (Cambridge, Mass.: MIT Press, 1993).

governance, I have been able to identify six distinct dimensions (there may be more) of effectiveness; I call them effectiveness as problem solving, effectiveness as goal attainment, behavioral effectiveness, process effectiveness, constitutive effectiveness, and evaluative effectiveness. A discussion of these perspectives on effectiveness will serve to avoid confusion and misunderstandings in our subsequent efforts to pin down factors that explain variations in levels of effectiveness attained by different international environmental governance systems.

Effectiveness as Problem Solving

First, and undoubtedly foremost, we want to know whether regimes are effective in the sense that they operate to solve the problems that motivate parties to create them in the first place. The problems that stimulate the formation of international regimes are diverse. They may, for example, involve the depletion of renewable resources as in the cases of stocks of fish or fur seals; the allocation of flow resources as in the case of water carried by rivers passing through several jurisdictions; the use of congestible common property resources as in the case of broadcast frequencies or orbital slots; or the conduct of scientific research in areas subject to jurisdictional differences as in the case of Antarctica. Also, the problem a regime addresses may be framed differently by various parties to the arrangement or be subject to redefinition over the life of the regime. The whaling regime began as a means of coping with stock depletions to ensure sustainable yields for consumptive users, for instance, but it has come to focus with the passage of time on the problem of protecting whales from all consumptive uses. Needless to say, judgments regarding the effectiveness of a regime may vary depending on how those making such judgments choose to frame the problem. What is more, the problem itself may change or take on new dimensions with the passage of time. So, for example, most wildlife management regimes originated as devices for avoiding severe stock depletions resulting from excessive harvesting on the part of human users. But over time, the problem of maintaining healthy stocks of wild animals has increasingly become a matter of coping with the consequences of habitat destruction.

Approached in this way, it is easy to see that the effectiveness of regimes varies greatly. In the fur seal case, the introduction of the regime set forth in the 1911 convention produced a striking rebound in the seal population by prohibiting pelagic sealing and regulating harvests on land. The Antarctic Treaty regime has proven remarkably effective in allowing scientific research and other cooperative activities to go forward, despite the inability of the parties to arrive at any final resolution of their jurisdictional differences. It is harder, though not impossible, to make a convincing case for the effectiveness of the regime set forth in the 1973 Convention on Trade in Endangered Species of Fauna and Flora as a means of solving the problem of maintaining healthy stocks of rhinoceros or elephants. For its part, the pollution-control regime developed under the Mediterranean Action Plan has not put an end to the problem of pollution in the Mediterranean Basin.

Effectiveness as Goal Attainment

Goal-oriented effectiveness, by contrast, is a measure of the extent to which a regime's (stated or unstated) goals are attained over time.[2] Of course, there is frequently a straightforward and easily identifiable relationship between goal attainment and the search for solutions to motivating problems. The management of stocks of wild animals for maximum sustainable yield or optimal sustainable population, to take a simple example, requires that solutions be found to the problem of severe depletions resulting from excessive harvests or the destruction of critical habitat. But goal attainment and problem solving need not go together. Putting in place an equitable process of allocating harvest quotas for wild animals (a specific goal of the fur seal regime) offers no assurance that a solution to the problem of stock depletions will be found. Controlling the trade in endangered species (a prime goal of the CITES regime) is not sufficient to protect the species in question from going extinct. Reducing sulfur dioxide emissions by 30 percent (the stated goal of the 1985 protocol to the Geneva Convention on Long-Range Transboundary Air Pollution) does not guarantee the biological recovery of German forests or Swedish lakes.

This distinction between effectiveness as problem solving and goal-oriented effectiveness becomes sharper when we broaden our perspective to consider unstated goals. More often than not, those engaged in regime formation are motivated by goals they do not feel comfortable articulating in public as well as by goals they deem appro-

[2] Oran R. Young, "The Political Economy of Fish," *Ocean Development and International Law* 10 (1982), 199–273.

priate for inclusion in public statements. Typically, these unstated goals deal with distributive concerns in contrast to the pursuit of some common good. To take a classic example, it is standard practice for those advocating expanded coastal state jurisdiction over fisheries to emphasize conservation in presenting their case in public. But it is common knowledge that they are motivated as well by a desire to protect their own fishers from competition on the part of foreign fishers. Similarly, the provisions of pollution-control regimes often owe as much to the efforts of the parties to protect certain industries as to a desire to promote the common good by avoiding or reducing environmental impacts. In such cases, the link between problem-solving effectiveness and goal-oriented effectiveness is apt to be particularly tenuous. As recent experience with the marine fisheries makes crystal clear, institutional arrangements may prove extremely effective in fulfilling the goal of protecting domestic fishers but contribute little toward solving the underlying problem of stock depletions caused by excessive harvests.

Behavioral Effectiveness

Yet another way of thinking about effectiveness is to ask whether the operation of a regime causes one or more of its members (or individuals, corporations, and organizations operating under the jurisdiction of the members) to alter their behavior, either by doing things they would not otherwise have done or by terminating or redirecting prior patterns of behavior.[3] The reduction of Japanese and Soviet investments in commercial whaling (by retiring existing whaling fleets without replacement) constitutes a behavioral change that is clearly related to the operation of the whaling regime, though some would argue that the causal connection is hard to demonstrate. The dramatic growth of American investment in capacity to harvest groundfish is unquestionably an outgrowth of the introduction of a regime featuring extended coastal state jurisdiction during the 1970s. Similarly, the striking increase in corporate research and development aimed at developing substitutes for CFCs occurred in the wake of the formation of the ozone regime under the provisions of the 1985 Vienna Convention for the Protection of the Ozone Layer and, especially, the 1987 Montreal Protocol on Substances That Deplete the Ozone Layer.

[3] See Young, "The Effectiveness of International Institutions," for emphasis on this dimension of effectiveness.

Although behavioral effectiveness may be correlated with problem-solving effectiveness or goal-oriented effectiveness, there is no basis for assuming that this will always be the case. As is now becoming clear, for example, the growth of American investment in the ground-fisheries of the Bering Sea region has simply substituted a new threat to the health of the fish stocks for the old threat posed by foreign fishers. The introduction of systems of transferable or tradable permits in marine fisheries typically has the effect of stimulating fishers to increase investments in sophisticated technologies, a behavioral response that can easily run counter to the requirements of both problem-solving and goal-oriented effectiveness. Similarly, there are reasons to doubt whether some of the chemicals developed as substitutes for CFCs will turn out to be environmentally benign in the long run. Equally troubling, the behavioral effects attributable to the establishment of an international regime may amount to a form of displacement in the sense that they create a new problem in the process of solving an old one. Banning the consumptive use of various species of great whales, for instance, has had the effect of increasing pressure on whale stocks not included in the ban. All told, therefore, it seems clear that the behavioral effects arising from the operation of a regime must be assessed on their own terms; they cannot be subsumed under the rubrics of effectiveness as problem-solving and goal-oriented effectiveness.

Process Effectiveness

A way of thinking that appeals to many administrators, lawyers, and political scientists treats effectiveness as a matter of the extent to which the provisions of an international regime are implemented in the domestic legal and political systems of the member states as well as the extent to which those subject to a regime's prescriptions actually comply with their requirements.[4] This approach has the virtue of suggesting relatively straightforward procedures for measurement. It is easy enough to determine whether individual states have ratified conventions or treaties setting forth the provisions of regimes and

[4] Peter H. Sand, *Lessons Learned in Global Environmental Governance* (Washington, D.C.: World Resources Institute, 1990); Edward Miles and Kai N. Lee, "Is There Intelligent Life on Earth? Learning about Global Change," paper presented at the annual convention of the American Political Science Association, August 1990; and Abram Chayes and Antonia H. Chayes, "Adjustment and Compliance Processes in International Regulatory Regimes," in Jessica Tuchman Mathews, ed., *Preserving the Global Environment* (New York: Norton, 1991), 280–308.

passed implementing legislation to put these provisions into practice within their own jurisdictions. An account of the extent to which such actions have led, in turn, to the promulgation of more detailed regulations designed to transform the provisions of a regime into a day-to-day routine is ordinarily feasible as well. Though monitoring compliance is apt to be a more complex process, there is little ambiguity at the conceptual level about what is at stake in such an approach to the assessment of effectiveness.

But what is the relationship between this conception of effectiveness as a political process centering on implementation and compliance and effectiveness in any of the previous senses? Although implementation and compliance are undoubtedly necessary to solving problems and attaining goals, the links between these measures and the other conceptions of effectiveness are far from straightforward. Perfect compliance is not sufficient to solve problems when key provisions of a regime are either inadequate or inappropriate. During the early years of the whaling regime, for example, compliance was high, but the International Whaling Commission set quotas for the harvesting of whales that were not restrictive enough to ensure the recovery of key stocks. Conversely, problem solving can occur even when levels of implementation and compliance are far from perfect. If the move to phase out the use of CFCs convinces the principal producers of these chemicals to close out their production lines and replace them with more benign substitutes, the problem of protecting the ozone layer from further damage may be effectively solved, even if some states participating in the arrangement are somewhat lax in implementing the rules of the regime. The potential for divergences between process effectiveness and behavioral effectiveness is even more apparent. Some shifts in behavior (for example, investments in advanced technologies on the part of those holding fishing permits) are clearly intended to soften the impact of a regime's rules without actually violating the rules. Other behavioral changes (for instance, increased efforts to harvest alternative species or to market unregulated chemicals) are not captured in statistics relating to implementation and compliance at all, though they may well be consequences of the establishment and operation of a regime.

Constitutive Effectiveness

Quite apart from its success in solving problems or facilitating the attainment of goals, a regime may be effective in constitutive terms in the sense that its formation gives rise to a social practice involving the expenditure of time, energy, and resources on the part of its members.[5] The Antarctic Treaty Consultative Meetings (ATCMs) and the activities they trigger, for example, have become a significant focus of attention for a number of parties even though the Antarctic regime is a rather modest international institution. The International Whaling Commission may or may not succeed in its efforts to protect stocks of certain species of whales, but participation in the political processes centered on the activities of the commission has become a major concern for countries including both the United States, which generally opposes the consumptive use of whales, and Japan and Norway, which have consistently resisted efforts to terminate consumptive use. It may well be that one of the factors that ultimately sank the regime for deep seabed mining articulated in Part XI of the 1982 Convention on the Law of the Sea was a reluctance on the part of some countries to commit themselves to a process that would have required the investment of considerable energy and resources on an ongoing basis.

Constitutive effectiveness differs, sometimes dramatically, from the other conceptions of effectiveness under consideration here. A social practice may flourish in the sense that it absorbs a sizable fraction of the attention and resources of those participating in it—it may even play a role in defining their identity—without becoming effective in the sense that its operation either solves the problem that stimulated its creation or attains the goals articulated by its founders.[6] This is, in fact, a central theme of the growing literature on government or nonmarket failure treated as a counterpart to market failure.[7] As experience with a variety of regimes dealing with the conservation or preservation of renewable resources (for example, stocks of fish or marine mammals) attests, this phenomenon is just as common in international society as it is in other social settings. Nor does the emergence of a social practice consuming significant amounts of time and energy offer any guarantee that parties will act to implement a re-

[5] For an argument that institutions can and often do play formative roles in establishing the identity and interests of the actors in a social setting see Alexander Wendt and Raymond Duvall, "Institutions and International Order," in Ernst-Otto Czempiel and James N. Rosenau, eds., *Global Changes and Theoretical Challenges: Approaches to World Politics for the 1990s* (Lexington, Mass.: Lexington Books, 1989), 51–73.

[6] On the social construction of political relationships see Alexander Wendt, "Anarchy Is What States Make of It: The Social Construction of Power Politics," *International Organization* 46 (Spring 1992), 391–425.

[7] Charles Wolf, Jr., *Markets or Governments: Choosing between Imperfect Alternatives* (Cambridge, Mass.: MIT Press, 1988).

gime's key provisions within their domestic jurisdictions or to ensure high levels of compliance with a regime's central rules. It is easy enough to find examples of this phenomenon involving natural resources and the environment; one good example is the problems of ensuring compliance with the rules of the CITES regime in a wide variety of domestic settings. But the classic examples of the phenomenon in international society undoubtedly occur in connection with regimes dealing with arms control and the protection of human rights.

Evaluative Effectiveness

For many observers, effectiveness is fundamentally a matter of performance rather than a simple measure of the consequences flowing from the operation of governance systems. Those who take this view generally do not ask whether a regime makes a difference in some generic sense. Instead, they want to know whether the regime produces results that are efficient, equitable, sustainable, or robust.[8] Specifically, the question is not just whether the whaling regime is succeeding in its effort to conserve whale stocks but whether it is operating in a cost-effective manner in the sense that comparable results could not be achieved at a lower cost or superior results achieved at a comparable cost by substituting some other institutional arrangements. The same is true regarding the extent to which the outcomes generated by international regimes (for example, the allocation of broadcast frequencies or the distribution of benefits flowing from the harvest of fish) are just or fair, either in end-state or in procedural terms.[9] Rapid changes involving international environmental problems (for instance, ozone depletion or climate change) have led many recent observers to place increased emphasis on adaptability to changing conditions as a performance criterion in assessing the effectiveness of regimes.[10]

Evaluative effectiveness taps a set of concerns that differ from

[8] For a general discussion of performance criteria see Robert Dorfman and Nancy S. Dorfman, "Introduction," in Dorfman and Dorfman, eds., *Economics of the Environment*, 2d ed. (New York: Norton, 1977), 1–37. The application of this reasoning to international institutions is discussed in Beth V. Yarborough and Robert M. Yarborough, "The New Economics of Organization," *International Organization* 44 (Spring 1990), 235–260.

[9] On the distinction between end-state and procedural conceptions of justice see Robert Nozick, *Anarchy, State, and Utopia* (New York: Basic Books, 1974), Part II.

[10] For a prominent example see Richard Elliot Benedick, *Ozone Diplomacy: New Directions in Safeguarding the Planet* (Cambridge, Mass.: Harvard University Press, 1991).

those underlying the conceptions above. A regime that is generally effective in solving a well-defined problem (for example, avoiding severe depletions of fish or animal stocks) may seem to many to operate in a manner that is inefficient, inequitable, or both. What is more, a regime that seems effective under current conditions may prove brittle in the face of relatively modest changes in the character of the problem (for instance, the emergence of new entrants or new harvesting technologies). If anything, the link between goal attainment and these performance criteria is even more tenuous. Although the ozone regime may set in motion a process leading relatively quickly to the phasing out of most uses of CFCs, for instance, there is ample room for questioning both the efficiency and the fairness of a process that relies on a (largely) uniform formula calling for equal percentage cuts in the consumption of CFCs. The distinction between evaluative effectiveness and constitutive effectiveness is even more dramatic. A regime is effective in the constitutive sense when it gives rise to a social practice that becomes a major focus of attention for its members. There is nothing in this conception that requires a strong performance with regard to criteria of efficiency and equity.

So far, I have taken pains not only to differentiate several dimensions of effectiveness but also to show that there is no basis for assuming that the different dimensions will co-vary in any simple or easily predictable manner. Yet this does not preclude the occurrence of interaction effects among the various dimensions in the sense that developments in some areas have discernible impacts on developments in others. Perhaps the most important of these interaction effects for scholars and practitioners interested in international environmental regimes are those involving causal links between effectiveness as problem solving on the one hand and effectiveness as goal attainment and process effectiveness on the other. For the most part, actors in international society are motivated to form regimes as a response to the emergence of more or less acute problems such as the progressive depletion of commercially valuable fish stocks, the realization that species playing central roles in important ecosystems may go extinct, or the anticipated consequences of a serious thinning of the protective layer of stratospheric ozone. In endeavoring to solve these problems, however, actors ordinarily specify goals (for example, a 30 percent reduction in sulfur dioxide emissions or a phase-out of the production of CFCs) and then devise sets of rules and policy instruments intended to bring behavior into line with the attainment of these goals. No doubt, such responses can and sometimes do serve to solve the problems that provoke them. But there is no guarantee that this will be the case. A 30 percent reduction in sulfur dioxide emissions may accompany or even cause a rise in emissions of other substances that are equally disruptive to the natural environment. Irreparable damage to the ozone layer may occur before the consumption of CFCs ceases. Though the emphasis that students of effectiveness place on implementation and compliance is perfectly understandable, therefore, the results should not be treated as a substitute for undertaking the more challenging task of investigating such matters as the causal links between process effectiveness and effectiveness as problem solving.

Whatever their effectiveness in the realm of intended consequences, international regimes—like all other governance systems—also produce side effects, results that their creators neither intend nor foresee at the time of their establishment. Sometimes side effects take the form of unforeseen distributive consequences as in the case of windfall profits accruing to those who receive tradable pollution rights or permits in an initial distribution or to those in possession of stocks of tradable goods following a decision to phase out future production. In other cases, side effects involve the operation of an institutional arrangement itself as in the case of the unforeseen capture of a regulatory system by those it is intended to regulate. Given the recent rise in levels of interdependence in international society, it is to be expected that side effects will become more ubiquitous in connection with the operation of international regimes and that these effects will often initiate chain reactions of considerable magnitude. As in other realms, there is an understandable tendency to focus on negative side effects in thinking about the unintended consequences flowing from the establishment and operation of international regimes. Yet these side effects clearly constitute a subset of the broader category of externalities, which suggests that we should be open to the prospect of positive as well as negative side effects. Both those responsible for designing international regimes and those seeking to provide overall assessments of their performance will surely want to be alert to the prospect of significant side effects. In individual cases, the impact of the relevant side effects may equal or even exceed the magnitude of the intended effects attributable to the operation of international regimes, a fact that should give pause to regime enthusiasts who advocate the creation of new institutions as a solution to every problem.[11]

DETERMINANTS OF EFFECTIVENESS

No doubt, our conceptions of effectiveness will continue to evolve as we conduct studies of the workings of specific international environmental regimes. But it is appropriate, at this stage, to turn to the other side of the equation, initiating an inquiry into the factors that operate as determinants of the effectiveness of governance systems in international society. The principal issue here centers on the tension between parsimony and explanatory power. Single-factor accounts are appealing both because they lend themselves to articulation in the form of necessary or sufficient conditions and because they hold the promise of reducing seemingly complex realities to a set of relatively simple and comprehensible propositions. In the social sciences, however, such accounts seldom fare well when they are tested against evidence derived from empirical observations. As a result, analysts typically find themselves fashioning explanatory accounts that include two or more independent variables and seeking to specify the relationships obtaining between or among these variables. There is no reason to expect studies of the determinants of institutional effectiveness to prove exceptional. Even so, differentiation of the types or categories of independent variables will provide a helpful backdrop for the growing body of case studies carried out by scholars working in this field.

One approach to this issue that will appeal to practitioners turns on the distinction between decision variables and structural variables. Decision variables are factors subject to conscious control or manipulation on the part of those responsible for designing and managing international regimes. The institutional arrangements embedded in governance systems (for example, their membership, decision-making procedures, and compliance mechanisms) belong to this category. Structural variables are features of the larger physical, biological, or

[11] Individual regimes also become components of larger systems of institutional arrangements or orders whose effects may prove highly significant at the macro level. Consider, for example, the macroeconomic argument articulated in Douglass C. North and Robert P. Thomas, *The Rise of the Western World: A New Economic History* (Cambridge, Eng.: Cambridge University Press, 1973).

social environment (for example, the distribution of power in international society) that are not subject to conscious control within any policy-relevant time frame. The study of decision variables holds an obvious attraction for those interested in the effectiveness of international regimes because it is easy to see ways to apply the findings of such research both to the management of existing institutions and to the design of new governance systems. Yet a note of caution is in order here. International governance systems are, for the most part, complex social institutions whose operation is not well understood. Nothing is more common than the establishment of regimes that prove ineffective in practice because they are based on premises that are either wrong or not applicable to the situation at hand.[12] By the same token, studies of structural determinants of effectiveness are by no means irrelevant from the point of view of those charged with establishing or managing international regimes. Practitioners who understand the key structural factors will surely have an advantage when creating regimes that are well-adapted to the environment in which they are expected to operate.

For analytic purposes, however, there is much to be said for a related distinction that separates endogenous variables, exogenous variables, and what I call linkage variables. Those who focus on endogenous variables seek to account for variations in the effectiveness of international governance systems by examining the character of the institutional arrangements themselves. The category of exogenous variables, by contrast, encompasses an array of physical, biological, and social conditions that make up the environment in which an international regime operates. Linkage variables have to do with the fit between the institutional character of a governance system and the environment in which it is expected to function.

Endogenous Variables

There is, to begin with, a debate concerning the extent to which international regimes require the services of organizations (in the sense of material entities possessing offices, personnel, equipment, budgets, and legal personality) to function effectively. Those who approach the issue from the perspective of business administration or

---

[12] Underdal, "Negotiating Effective Solutions"; and Oran R. Young, *International Cooperation: Building Regimes for Natural Resources and the Environment* (Ithaca: Cornell University Press, 1989), chap. 9.

public administration, whose primary concern is the performance of organizations, exhibit a tendency to shift the focus of analysis from the effectiveness of international regimes to the effectiveness of international organizations.[13] This is, in my view, a mistake. With all due respect for the roles organizations play, there is great variation among international governance systems in the extent to which their operation requires the services of some administrative apparatus, and there is no obvious correlation between the presence of organizations and the effectiveness of regimes. As numerous observers have pointed out, moreover, both material and intangible costs are associated with the operation of organizations, which suggests the value of a close examination of the factors that determine when and what sort of organizations are required to make international regimes effective.

Quite apart from the matter of organization, there is much to be said for studies of decision procedures, revenue sources, and compliance mechanisms in efforts to pinpoint the determinants of institutional effectiveness in international society.[14] In the case of decision procedures, the problem is to devise some process that makes it possible to avoid the twin pitfalls of paralysis and defection. Ingenious devices, such as the International Whaling Commission's procedure of combining majority rule with a system of individual objections, are surely worthy of study in this connection. The fundamental question regarding revenue sources, concerns the extent to which a regime is able to obtain revenue directly rather than via some pass-through arrangement under which members make periodic contributions. The controversy surrounding efforts to create independent revenue sources in specific cases, such as the proposed International Seabed Authority, indicates how sensitive this issue is. With regard to compliance, the problem centers on the need to secure compliant behavior on the part of a regime's members in a social setting in which enforcement capabilities are largely under the control of the members themselves. Recently, this issue has given rise to interesting work both on the idea of transparency (that is, the formulation of rules in such a way as to facilitate efforts to observe or measure compliance) and on

[13] Much of the debate in recent years regarding the reform of the United Nations System reflects this way of thinking. For a recent review touching on a wide range of proposed reforms in the various components of the United Nations System see Johan Kaufman and Nico Schrijver, *Changing Global Needs: Expanding Roles for the United Nations System* (Hanover, N.H.: Academic Council on the United Nations System, 1990).

[14] For a particularly sophisticated account of this type see Sand, *Lessons Learned in Global Environmental Governance*, Part II.

the use of sophisticated technologies to monitor compliance on the part of individual members in a nonintrusive manner.[15]

The growing awareness that change is one of the dominant characteristics of today's world has led also to an increasing concern for robustness and, more specifically, for adaptability or flexibility among those who think about the effectiveness of international regimes. The idea here is that a regime cannot remain effective for long unless it has some built-in capacity to adjust to changes in the issue area to which it pertains or the behavior it is designed to regulate. Because authority is decentralized in international society, there is no simple way to solve the problem of building flexibility into regimes. Yet ingenious responses to this problem have been developed in some cases. Allowing for the accession of new members (as in the cases of the whaling regime and the Antarctic Treaty regime), for example, can bring about changes in the functioning of a regime without requiring any formal alterations in its constitutive provisions. Providing for changes in the schedule of the whaling regime and the appendixes of the CITES regime without requiring formal ratification has had the effect of introducing considerable flexibility into these governance systems. Equally interesting is the process now emerging in connection with the ozone regime in which the annual review conferences, held under the auspices of the arrangements set forth in the Montreal Protocol, are empowered to make significant changes in the workings of the regime that do not require ratification.[16]

Exogenous Variables

The category of exogenous variables thought to have a bearing on the effectiveness of international regimes covers a wider array of factors than the category of endogenous variables. Whereas endogenous factors are limited, by definition, to attributes or properties of

[15] Recent work on compliance with international environmental agreements is reviewed in Jesse H. Ausubel and David G. Victor, "Verification of International Environmental Agreements," *Annual Review of Energy and Environment* 17 (1992), 1–43.

[16] Thus the review conferences can accelerate the phase-out schedule for chemicals already covered by the regime without ratification. The addition of new chemicals to the category of those to be phased out, on the other hand, does require ratification by the regime's members. At the 1990 meeting in London, for example, the parties agreed to shorten the phase-out period for a number of CFCs without triggering a requirement for ratification. They also decided to expand the scope of the regime to cover additional chemicals (for instance, carbon tetrachloride), an action requiring ratification by the members.

the regimes themselves, exogenous variables may range across the full spectrum of driving forces that analysts expect to influence the course of collective outcomes in international society. Thus, not surprisingly, a broad range of factors must be considered by those endeavoring to account for variations in the effectiveness of regimes. Yet these factors do divide into several major clusters associated with different schools of thought about the forces at work in international relations more generally. Three of these clusters, in particular, seem noteworthy as guides to our thinking about the determinants of institutional effectiveness: power factors, interest factors, and knowledge factors.

Those who call themselves realists or structuralists approach institutions as reflections of the underlying configuration of power in international society.[17] This way of thinking may seem most familiar in connection with discussions of regime formation, but it applies just as well to analyses of the effectiveness of governance systems. A particularly prominent strand of this reasoning involves hegemonic stability theory, which suggests that the presence of a hegemon in the sense of a dominant actor or a party possessing a preponderance of material resources is necessary for a regime to function effectively.[18] The decline or fall of the relevant hegemon, on this account, is likely to lead inexorably to a reduction of the regime's effectiveness and, in extreme cases, to its transformation. This is, however, not the only power-based argument that is relevant to a discussion of the determinants of regime effectiveness. An alternative view, which is especially interesting because it runs counter to the argument embedded in hegemonic stability theory, suggests that institutions work best or are most effective when they operate in an environment characterized by some rough balance of power among their principal members. A little thought will suggest a number of additional power-based ideas that could prove relevant in analyzing the effectiveness of international governance systems.

Arguments centering on interests rest on a view of international society that emphasizes interactive decision making and collective action among groups of autonomous actors. On this account, regimes

[17] Susan Strange, "*Cave! hic dragones*: A Critique of Regime Analysis," in Stephen D. Krasner, ed., *International Regimes* (Ithaca: Cornell University Press, 1983), 337–354; and Krasner, "Global Communications and National Power: Life on the Pareto Frontier," *World Politics* 43 (April 1991), 336–366.

[18] For a clear exposition see Robert O. Keohane, *After Hegemony: Cooperation and Discord in the World Political Economy* (Princeton: Princeton University Press, 1984), chap. 3.

are social institutions that emerge to circumvent or mitigate the collective-action problems that plague all social settings featuring interactive decision making in the absence of a central public authority or system of rules to guide the behavior of the participants.[19] In thinking about regime effectiveness, those who focus on interests tend to emphasize factors relating to the configuration of interests among the players as well as factors relating to the extent to which institutional arrangements offer appropriate solutions to the relevant collective-action problems. Studies of the configuration of interests highlight not only the locus of a given issue area on the spectrum from pure cooperation (that is, coordination games) to pure conflict (that is, zero-sum games) but also other factors such as the existence of a stable equilibrium.[20] With regard to solutions, the issue concerns the extent to which institutional arrangements are well adapted to the problem at hand, a subject to which I shall return shortly in discussing linkage variables.

Those who look to knowledge in thinking about regime effectiveness rest their case on the proposition that ideas matter independently of configurations of power and interests.[21] Their view, developed in many cases in counterpoint to the arguments of the realists or structuralists, suggests that governance systems—in international society as elsewhere—are reflections of deeper worldviews or intellectual paradigms that structure the way people think about relations among states. On this account, a regime is likely to be effective, in at least some of the senses articulated earlier in this chapter, when it rests on a common conception of the problem to be solved and some degree of consensus regarding what is needed to fashion a solution. A particularly provocative line of thinking in this connection centers on the idea of hegemony in the cognitive or Gramscian sense.[22] The idea here is that a system of thought, which may or may not be an outgrowth of the views of an actor that is a hegemon in the material sense, can hold sway over the thinking of policymakers in many dif-

[19] Young, *International Cooperation*.

[20] An equilibrium is stable to the extent that a system tends to revert to that condition in the aftermath of displacements or perturbations.

[21] For extended accounts of the role of ideas in the operation of international institutions see Ernst B. Haas, *When Knowledge Is Power: Three Models of Change in International Organizations* (Berkeley: University of California Press, 1990); and Peter M. Haas, ed., *Knowledge, Power, and International Policy Coordination*, a special issue of *International Organization* 46 (Winter 1992).

[22] Robert W. Cox, "Gramsci, Hegemony and International Relations: An Essay in Method," *Millennium: Journal of International Studies* 12 (Summer 1983), 162–175.

ferent national settings and that the presence of some such cognitive construct is critical to the success or failure of international regimes created to cope with specific problems. Yet there is no reason to confine our thinking about knowledge as a source of effectiveness to such a grand theory. It may well be that more mundane considerations regarding knowledge are relevant as well in efforts to explain variations in observed levels of institutional effectiveness.

Linkage Variables

Some students of international regimes have suggested that effectiveness depends on the difficulty or the "malignness" of the problem an institutional arrangement is intended to solve.[23] This intuitively appealing idea rests on the assumption that we can rank problems from those that are easiest to solve or most benign to those that are most difficult to solve or most malign. So, for example, coordination problems, which require only some adjustment of behavior to avoid common aversions, seem easier to solve than cooperation problems, which require both active collaboration and some mechanism for ensuring compliance to produce some valued products.[24] On reflection, however, it is by no means clear how far this line of reasoning can carry us in explaining or predicting levels of effectiveness. The idea of difficulty, in the hands of many, is a measure of the intensity of the conflicts of interest among those engaged in interactive decision making. To the extent that this is the case, the argument might better be left to interest-based thinking, which offers more sophisticated analytic tools than the simple notion of difficulty. Approached from another angle, regimes involve efforts to solve problems that are hard to classify on a scale of difficulty, except in very gross terms. In all but the simplest of situations, in fact, the degree of difficulty of the problem to be solved is likely to become a subject of lively debate rather than something to be treated as an objective condition. The current controversy over the extent to which the problem of climate change is

[23] The term *malignness* originated with Steinar Andreson and Jorgen Wettestad of the Fridtjof Nansen Institute in Oslo. For a discussion that relies on a typology of conflicts to make a similar point see Volker Rittberger and Michael Zurn, "Regime Theory: Findings from the Study of 'East-West Regimes,'" *Conflict and Cooperation* 26 (1991), 165–183.
[24] In this connection, see also the distinction between common aversions and common interests in Arthur A. Stein, "Coordination and Collaboration: Regimes in an Anarchic World," in Krasner, ed., *International Regimes*, 115–140.

more difficult to solve than the problem of ozone depletion illustrates this point aptly.[25]

Another approach to this general topic, which captures some of what is at stake in the discussion of difficulty, focuses on the fit between the character of an international regime and the problem it is intended to solve. Whereas some problems (for example, the conservation of polar bears) can be solved through the elaboration of coordination regimes featuring common rules coupled with decentralized administration, other problems (for example, the setting and allocation of catch quotas for krill in the Southern Ocean or the allocation of broadcast frequencies in the electromagnetic spectrum) can be solved only through the establishment of some social choice mechanism capable of making collective decisions on a continuing or recurrent basis. Regimes for high seas fisheries, in which it is relatively hard to monitor compliance with specific regulations, pose different requirements than regimes for nuclear safety, in which it is virtually impossible to hide serious accidents. Governance systems that work well when the members are modern states with strong central governments frequently fail when the governments of the participating states have a more limited capacity to control what goes on within their own jurisdictions (for example, the activities of poachers engaged in practices banned under the terms of the CITES regime). Similarly, the need for built-in flexibility is greater with regard to problems in which scientific understanding is changing rapidly (for example, ozone depletion or climate change) than for problems whose levels of uncertainty are much lower (for example, regimes to allocate the flow of water in shared river basins).

Overall, there is much to be said for the view that the ability to customize the provisions of a regime to fit the circumstances at hand constitutes an important determinant of institutional effectiveness. This is, of course, easier said than done. Not only is it difficult to foresee how complex institutional arrangements will work in practice, but also individual participants are subject to continual pressure both from incentives to capture short-term gains to the detriment of longer-term considerations relating to institutional effectiveness and from the maneuvers of those endeavoring to protect special interests in a way that detracts from regime performance. Then, too, there is the problem of making appropriate adjustments over time. Institu-

[25] See, for example, Jessica T. Mathews et al., *Greenhouse Warming: Negotiating a Global Regime* (Washington, D.C.: World Resources Institute, 1991).

tions are like relationships among individuals; they require continuous monitoring and adjustments to remain viable. It is not sufficient simply to wind them up and set them in motion on the assumption that they will adjust to changing circumstances on their own in the absence of conscious interventions. It follows that any clear-cut conclusions we are able to reach about linkages between endogenous factors in the sense of attributes or properties of the regimes themselves and exogenous factors in the sense of features of the physical, biological, and social environment should prove directly relevant to the search for effectiveness in the establishment and management of a wide range of governance systems in international society.

CONCLUSION

Effectiveness, it is clear, is not a simple matter when we are assessing the consequences of international environmental governance systems. Not only is it possible to conceptualize effectiveness in different ways, but it is also common to look to a variety of factors in efforts to explain the levels of effectiveness attained by specific regimes. What is more, much of the variance in our thinking about effectiveness is surely attributable to the disciplinary perspectives and larger worldviews that we as analysts bring to the study of this subject. Thus it will come as no surprise that our understanding of the determinants of effectiveness in international governance systems is rudimentary at this stage. Nonetheless, the effort to improve knowledge of this complex subject must be placed at the top of the agenda for students of international governance. The study of governance systems in international society cannot prosper in the absence of a better understanding of the determinants of effectiveness. Those responsible for designing governance systems to cope with growing threats to the earth's habitability demand knowledge that they can use to devise regimes that will prove effective. It is time, therefore, to get on with the task of studying effectiveness in a systematic and empirically grounded fashion.

CONCEPTUAL
LINKAGES

CHAPTER SEVEN

Governance Systems and International Organizations

The point of differentiating between institutions and organizations in a variety of social settings is not to build a case for granting priority to one or the other in the study of international affairs. On the contrary, the distinction opens up a new and important research agenda centering on the interplay between institutions and organizations in efforts to meet the demand for governance at the international level. To concretize this proposition and, in the process, to delineate the points of tangency between the research programs of those who think about international regimes or governance systems and those who study international organizations, I explore in this chapter the roles accorded to intergovernmental organizations in institutional bargaining pertaining to natural resources and the environment at the international level.

To set the stage for this analysis, recall the distinction between institutions and organizations introduced in Chapter 1. Governance systems or regimes are constellations of rules of the game that guide the interactions of actors in specific issue areas. Organizations, by contrast, are material entities possessing offices, personnel, equipment, budgets, and legal personality. The United Nations Environment Programme is an organization; the environmental protection arrangements for the Mediterranean Basin set forth in the 1976 Bar-

An earlier version of this chapter appeared as Oran R. Young, "Perspectives on International Organizations," Gunnar Sjostedt, ed., *International Environmental Negotiation* (Newbury Park, Ca.: Sage Publications, 1993), 244–261.

celona Convention for the Protection of the Mediterranean Sea against Pollution and Its Related Protocols as well as those for stratospheric ozone formalized in the 1985 Vienna Convention for the Protection of the Ozone Layer together with the 1987 Montreal Protocol on Substances That Deplete the Ozone Layer (as amended in 1990) are international regimes. The Economic Commission for Europe (ECE) is an organization; the 1979 Geneva Convention on Long-Range Transboundary Air Pollution, coupled with its 1985, 1988, and 1991 protocols on sulfur emissions, nitrogen oxide emissions, and volatile organic compounds, lays out the terms of an international regime. The same relationship exists between the International Commission for the Protection of the Rhine against Pollution (ICPR) and the Rhine River regime articulated in the provisions of the 1976 Bonn conventions on the protection of the Rhine River against chemical pollution and against chloride pollution and in the terms of the 1987 Rhine Action Programme.

International organizations figure prominently in two distinct capacities in the creation of international governance systems. Organizations such as the UNEP, the ECE, and the ICPR can and often do become instruments of regime formation in the sense that they play significant roles in energizing the institutional bargaining processes that produce constitutional contracts giving rise to environmental regimes.[1] Those engaged in negotiations regarding the provisions of international regimes, by contrast, frequently foresee a need for organizations to implement and administer the provisions of the governance systems they create so that the character of the organizations to be established in connection with environmental regimes regularly becomes a prominent agenda item in institutional bargaining processes. Some organizations—UNEP is a striking example—figure in both capacities, serving initially as instruments of regime formation and subsequently assuming roles in the administration of the governance systems they help to establish. For purposes of analysis, I call these two sets of concerns international organizations as instruments and international organizations as objects.

---

[1] Although we often associate constitutional contracts with formal statements of the provisions of regimes in treaties or conventions, the concept applies as well to informal practices centered on unwritten networks of rights and rules. Many regimes encompass both formal and informal elements. See James M. Buchanan, *The Limits of Liberty: Between Anarchy and Leviathan* (Chicago: University of Chicago Press, 1975), esp. chap. 4.

INTERNATIONAL ORGANIZATIONS AS INSTRUMENTS

We live in an era marked by rapid growth in the number and variety of intergovernmental organizations.[2] This growth is in part a reflection of rising interdependence in international affairs and the resultant need for organizations to manage complex webs linking the members of international society.[3] In part, it is a product of the emergence during the postwar period of a worldview highlighting benefits expected to accrue to individual members of international society from intensive interactions with others while, at the same time, deemphasizing the dangers of foreign entanglements and the attractions of autarky.

A Choice of Organizations

A variety of international organizations can and do become actively involved in environmental negotiations. Multipurpose organizations such as the ECE and the Organization for Economic Cooperation and Development assume leading roles in some environmental negotiations; organizations whose mandate is limited to environmental issues, like UNEP, take on these roles in other cases. Even among environmental organizations, there is an important distinction between those focused on a single issue area and those whose concerns extend to a broad spectrum of issues. Whereas the ICPR has played a key role in devising the terms of the Rhine River regime, for example, UNEP has emerged as an important player in the development of regimes to control regional pollution, protect the ozone layer, regulate transboundary shipments of hazardous wastes, and, most recently, preserve biological diversity.

Nor is participation in negotiations concerning specific environmental issues limited to a single international organization. UNEP, the Food and Agriculture Organization (FAO), the International Maritime Consultative Organization (now simply the International Maritime Organization or IMO), the International Atomic Energy Agen-

[2] Clive Archer, *International Organizations* (London: George Allen & Unwin, 1983); and Paul Taylor, *International Organization in the Modern World: The Regional and the Global Process* (London: Pinter, 1993).

[3] Robert O. Keohane and Joseph S. Nye, *Power and Interdependence*, 2d ed. (Glenview: Scott, Foresman, 1989).

cy (IAEA), the World Meteorological Organization, and the World Health Organization (WHO), for example, joined forces to develop the Mediterranean Action Plan in the 1970s. Similarly, in the ongoing effort to form an international regime to cope with climate change, UNEP and WMO have worked together to structure and facilitate the course of institutional bargaining, which has actually taken place under the auspices of yet another organization, the Intergovernmental Negotiating Committee on Climate Change established by the United Nations General Assembly specifically to develop a climate regime. Among other things, these alliances can give rise to new organizational arrangements, such as the Joint Group of Experts on the Scientific Aspects of Marine Pollution (GESAMP) in the Mediterranean case and the joint UNEP/WMO Intergovernmental Panel on Climate Change in the climate change case.

What accounts for the choice of international organizations to become involved in environmental negotiations? Some organizations are endowed with legal or constitutional mandates giving them strong claims to participate in any negotiations taking place in a more or less well-defined issue area. It would be awkward, for instance, to proceed with negotiations relating to high seas fisheries issues without the participation of FAO or with negotiations dealing with atomic energy in the absence of IAEA as a significant player. In other cases, the choice is determined more by suitability or the fit between an organization's membership, functional scope, or geographic reach and the issues under consideration. This accounts, for example, for the choice of the ECE rather than the European Community (EC), the OECD, or the Conference on Security and Cooperation in Europe (CSCE) as the organizer of the negotiations leading to the 1979 Geneva Convention on Long-Range Transboundary Air Pollution. The membership of the EC was too narrow and that of the OECD too broad, while the CSCE had not emerged as an effectual organization at the time. The UNEP was chosen over the OECD in the negotiations leading to the 1989 Basel Convention on the Control of Transboundary Movements of Hazardous Wastes because relations between developed and developing countries became a central issue in these negotiations, and UNEP was better situated than the OECD to operate as an instrument of regime formation in this connection.

Frequently, however, the choice of organizations to become active players in environmental negotiations involves political considerations as well. Before 1986, for example, the United States and some of its allies preferred the OECD's Nuclear Energy Agency over the IAEA as an arena for negotiations relating to nuclear issues not only because of its technical sophistication but also because of the political compatibility of the countries participating in the work of this agency. Though the members of the Antarctic club have long maintained that the Antarctic Treaty Consultative Meetings are more suitable than various United Nations organs as a forum for efforts to work out additional elements of the Antarctic Treaty System, it is no secret that the Antarctic Treaty Consultative Parties have a strong preference for the ATCMs in part, at least, because this forum maximizes their control over the negotiating process and blunts efforts to apply the doctrine of the common heritage of mankind to Antarctic activities. Similar observations apply to the roles of the United Nations Conference on Trade and Development (UNCTAD), the World Bank, and the United Nations Development Programme. Whereas many developing countries prefer UNCTAD because it tends to mirror their views on North-South issues, the developed countries are far more comfortable with the bank, in which their influence is greater. These conflicting preferences have strengthened the role of UNDP in some environmental negotiations because this organization has endeavored, with some success in the eyes of many observers, to steer a middle course between the preferences of the developing countries and those of the developed countries.[4]

One of the more striking developments of the last two decades in the realm of international environmental affairs is the emergence of UNEP as a prominent and effectual player in international environmental negotiations. Given the modest political and material resources at its disposal, the success of UNEP in launching the Regional Seas Programme, promoting the ozone protection regime, and sponsoring the negotiations on transboundary movements of hazardous wastes is remarkable. What accounts for this success? It seems clear that a combination of endogenous and exogenous factors has facilitated the work of UNEP. The organization itself has achieved a reputation not only for technical competence but also for strong leadership. At the same time, UNEP's strategy of bringing science to bear and stressing the technical aspects of such issues as marine pollution, ozone depletion, and hazardous wastes has served it well, in part at

---

[4] This is not to say that UNDP has been particularly well managed or effective in its major undertakings. There is, in fact, considerable controversy regarding UNDP's performance.

least because the countries involved in these negotiations have found it expedient to downplay the political dimensions of the issues at stake.

Will UNEP be able to play an equally central role as attention focuses increasingly on efforts to come to terms with global environmental issues such as climate change and the loss of biological diversity? There can be no doubt about UNEP's technical competence to participate in negotiations regarding these matters.[5] Yet it is hard to deemphasize the underlying socioeconomic and political issues at stake in negotiations over climate change and biological diversity.[6] Coping with climate change may require drastic alterations in our thinking about economic growth; coming to terms with the loss of biological diversity is likely to necessitate actions that seem highly intrusive to countries that, like Brazil, possess large tracts of moist tropical forests. In both cases, negotiators will face profound questions relating to the links between environment and development and to relations between developing countries and advanced industrial countries.

Under the circumstances, the relatively apolitical approach UNEP has adopted successfully in dealing with regional seas, hazardous wastes, and even ozone depletion is not likely to prove tenable as a way of handling issues like climate change. This is surely one of the lessons to be drawn from the controversy surrounding Resolution 44/228, which the United Nations General Assembly passed in December 1989 and which set forth the terms of reference for the 1992 United Nations Conference on Environment and Development. Similar concerns undoubtedly account for the decision of the General Assembly (articulated in Resolution 45/212 of December 1990) to establish a separate entity (the INC) to handle the climate change negotiations. This is not to say that UNEP's role in international environmental negotiations will now evaporate; the organization has served, for instance, as the principal negotiating forum in the effort to devise a regime dealing with biological diversity. But it does seem clear that we are entering a new phase in the establishment and implementation of international environmental regimes.

[5] This does not mean that UNEP's internal management has been particularly efficient. There are those who maintain that UNEP has succeeded in some of its undertakings despite weak or inefficient management.

[6] For a sophisticated account that reaches somewhat different conclusions see Richard Elliot Benedick, *Ozone Diplomacy: New Directions in Safeguarding the Planet* (Cambridge, Mass.: Harvard University Press, 1991).

Roles for International Organizations

What specific roles do international organizations play when they become involved in institutional bargaining dealing with environmental issues? It is customary in many quarters to stress the technocratic or apolitical nature of these roles. This approach is certainly understandable as a form of deference to states that have long been regarded as the primary, if not exclusive, members of international society and that exhibit a pronounced tendency to react negatively to perceived encroachments on their primacy in international affairs. Nonetheless, as we move further into an era of complex interdependence, it is apparent that international organizations cannot and will not confine themselves to narrowly technical roles. Nowhere is this change more evident than in the realm of international environmental affairs.

International organizations—sometimes in combination with nongovernmental organizations—frequently act as catalysts in environmental negotiations, influencing the way the issues are conceptualized or framed and propelling them toward the top of the international policy agenda. Capitalizing on the momentum generated by the 1972 United Nations Conference on the Human Environment, for example, UNEP has had remarkable success in advancing one issue after another to the top of the international agenda. In the Regional Seas Programme, for example, the organization has contributed substantially to the fund of intellectual capital (for example, by developing the concept of an ecological region) available to those engaged in environmental negotiations. Similarly, international organizations can and often do keep international environmental issues alive during periods when one or more of the major states have reasons to deemphasize them. The role the IPCC (a joint enterprise of UNEP and WMO) has played in countering efforts on the part of some states (including the United States) to slow the pace of international negotiations pertaining to climate change on grounds of scientific uncertainty is particularly instructive in this regard.[7]

Increasingly, international organizations have also assumed a coordinating role in environmental negotiations. Because environmental

[7] On the politics of regime formation in the case of climate change see Eugene B. Skolnikoff, "The Policy Gridlock on Global Warming," *Foreign Policy* 79 (Summer 1990), 79–93; and James K. Sebenius, "Negotiating a Regime to Control Global Warming," in Jessica Tuchman Mathews et al., *Greenhouse Warming: Negotiating a Global Regime* (Washington, D.C.: World Resources Institute, 1991), 69–98.

issues cut across many other concerns, efforts to form environmental regimes typically touch on the interests of a variety of functionally oriented agencies. At the international level alone, for example, those agencies concerned with Mediterranean pollution during the 1960s and 1970s included the International Maritime Consultative Organization (IMCO), the United Nations Educational, Scientific, and Cultural Organization (UNESCO), FAO, WMO, WHO, IAEA, and (following its establishment in 1973) UNEP. Under the circumstances, the significance of GESAMP's role as a coordinating mechanism becomes clear. And part of the genius of UNEP's effort in the period immediately preceding the signing of the 1976 Barcelona Convention surely lies in the organization's success in coordinating the activities of an array of interested agencies.

More and more, international organizations have become a source of leadership in environmental negotiations, a development that makes it appropriate to speak of them as architects of the institutional arrangements emerging from these negotiations.[8] Partly, this is a matter of developing negotiating texts on key issues. There is nothing new about this source of influence, but international organizations are now increasingly active in formulating negotiating texts, often during the period preceding the initiation of formal negotiations. Their prior involvement means that organizations such as UNEP can exercise considerable influence over the course of environmental negotiations, even when they are not key players during the negotiation stage. Individuals acting in the name of international organizations, such as Maurice Strong and Mostafa Tolba at UNEP, Janos Stanovnik at the ECE, and Hans Blix at IAEA, have become influential leaders in environmental negotiations, playing roles that go beyond purely technical considerations.[9] Whether observers regard the results as good, bad, or indifferent, then, it is clear that international organizations are now in the thick of environmental negotiations; no account of specific negotiations is likely to make sense today unless it considers the roles these organizations play.

International organizations, like states, may sometimes emerge as

[8] For a study that focuses on the concept of architecture in this context see Alan K. Henrikson, ed., *Negotiating World Order: The Artisanship and Architecture of Global Diplomacy* (Wilmington: Scholarly Resources, 1986).

[9] For a general account of the roles that individual leaders play in institutional bargaining see Oran R. Young, "Political Leadership and Regime Formation: On the Development of Institutions in International Society," *International Organization* 45 (Summer 1991), 281–308.

obstacles to the negotiation and implementation of environmental regimes. Institutional arrangements espoused by some actors may either impinge on the interests of particular organizations or require an assessment of the principal forces at work that conflict with the premises on which existing organizations operate. It is sometimes said, for instance, that the World Bank has been part of the problem rather than of the solution in efforts to reconcile the demands of development and environmental protection in the Third World because it has relied on a theory of economic development that fails to account properly for the value of standing stocks of natural resources and does not accord adequate weight to environmental externalities such as the loss of biological diversity arising from the destruction of moist tropical forests.[10] We cannot assume that the influence of international organizations on environmental negotiations will always be constructive. Like states, these organizations have interests that may or may not provide them with incentives to occupy a place in the vanguard regarding specific transboundary environmental issues.

Some observers have suggested as well that international organizations loom larger in some stages of the negotiating process than in others. Specifically, the idea has surfaced that international organizations are more central to the preparatory or prenegotiation phase and to the implementation phase than they are to the actual bargaining phase.[11] There is some merit to this idea. The experience of UNEP leaves little doubt that international organizations can and often do exercise considerable influence over the formulation of environmental issues before negotiations actually get under way. And depending upon the character of the regimes formed, organizations may be critical to the implementation or administration of the mechanisms established. Even so, it would be a mistake to overlook the growing importance of international organizations during the course of institutional bargaining over the provisions of environmental regimes per se (for example, the ongoing efforts to develop effective governance systems to control climate change and protect biological diversity). It seems fair to conclude that if international organizations

[10] On the need for an accounting system that incorporates the value of standing stocks of natural resources see Robert Repetto, "Balance-Sheet Erosion—How to Account for the Loss on Natural Resources," *International Environmental Affairs* 1 (Spring 1989), 103–137.

[11] On the concept of prenegotiation see Janice Gross Stein, ed., *Getting to the Table: The Process of International Prenegotiation* (Baltimore: Johns Hopkins University Press, 1989).

were not available to participate in institutional bargaining, we would have to invent them.

The Effectiveness of International Organizations

How effective are international organizations as instruments of regime formation with regard to environmental issues? Not surprisingly, a review of the record yields a mixed picture. UNEP has been, for the most part, a success story. So, too, have been the ECE with regard to transboundary air pollution, the International Maritime Organization (IMO) in the case of the regime established under the terms of the 1973/1978 Convention for the Prevention of Pollution from Ships, and the International Union for the Conservation of Nature and Natural Resources—a hybrid that is a cross between a nongovernmental organization and an intergovernmental organization—in connection with biological conservation regimes such as the arrangements for trade in endangered species set up under the 1973 Washington Convention on International Trade in Endangered Species of Fauna and Flora.

In other cases, international organizations have been less successful. The OECD encountered significant limits in dealing both with nuclear issues and with transboundary movements of hazardous wastes. The IAEA may well have set its sights too low in pushing, in the immediate aftermath of the Chernobyl accident, for the adoption of the 1986 Vienna conventions on notification and assistance in the event of a nuclear accident. The FAO has had a hand in establishing international regimes dealing with fisheries, but the regimes themselves have not proven particularly effective once in place. The role of UNCTAD in establishing commodity regimes to regulate international trade in primary products, including tin, coffee, sugar, and wheat, has been similarly problematic.[12] There are also hints in some recent cases that international organizations can become overactive participants in environmental negotiations, exacerbating the collective-action problems associated with such negotiations rather than helping to solve them or pushing for arrangements that seem attractive on paper but that are unlikely to prove workable in practice. Although the evidence is far from clear-cut, such problems seem to have oc-

[12] Jock A. Finlayson and Mark W. Zacher, *Managing International Markets: Developing Countries and the Commodity Regime* (New York: Columbia University Press, 1988).

curred in the negotiations that produced some of the contemporary regimes dealing with the conservation of species and ecosystems.

What accounts for this variation in the effectiveness of international organizations in environmental negotiations? The answer to this question undoubtedly turns on a combination of exogenous and endogenous factors. In the case of ozone depletion, for example, UNEP benefited from strong public interest, the development of a relatively high degree of consensus among scientists regarding the issue, and the emergence of the necessary political will among the participating states. Yet it is undeniable that UNEP was also able to capitalize on the reputation for efficacy it had developed through prior activities (for example, the Regional Seas Programme) and that Mostafa Tolba, UNEP's executive director, played a skillful leadership role, particularly in the crucial negotiations eventuating in the 1987 Montreal Protocol on Substances That Deplete the Ozone Layer. Many of the same comments apply to the regime for transboundary movements of hazardous wastes articulated in the 1989 Basel Convention. What is needed, then, is a convergence of exogenous and endogenous factors to maximize the effectiveness of international organizations in environmental negotiations.

Are such convergences likely to occur regularly in the future and, in particular, can we expect them to occur in conjunction with evolving issues of global environmental change, including climate change and biological diversity? There is, in my judgment, no basis for taking such convergences for granted. As the 1989 United Nations debate on UNCED and the 1990 decision to establish the INC as a separate entity suggest, these issues may become too important and too politicized to be left to an organization like UNEP, no matter how technically competent it is. The issues themselves may raise questions, such as the responsibility of states for environmental destruction occurring within their own jurisdictions or the obligations of developed countries to assist developing countries in dealing with their environmental problems, that can be resolved only at the highest political levels. Yet it would be inappropriate to arrive at bleak conclusions about the probable roles of international organizations as instruments of environmental regime formation during the near future. Just as the 1972 United Nations Conference on the Human Environment set in motion a train of events that facilitated the work of UNEP during the 1970s and 1980s, the accomplishments of UNCED may propel organizations like UNEP, WMO, or the recently established United Nations Commission on Sustainable Development to the forefront in dealing with issues of global environmental change during the 1990s. The roles international organizations play in specific environmental negotiations are closely linked to broader political developments. To the extent that these larger trends are favorable, therefore, international organizations may emerge as key players in a variety of environmental negotiations during the next decade.

INTERNATIONAL ORGANIZATIONS AS OBJECTS

So far, I have been examining roles international organizations play in the institutional bargaining that gives rise to environmental regimes without paying much attention to the specific issues at stake. But organizations must also be viewed as objects, and we need to address some questions relating to efforts during the course of environmental negotiations to design international organizations intended to implement or administer the provisions of environmental governance systems. The cases referred in the preceding discussion suggest some interesting observations about the creation of international organizations as products of the institutional bargaining eventuating in the formation of environmental regimes.

The Demand for Organizations

When are organizations needed to implement or administer the provisions of international regimes dealing with environmental matters? It is clear both that some regimes are capable of operating successfully with little or no assistance from organizations and that there is considerable variation among regimes in this area. The core regime for Antarctica established under the terms of the Antarctic Treaty of 1959 has no administrative apparatus; the complementary regime for living resources created under the terms of the 1980 Convention on the Conservation of Antarctic Marine Living Resources is administered by a commission assisted by a scientific committee and backstopped by a secretariat. Though the regime for whales set up under the 1946 International Convention for the Regulation of Whaling features some significant standing organizations, the international regime for the conservation of polar bears relies entirely on administrative mechanisms operating within the range states. Similarly, for the regime for the protection of stratospheric ozone, it made perfect sense to rely on national governments to administer the provisions of the 1987 Montreal Protocol, but the administration of the compensation fund established under the 1990 London Amendments has been entrusted to an international organizational mechanism known as the Executive Committee.

An examination of actual practice at the international level suggests the value of differentiating among various functions that may justify the creation of organizations to administer the provisions of environmental regimes. The need to gather, analyze, and disseminate information, a function that encompasses but is not restricted to research, seems to many to constitute an undeniable, albeit circumscribed, basis on which to build the case for establishing organizations in conjunction with international regimes. How could the International Whaling Commission set quotas for harvests or establish moratoria, the World Heritage Committee make decisions about sites to be included on the World Heritage List, or the biennial CITES conferences reach conclusions regarding the placement of species on Appendices I and II without a ready source of credible information? But even this argument is not ironclad. The core Antarctic Treaty regime has functioned well without an apparatus of its own for gathering and disseminating information.[13] Much the same is true of the polar bear regime and the regime for North Pacific fur seals (though the latter arrangement collapsed in the 1980s for other reasons).

Other functions that seem to require an administrative apparatus, include authoritative decision making, raising and disbursing revenues, handling transfer payments (including technology transfers), managing buffer stocks, eliciting compliance, resolving disputes, and evaluating outcomes. Given the way the regimes in question are structured, it seems natural to turn to organizations to handle such tasks as deciding whether Antarctic marine living resources are sufficiently abundant to allow commercial harvests, handling economic returns and rents accruing from deep seabed mining, managing the compensation fund for developing countries endeavoring to phase out their use of chlorofluorocarbons, certifying compliance with the terms of rules pertaining to the peaceful uses of atomic energy, and so forth. But imaginative negotiators can and often do succeed in devising ways to perform these tasks that eliminate or minimize the need to

---

[13] This situation has undoubtedly contributed to the development of a significant role for the Scientific Committee on Antarctic Research, a nongovernmental organization that belongs to the International Council of Scientific Unions and has no formal link to the Antarctic Treaty System.

create new international organizations. To illustrate, the across-the-board reductions in the production and consumption of CFCs mandated under the terms of the Montreal Protocol are being carried out under the supervision of national administrative agencies operating within each participating country. National administrators can take responsibility for implementing common rules within their own jurisdictions, as in the case of polar bears, without any need for an international organization to oversee the administration of a regime. And the mutual inspection provisions of the 1959 Antarctic Treaty offer an ingenious device for ensuring compliance without creating a specialized international organization to handle this function.

What can we conclude from these observations? Although the establishment of organizations is certainly justifiable in connection with some international environmental regimes, it is worth emphasizing the extent to which ingenious negotiators can devise institutional arrangements that operate effectively in the absence of international organizations to administer their provisions. There is a sense, moreover, in which the burden of proof rests with those who advocate the creation of international organizations in conjunction with environmental regimes. All organizations are costly to operate, whether these costs are measured in straightforward monetary terms or in terms of more intangible consequences such as opportunities lost as a result of bureaucratization or the inefficiencies arising from co-optation by special interests. It follows that when it is possible to eliminate or minimize reliance on organizations without sacrificing effectiveness, the case against the creation of new international organizations is compelling. In the more typical case in which there are trade-offs between the usefulness of organizations in the pursuit of effectiveness and the costs of operating these organizations, on the other hand, there is a need for clear-sighted analysis to make appropriate decisions. In some instances, the parties engaged in institutional bargaining regarding international environmental regimes will have conflicting preferences regarding these trade-offs. Yet in many cases, the problem is more a matter of using analytic techniques to arrive at well-reasoned conclusions about the character of suitable organizations than of bargaining to resolve conflicts of interest.

Types of Organization

A conclusion that some sort of organization is needed to implement or administer the provisions of an international governance system does not resolve the issues at stake. On the contrary, such a decision leads to several additional sets of considerations. There is, to begin with, the question of whether to create an independent organization to administer a new regime or to piggyback on an existing organization created initially for some other purpose or even to form a coalition with others for the purpose of sharing administrative mechanisms among several distinct regimes. The CITES regime, for instance, delegates many of the relevant administrative chores to UNEP, which has handed them over in turn to IUCN and the World Wildlife Fund. For many years, the Bureau of Whaling Statistics, which antedated the 1946 convention on whaling and was never formally a component of the international whaling regime, was able to handle much of the collection and dissemination of information about whaling. The IAEA, an organization created some time ago for other reasons, has administered the provisions of the 1986 conventions dealing with notification and assistance in the event of nuclear accidents.

Though we live in an era marked by rapid growth in the ranks of international organizations, there is much to be said for taking seriously the ideas of piggybacking on existing organizations or sharing organizational arrangements among regimes. The downside of this approach is that the resultant arrangements cannot be tailored to fit the needs of particular regimes. In some cases, this may seem a significant drawback. But those negotiating the terms of environmental regimes are well aware that it is difficult in today's world to provide secure funding for international organizations and that a diversified portfolio of functions may contribute to the financial stability of any organizations they establish. Here, again, there may be conflicts of interest among the participants in institutional bargaining relating to the formation of international environmental regimes. More often than not, however, this issue is likely to become a topic for joint problem solving, as the participants seek to devise administrative mechanisms capable of handling tasks effectively, while minimizing the financial burden placed on the members of the resultant regimes.[14]

It is apparent as well that the nature of the organizations needed will be closely tied to the character of the governance systems or

[14] For a helpful account of problem solving or integrative bargaining in contrast to distributive bargaining see Richard E. Walton and Robert B. McKersie, *A Behavioral Theory of Labor Negotiations: An Analysis of a Social Interaction System* (New York: McGraw-Hill, 1965), chaps. 4 and 5.

regimes they are intended to serve. Any regime calling for authoritative decisions about catch quotas or harvest limits, the inclusion of species on protected lists, measures to protect migration routes, and the like will require a sophisticated capability for making scientific judgments about the population dynamics of individual species (not to mention other species with which they interact) and for monitoring the results of these decisions over time. A regime that relies on command-and-control regulations, such as the arrangements governing sulfur and nitrogen oxide emissions under the protocols to the 1979 Geneva Convention, calls for different administrative capabilities than a regime that makes use of incentive systems such as transferable fishing permits or permits for the emission of various pollutants. Regimes that contemplate the raising or distribution of revenues, for example, the ozone compensation fund or the revenue-generating provisions of the now defunct Convention for the Regulation of Antarctic Mineral Resource Activities (CRAMRA), require administrative mechanisms that are not needed when there are no issues pertaining to revenues (other than the costs of administration). Even more dramatically, the Enterprise, envisioned as an operating authority under the deep seabed mining provisions set forth in Part XI of the 1982 Convention on the Law of the Sea, would differ profoundly from the International Seabed Authority (ISA), treated as an agency with regulatory authority but no capacity to engage in mining operations in its own right.

It is easy to imagine the emergence of conflicts of interest regarding the nature of the organizations to be established in conjunction with environmental regimes because such matters are closely tied to the underlying character of the regimes themselves. Given the clash between the United States and the Group of 77 over the fundamental character of a regime for deep seabed mining, for example, it is hardly surprising that it was ultimately impossible to reach agreement on organizational details pertaining to the International Seabed Authority and the Enterprise. The sharp differences between environmentalists and others that surfaced regarding the governance system envisioned in CRAMRA created similar problems. Because organizations are material entities that are relatively easy to grasp in concrete terms, it is to be expected that those participating in negotiations aimed at creating environmental regimes will bargain particularly hard over the character of the organizations set up to implement and administer the institutional arrangements they create.

Avoiding Perennial Problems

Though the establishment of organizations may make perfectly good sense under the circumstances at hand, any move to set up new organizations triggers concern about a number of classic problems that are just as relevant to international environmental governance systems as they are to any other social institutions. These include paralysis, underfunding, co-optation, intrusiveness, and bureaucratization. There are no magic solutions to these problems. But those engaged in institutional bargaining at the international level would do well to foresee the relevance of such matters to the specific situations they are confronting and to take steps in advance to mitigate their impact.

The problems of paralysis and underfunding emerge again and again in connection with international organizations. Paralysis typically occurs when those setting up an organization insist on a decision-making procedure requiring unanimity so that they are assured the power to veto actions they dislike even after the organization is up and running. There are examples of imaginative ways to alleviate this problem in conjunction with international environmental regimes. One constructive device is to rely on a majoritarian decision rule with a provision for a limited veto, as in the case of CRAMRA, or a provision allowing individual members to opt out of specific decisions, as in the cases of the whaling regime and CITES. Another is to combine a majoritarian rule with some form of weighted voting, as in the case of the International Monetary Fund. The problem of underfunding can be at least as serious as the danger of paralysis in limiting the effectiveness of international organizations. The common tendency of member states to refuse to grant international organizations a means of generating their own revenues and, therefore, to compel them to rely exclusively on dues or voluntary contributions from individual members has proven particularly debilitating. Yet the development of environmental regimes offers some attractive options for mitigating this problem. The idea of allowing organizations, acting in the name of the common heritage of mankind, to collect economic royalties or rents, as envisioned in the cases of the International Seabed Authority and the commission called for under CRAMRA, is an interesting one. So also is the idea of allowing organizations to collect revenues through the sale of permits for the harvest of renewable resources or the emission of various effluents.

The danger of co-optation or the capture of administrative agen-

cies by special interests is just as relevant, though perhaps less familiar, at the international level as it is in domestic society. The developing countries have long complained about the capacity of affluent
countries in general and the United States in particular to control
IMF decisions. The United States has taken a similar view of the role
of the Group of 77 in UNCTAD and the potential role of this group
in the activities of the ISA. The Antarctic Treaty Consultative Parties
claim that any move to bring the Antarctic Treaty System under the
umbrella of the United Nations would play into the hands of the
special interests of the developing countries. And many environmentalists asserted that mining interests would have been able to exercise
undue influence over the behavior of the organizational mechanisms
(especially the regulatory committees) envisioned under CRAMRA.
No doubt, there is an element of truth to some of these charges; few
organizations are immune to pressure from special interests. Yet steps
taken to minimize the problem of co-optation, such as insisting on
unanimity as a decision rule, run the risk of exacerbating other classic
problems, including paralysis.

Intrusiveness and bureaucratization are other problems well-
known to those who have studied the behavior of administrative agencies in domestic society. The administration of complex regimes requires the promulgation of implementing regulations, which may in
turn become bones of contention both among those who believe that
they are not being implemented in a manner consonant with the
intent of a regime's creators and on the part of those who argue that
the resultant red tape constitutes an inefficient and unjust burden on
actors whose activities they regulate. Although there is no final solution to such problems, experience in the domestic realm does suggest
lessons that are worth considering in creating organizations to administer international environmental regimes. Systems relying on transferable use rights in contrast to command-and-control regulations,
for example, leave more room for discretionary action on the part of
subjects and encourage efficiency by allowing subjects to meet requirements in the least expensive manner. Similarly, devices designed
to maximize transparency as a means of ensuring compliance have the
virtue of reducing the need for intrusive monitoring and avoiding
inconclusive arguments regarding the extent to which subjects have
or have not complied with applicable rules in specific situations.[15]

[15] Abram Chayes and Antonia H. Chayes, "Adjustment and Compliance Processes in
International Regulatory Regimes," in Jessica Tuchman Mathews, ed., *Preserving the Global
Environment: The Challenge of Shared Leadership* (New York: Norton, 1991), 309–323.

It is to be hoped that those responsible for negotiating the terms of international environmental regimes will give sustained thought to alleviating these perennial problems. There is no guarantee that the resultant negotiations will be trouble free; conflicts of interest are likely to arise. Those who fear co-optation are likely to push for unanimity as the applicable decision rule, whereas those more concerned about paralysis will favor some form of majoritarian rule. Negotiators hailing from capitalist countries are apt to be more resistant to arrangements based on command-and-control regulation than those who come from socialist countries. Those concerned about the deadening effects of bureaucratic red tape are likely to resist efforts to provide international organizations with sizable revenue streams that they can control on their own. There are no correct answers to differences of opinion regarding these matters. Negotiations about them are therefore apt to take on the mixed-motive character long familiar to students of bargaining.[16] Yet we should not conclude that the search for solutions to these perennial problems of administration offers no opportunities for imaginative and mutually beneficial problem solving. In fact, there is much to be said for the proposition that this is an area with considerable scope for inventiveness on the part of those who think about questions of institutional design coupled with leadership on the part of those who participate directly in institutional bargaining concerning international environmental regimes.[17]

CONCLUSION

We live in an era of increasing international interdependencies that give rise to growing demands for governance systems to manage human activities that would otherwise interfere with and produce harmful effects on each other. Nowhere is this more apparent than in the realm of natural resources and the environment. In this connection, the anarchical character of international society will strike many as an obstacle to progress. But this is not the only perspective from which to approach issues relating to the management of environmental interdependencies. The absence of a central government at the interna-

[16] For a seminal account of bargaining as a form of mixed-motive interaction see Thomas C. Schelling, *The Strategy of Conflict* (Cambridge, Mass.: Harvard University Press, 1960).
[17] On leadership in the context of institutional bargaining see Young, "Political Leadership and Regime Formation."

tional level does not rule out the prospect of creating international environmental regimes and the organizations needed to implement and administer them. Equally important, the absence of an established central government makes it possible to avoid the difficulties of establishing new arrangements in the face of parochial opposition on the part of interests entrenched in existing organizations. A review of recent experience makes it abundantly clear that the resultant opportunities have given rise to considerable ferment with regard to the development of international environmental regimes. Although recent initiatives in this realm vary greatly in their effectiveness and attractiveness on other grounds, there is room for cautious optimism among students of international environmental affairs.[18]

At the same time, new challenges may soon make the issues of the recent past seem elementary by comparison. The advent of an era of global environmental changes—most of them largely anthropogenic in nature—is particularly striking in this regard. Some of these changes, including the climate-altering potential of the greenhouse effect, may well require fundamental revisions in the way we think about economic growth and force us to confront seriously North-South issues as they have arisen in discussions of environment and development in forums like UNCED.[19] Others, such as the loss of biological diversity, raise complex questions regarding the stakes of outsiders in activities occurring largely within the borders of individual states and the justifiability of various forms of intervention on the part of outsiders claiming to act in the name of international society. Although the potential for conflicts of interest over such matters is great, there are also opportunities for international cooperation that can provide a basis for the establishment of important new international governance systems and the organizations needed to make them function effectively. To the extent that such opportunities come into focus during the foreseeable future, it will be essential to draw lessons from the experiences of the recent past about what works and what does not work in linking institutions and organizations in the interests of solving large-scale environmental problems. Only by con-

---

[18] For a sophisticated assessment of recent experience in this realm see Peter H. Sand, *Lessons Learned in Global Environmental Governance* (Washington, D.C.: World Resources Institute, 1990).

[19] See Michael Grubb, *The Greenhouse Effect: Negotiating Targets* (London: Royal Institute of International Affairs, 1989); and the review of this work in James K. Sebenius, "Report on Reports," *Environment* 32 (November 1990), 25–30.

ducting such analyses and, in the process, fostering the intellectual cooperation between students of international institutions and international organizations needed to carry them out successfully can we learn from our experiences and prepare ourselves to deal constructively with the challenges that lie ahead.

CHAPTER EIGHT

Governance Systems and International Legal Regimes

In this concluding chapter, I seek to foster linkages between two sizable but largely disjoint streams of analysis pertaining to international governance: the perspectives of law and the contributions of the social sciences. These bodies of knowledge and the communities of scholars who have produced them have great potential for mutual enrichment. Yet they have not joined in any systematic way to develop a comprehensive account of international institutions or governance systems. What accounts for this failure, and how can we solve this problem in the future? In addressing this topic, I again take examples from institutional arrangements for natural resources and the environment. But the analysis is generic; it should attract the attention of those whose studies of international governance systems pertain to security, economics, or human rights as well as those concerned with the rapidly growing agenda of international environmental issues.

IDENTIFYING LEGAL REGIMES

To introduce this complex subject, I ask, What makes an institution or some of its elements legal? Is it reasonable to expect that we can

Earlier versions of this chapter were prepared for presentation at the annual conventions of the International Studies Association, Vancouver, B.C., 20–23 March 1991, and the American Society of International Law, Washington, D.C., 1–3 April 1992.

formulate a concrete distinction between legal regimes on the one hand and illegal regimes or nonlegal regimes—including economic, political, and social arrangements—on the other? Are we better off seeking to draw an analytic distinction between the legal and the economic, political, and social aspects of the same international institutions on the understanding that a single governance system may encompass several or all of these aspects? Alternatively, does the distinction we are looking for lie more in the modes of reasoning characteristic of law and the social sciences than in their subject matter?

There is no litmus test that we can apply to specific international institutions with reasonable confidence that it will yield simple and unambiguous answers to the questions I have posed. To come to terms with this subject, then, we must start by unpacking the basic issue and then proceed to address subsidiary questions that emerge in the process. In this section, I explore a range of these questions. In the next section, I examine the implications of the argument presented for the prospects of joining the contributions of legal scholars and social scientists to broaden and deepen our understanding of international governance systems.

Do legal regimes differ from other international governance systems because their membership is limited to sovereign states or because they can enter into force only when ratified by states? A model of international law centered on rules developed over time to guide the interactions of sovereign states as the members of international society[1] has the virtues of simplicity and receptivity to comforting analogies between domestic society and international society and also of compatibility with the interests of the most powerful members of international society. Analytically, nothing could be simpler than a system whose members all occupy the same basic role (that is, they are all sovereign states) and enjoy a fundamental legal equality (that is, they are subject to the same rules and share the same rights and duties). The analogy between the role of individual states as the members of international society and the role of individual persons as the members of domestic society adds to the illusion of simplicity by making it easy to deem-

---

[1] As J. L. Brierly puts it in his well-known text, international law "may be defined as the body of rules and principles of action which are binding upon civilized states in their relations with one another" (*The Law of Nations*, 6th. ed. [New York: Oxford University Press, 1963], 1).

phasize or even to overlook complications arising from the fact that states are collective entities.[2] Equally important, powerful states, which invariably benefit from economic and political inequalities in international society, have obvious incentives to support a legal system that operates to maintain and secure their advantages.[3]

Whatever its merits as a characterization of the international legal system and, more generally, international society in earlier eras, this superficially appealing model is wholly inadequate as the foundation of a general account of international law today.[4] It cannot provide a useful means of distinguishing between legal regimes and other international governance systems. Just as municipal law accords legal personality to a variety of collective entities, including government agencies, business corporations, and a multiplicity of associations, contemporary public international law recognizes entities other than states, including intergovernmental organizations, nongovernmental organizations, and even individuals, as actors capable of participating in the formation and administration of international regimes in their own right.[5] It would be impossible under any other assumption, for example, to develop a convincing account of the roles the United Nations Environment Programme and its executive directors Maurice Strong and Mostafa Tolba have played in the formation and operation of regimes to control pollution in the Mediterranean Basin, phase out the production and consumption of chlorofluorocarbons worldwide, and regulate transboundary movements of hazardous wastes.[6] When we turn from the concerns of public international law

[2] On the analytic issues arising from the fact that the members of international society are collective entities see Robert D. Putnam, "Diplomacy and Domestic Politics: The Logic of Two-Level Games," *International Organization* 42 (Summer 1988), 427–460.

[3] This legal "conservatism" is a source of the doubts many have raised about Bull's well-known effort to treat the protection of property as one of the basic values or goals of international society. See Hedley Bull, *The Anarchical Society: A Study of Order in World Politics* (New York: Columbia University Press, 1977), chap. 1.

[4] See K. J. Holsti, "Governance without Government: Polyarchy in Nineteenth Century European International Politics," and Mark W. Zacher, "The Decaying Pillars of the Westphalian Temple: Implications for International Order and Governance," in James N. Rosenau and Ernst-Otto Czempiel, eds., *Governance without Government: Change and Order in World Politics* (New York: Cambridge University Press, 1992), 30–101.

[5] Rosalyn Higgins, "Conceptual Thinking about the Individual in International Law," in Richard Falk, Friedrich Kratochwil, and Saul H. Mendlovitz, eds., *International Law: A Contemporary Perspective* (Boulder: Westview Press, 1985), 476–494.

[6] For a detailed account of the Mediterranean case see Peter M. Haas, *Saving the Mediterranean: The Politics of International Environmental Cooperation* (New York: Columbia University Press, 1990).

to the regimes that populate the world of private international law, moreover, the scene is dominated by efforts to regulate the behavior of a wide variety of nonstate actors—including private and public corporations, banks and insurance companies, airlines and shipping companies—that engage in extensive transboundary activities.

Nor is it helpful to maintain the fiction that the provisions of international regimes can become legal rights and duties only through ratification by member states. Virtually everyone acknowledges that many, perhaps most, of the provisions of the 1982 Convention on the Law of the Sea became part of the corpus of international law well before the convention received the requisite number of ratifications to enter into force formally. Similarly, it is hard to deny that a number of principles pertaining to responsibility for transboundary environmental impacts—originating with the Trail Smelter case of the 1920s and 1930s and finding fuller expression in the declaration of the 1972 United Nations Conference on the Human Environment, the 1987 report of the World Commission on Environment and Development, and the 1992 declaration of the United Nations Conference on Environment and Development—have begun to acquire the status of law, even though states have not adopted them in any formal sense.[7] Conversely, ratification by the relevant states offers no guarantee that an incipient international regime will achieve acceptance as an effective component of the international legal order. History is replete, for instance, with legal arrangements intended to control or eliminate the international traffic in narcotics that have ended up as dead letters.[8]

Do the generative sources of the legal prescriptions embedded in international regimes differ from those of nonlegal prescriptions? The field of international law is not characterized by consensus concerning the generative sources of legal prescriptions or the "creation stories" devised to explain the origins of law in international society.[9] This point can be

---

[7] Jan Schneider, "State Responsibility for Environmental Protection and Preservation," in Falk, Kratochwil, and Mendlovitz, eds., *International Law*, 602–633.

[8] See Ethan A. Nadelmann, "Global Prohibition Regimes: The Evolution of Norms in International Society," *International Organization* 44 (Autumn 1990), 479–526; and Janice E. Thompson, "The Genesis and Internationalization of Norms," in Rosenau and Czempiel, eds., *Governance without Government*, 195–218.

[9] For a particularly influential modern exchange on this subject see the debate between H. L. A. Hart, "Positivism and the Separation of Law and Morals," *Harvard Law Review* 71 (1958), 593–629, and Lon L. Fuller, "Positivism and Fidelity to Law: A Reply

illustrated by considering the constellation of prescriptions known collectively as the law of the sea, both before and after the Third United Nations Conference on the Law of the Sea (UNCLOS III).[10] Natural law thinkers see these prescriptions as applications to marine issues of underlying principles that exist independently of human thought or action so that the development of international law in this issue area is a matter of developing appropriate procedures for discovering and translating these principles into specific legal prescriptions. Legal positivists, by contrast, operate from a contractarian vantage point that envisions the prescriptions making up the law of the sea as social artifacts in the sense that they add up to a social or constitutional contract resting on the consent (implied if not explicit) of those whose activities they govern. For their part, legal scholars influenced by the contemporary law and society movement tend to treat the law of the sea as an evolving system of prescriptions reflecting underlying socioeconomic or political conditions and arising from the flow of authoritative decisions occurring within a variety of overlapping arenas.[11]

Though they differ among themselves on matters relating to regime formation and the effectiveness of international regimes, most social scientists who have contributed to the rapidly growing literature on regimes approach institutional arrangements as devices for solving collective-action problems at the international level.[12] They are inclined to look for the origins of the law of the sea in efforts to solve problems associated with the human use of shared (or transboundary) resources or international commons. These scholars differ in their perspectives on the ontological status of international regimes and,

---

to Professor Hart," *Harvard Law Review* 71 (1958), 630–671. For an account that refers specifically to "creation stories" see Ronald R. Garet, "Natural Law and Creation Stories," in J. Roland Pennock and John W. Chapman, eds., *Religion, Morality, and the Law (NOMOS XXX)* (New York: New York University Press, 1988), 218–262.

[10] For an insightful account of recent developments in the law of the sea presented from a regime perspective see Robert L. Friedheim, *Negotiating the New Ocean Regime* (Columbia: University of South Carolina Press, 1993).

[11] For a brief and accessible introduction to what is often called the New Haven school of thought on international law see Myres S. McDougal and Harold D. Lasswell, "The Identification and Appraisal of Diverse Systems of Public Order," in Falk, Kratochwil, and Mendlovitz, eds., *International Law*, 163–187.

[12] Stephen D. Krasner, ed., *International Regimes* (Ithaca: Cornell University Press, 1983); Robert O. Keohane, *After Hegemony: Cooperation and Discord in the World Political Economy* (Princeton: Princeton University Press, 1984); and Oran R. Young, *International Cooperation: Building Regimes for Natural Resources and the Environment* (Ithaca: Cornell University Press, 1989).

consequently, in their views regarding appropriate epistemologies for the study of regimes. The central debate arrays those who think in behavioral terms and subscribe to some variety of positivism or neo-positivism against those who emphasize the subjective character of social institutions and call for the deployment of nonpositivist procedures (for example, what some have characterized as an "interpretive epistemology") in the effort to understand regimes.[13]

These jurisprudential and epistemological concerns overlap or intersect at some points and diverge at others. The contractarian perspective of legal positivism, for example, fits comfortably with the collective-action viewpoint developed by political scientists and economists interested in international governance systems. There is little in the social science literature, by contrast, that maps easily onto the essentialist concerns of those engaged in natural law thinking. But more to the point, this discussion offers no support for the view that the generative sources of legal prescriptions differ in some fundamental way from those of other prescriptions. Arguably, natural laws differ from other rules, norms, or social conventions because they exist independently of human thought or action. But natural law thinking does not dominate the field of international law. In any case, natural law analyses are notoriously difficult to operationalize so that it is commonplace to encounter sharp disagreements about the legal status of specific prescriptions among those who share a commitment to the basic tenets of the natural law perspective.

Do legal regimes exhibit a higher degree of formalization than other regimes? A superficially attractive response to our basic question arises from the idea that international prescriptions become legal when they are incorporated explicitly into the provisions of formal instruments such as conventions, treaties, and protocols. This is the international law equivalent of equating law in municipal systems with what is commonly known as "black letter" law or the provisions of statutes. In both cases, the problem is the same; this tack confuses a particular variety

[13] Friedrich V. Kratochwil and John Gerard Ruggie, "International Organization: A State of the Art or an Art of the State," *International Organization* 40 (Autumn 1986), 753–776. For thoughtful discussions of nonpositivist approaches consult Friedrich V. Kratochwil, *Rules, Norms, and Decisions: On the Conditions of Practical and Legal Reasoning in International Relations and Domestic Affairs* (Cambridge, Eng.: Cambridge University Press, 1989); and Nicholas Greenwood Onuf, *World of Our Making: Rules and Rule in Social Theory and International Relations* (Columbia: University of South Carolina Press, 1989).

or type of law with law in general. As a result, it fails to direct our attention to any generic features of law that would make it possible to distinguish between legal regimes and other regimes or between legal and nonlegal prescriptions at the international level.

Life would be simpler—not least for students of international affairs—if the entire body of international law were set forth in a collection of treaties or conventions. Those who devote themselves to the codification of international law seem to be motivated in part by a vision of this sort.[14] But a moment's thought will remind us that much of international law takes the form of customary law and, increasingly, of what has come to be known as "soft law." The concept of customary law is straightforward enough; it refers to prescriptions that can be inferred from social practices at the international level even though they have never been set forth formally in a treaty or a convention. Soft law is a more subtle phenomenon whose growing significance correlates with the decline of the model of international law as a constellation of rules applicable to a society composed exclusively of sovereign states.[15] The category encompasses prescriptions such as resolutions of the United Nations General Assembly, declarations of multinational conferences (for example, the 1972 United Nations Conference on the Human Environment and the 1992 United Nations Conference on Environment and Development), and decisions of supranational bodies (for example, the annual review conferences organized under the terms of the ozone regime) that are not legally binding in any formal sense but that are often accepted as playing a regulative role in international society.

To make matters more complex, legal institutions share with all other social institutions a propensity to acquire informal dimensions or elements with the passage of time.[16] Partly, this is a result of the development of common understandings concerning what formal,

---

[14] In recent decades, the International Law Commission, operating under the auspices of the United Nations General Assembly, has become the principal forum for codification efforts. See Nicholas Greenwood Onuf, "International Codification: Interpreting the Last Half-Century," in Falk, Kratochwil, and Mendlovitz, eds., *International Law,* 264–279.

[15] For a sophisticated discussion of what counts as international law under contemporary conditions consult Anthony D'Amato, "What 'Counts' as Law?" in Nicholas G. Onuf, ed., *Lawmaking in the Global Community* (Durham: Carolina Academic Press, 1982), 83–107. For an account that stresses the role of soft law options regarding environmental issues see Peter S. Thacher, "Alternative Legal and Institutional Approaches to Global Change," *Colorado Journal of International Environmental Law and Policy* 1 (Summer 1990), 101–126.

[16] James G. March and Herbert A. Simon, *Organizations* (New York: Wiley, 1958).

but often imprecise, formulas are taken to mean in practice. It is hard to imagine making effective use even of analytically well-defined concepts, such as maximum sustainable yield or endangered species, much less more nebulous concepts, like sustainable development, in the absence of such common understandings. In part, it is a matter of filling in gaps left in the formalization of legal regimes. The 1973 five-nation regime for the protection of polar bears, for example, has little to say about procedures for dispute resolution or for dealing with proposals concerning changes in the provisions of the regime itself.[17] But an examination of the social practice that has grown up around this regime reveals that the informal views of the parties on such matters are generally compatible so that these gaps need not be regarded as flaws in the regime.

Are some issue areas better suited to legal regulation or control than others? There is an understandable tendency to try to solve the problem of distinguishing between legal and nonlegal prescriptions by simply saying that some issues or issue areas are inherently legal in character, while others are not. This way of thinking is attractive because it suggests a method of differentiating between legal regimes and other regimes that is both clear-cut and generic. But is it possible to formulate a criterion that will allow us to divide subjects neatly into those that are legal and those that are? Perhaps the most sophisticated effort to pursue this line of thinking is reflected in the long-running debate about the concept of justiciability as a means of separating legal issues from issues that are essentially political and therefore not amenable to regulation or resolution through the articulation and application of legal prescriptions.[18] But as the history of this debate clearly indicates, the idea that this strategy offers a simple solution to our underlying problem is illusory. Not only is it possible to cast most matters either as legal or as political issues depending upon the purpose at hand, but it is also apparent that what are treated as legal issues in some eras and in some social settings are cast as political matters at other times and in other places.

The current efforts to develop international regimes dealing with

[17] The relevant article of the Agreement on the Conservation of Polar Bears of 15 November 1973 says only that "the Contracting Parties shall continue to consult with one another with the object of giving further protection to polar bears."

[18] P. E. Corbett, *Law and Society in the Relations of States* (New York: Harcourt, Brace, 1951), esp. 77–79. An analogous exercise might focus on separating legal issues from issues that are moral or ethical in character.

climate change and the loss of biological diversity are cases in point. Much time and energy is now going into working out provisions of institutional arrangements in these areas suitable for inclusion in international treaties or conventions.[19] Recently, these matters have become prominent on the international agenda as a result of the effort required to reach agreement—at least on framework conventions—in time to be opened for signature at the June 1992 United Nations Conference on Environment and Development. But what does this tell us about the distinction between legal issues and nonlegal issues? Few would question that climate change and biological diversity are appropriate topics for treatment in legal instruments such as treaties or conventions. But it is equally apparent that these issues are profoundly political because they raise basic questions about the responsibility of states for the impacts on others of activities taking place within their own jurisdictions and the terms on which North-South bargaining over global environmental issues will proceed.[20] In these cases, which are far from atypical, it is not possible to designate the relevant issues as essentially legal or nonlegal. The legal, political, economic, and even cultural dimensions of the issues are so bound up with each other that it is difficult to devise useful analytic distinctions among the various aspects of the issues, much less concrete distinctions dividing these issue areas into legal and nonlegal components.

Is the nature of the obligation to comply with legal prescriptions different from the obligation to comply with other prescriptions? The obligation to comply with the prescriptions of a governance system may arise, sometimes simultaneously, from several differentiable sources. Subjects may feel an obligation to comply with the prescriptions embedded in a regime because they see it as the proper thing to do on moral or ethical grounds (that is, for moral reasons), because compliance with the prescriptions constitutes a principle of right action regarded as binding upon the members of the group (that is, for normative reasons), because compliance is required by the terms of a constitutional contract they have entered into (that is, for contractual reasons), or be-

[19] Jessica Tuchman Mathews, ed., *Preserving the Global Environment: The Challenge of Shared Leadership* (New York: Norton, 1991).

[20] Ronnie D. Lipschutz and Ken Conca, eds., *Environmental Dramas on a Hundred Thousand Stages: Society, Politics, and Global Ecological Interdependence* (New York: Columbia University Press, 1993).

cause they have concluded on the basis of rule utilitarian calculations that it is in everyone's best interest to ensure the viability of international institutions by complying with their prescriptions (that is, for utilitarian reasons). Independently, though often concomitantly, subjects may feel an obligation to comply because prescriptions (along with the more detailed regulations promulgated to implement them) are authoritative, either because an acknowledged public authority has articulated them or because the prescriptions are the product of a process or procedure deemed authoritative (that is, for legal reasons).[21]

It is difficult to separate out the effects of these distinct sources of obligation in examining the thinking or behavior of individual subjects about the prescriptions of actual regimes. To what extent does the sense of obligation to comply with the provisions of the evolving international regime to protect stratospheric ozone, for example, rest on the enlightened self-interest of rule utilitarianism in contrast to some sense of normative or contractual obligation that stresses the importance of complying with a set of rights and rules entered into freely or voluntarily? Nonetheless, those who characterize certain prescriptions as legally binding typically have in mind rights and rules that subjects are obligated to comply with because they are authoritative in nature. Underlying this characterization in the minds of some, but by no means all, subjects is some form of contractarian reasoning. That is, some subjects will accept a set of rules as authoritative because processes acknowledged to be authoritative have resulted in their articulation in the form of a constitutional contract. Yet a moment's reflection will demonstrate that this is not the only possible source of authoritativeness.[22]

This way of thinking about the sources of the obligation to comply is certainly helpful. It allows us, for instance, to draw an important—and all too often misunderstood—distinction between norms that rest on the acceptance of socially defined principles of right action as

[21] J. Roland Pennock and John W. Chapman, eds., *Political and Legal Obligation (NOMOS XII)* (New York: Atherton Press, 1970).

[22] Some monarchs, for example, claim authority as a matter of divine right. For a discussion of the role of religion as a source of authority see Lisa Newton, "Divine Sanction and Legal Authority: Religion and the Infrastructure of the Law," in Pennock and Chapman, eds., *Religion, Morality, and the Law*, 179–200. For a range of perspectives on the sources of authority see J. Roland Pennock and John W. Chapman, eds., *Authority Revisited (NOMOS XXIX)* (New York: New York University Press, 1987).

a source of obligation and legal rules that acquire their obligatory character by virtue of their authoritativeness.[23] Similarly, it clarifies the distinction between legal rules and social conventions (for example, rules governing the right-of-way in transportation systems), which require nothing more than simple calculations of enlightened self-interest to make them seem obligatory.[24]

Even so, complications plague efforts to apply such reasoning, especially in social systems such as international society that are highly decentralized. Interested parties often have incentives to muddy the waters by conflating the different sources of obligation so as to elicit compliance with actual prescriptions. It may seem (for good reasons) easier, for example, to promote compliance when subjects can be persuaded that they are obligated to comply for moral or normative reasons than when their sense of obligation is based solely on utilitarian considerations. What is more, most of us are accustomed to associating authority with an easily identifiable actor or agency (for example, a monarch, an elected head of state, or a legislature), which helps to account for the difficulties often experienced in making clear-cut decisions regarding the authoritativeness of international prescriptions. This may explain why some students of international affairs devote as much or more attention to contractual rather than legal reasons in discussing the obligation to comply with the prescriptions of international governance systems. To the extent that this is true, it becomes easier to understand some of the paradoxes associated with our basic question.

Do subjects actually comply with legal prescriptions for reasons other than those that lead them to comply with nonlegal prescriptions? Many students of law place great emphasis on what they characterize as the force of law, an idea suggesting that subjects experience pressures to comply with legal prescriptions that differ from the pressures to comply with nonlegal prescriptions, whatever they may think about the sources of obligation discussed in the preceding paragraphs. For the most part, this argument flows from a model of human behavior that emphasizes the role of enforcement in eliciting compliance and, therefore, the importance of devising sanctions that not only are likely to be im-

---

[23] For a range of perspectives on norms consult the essays in the "Symposium on Norms in Moral and Social Theory," *Ethics* 100 (July 1990).

[24] David K. Lewis, *Convention: A Philosophical Study* (Cambridge, Mass.: Harvard University Press, 1969).

posed under specifiable circumstances but that also are likely to prove effective when they are imposed. It is this line of thought that has led some students of international affairs to question whether international law is law at all in any meaningful sense of the term.[25] Because enforcement in domestic legal systems is the responsibility of designated central authorities (typically one or another government agency) and because international society lacks central authorities, it is easy to reach the conclusion that international prescriptions cannot acquire the force of law and, therefore, cannot coalesce into a legal system.

Some analysts have sought to circumvent this problem by developing the concept of self-help or decentralized enforcement mechanisms; others have focused on the idea of collective security organized through international organizations such as the United Nations as a mechanism for mounting authoritative sanctions in international society.[26] A more fundamental way of dealing with the problem, however, flows from the distinction between compliance and enforcement coupled with the observation that sanctions or even threats to impose sanctions seldom constitute the most important determinant of observed levels of compliance with institutionalized rights and rules on the part of members of subject groups.[27] Even in domestic society, public authorities would soon find themselves overwhelmed if they had to rely primarily on enforcement to induce subjects to comply with prescriptions. This argument deemphasizes the importance of the distinction between domestic society and international society with regard to the centralization of public authority and, in the process, takes a lot of the bite out of the view that international law is not actually law in the proper sense because of the underdeveloped nature of enforcement mechanisms at the international level. As a byproduct, it also undermines the case for an affirmative answer to the question of whether subjects typically comply with legal prescriptions

[25] Wolfgang Friedmann, *The Changing Structure of International Law* (New York: Columbia University Press, 1964), chap. 8.

[26] Inis L. Claude, Jr., *Power and International Relations* (New York: Random House, 1962), chaps. 5–6; and Ernst A. Haas, "Collective Security and the Future of the International System," in Richard A. Falk and Cyril E. Black, eds., *Trends and Patterns*, Vol. 1 of *The Future of the International Legal Order* (Princeton: Princeton University Press, 1969), 226–316.

[27] For general treatments of compliance in international society see Oran R. Young, *Compliance and Public Authority, a Theory with International Applications* (Baltimore: Johns Hopkins University Press, 1979); and Roger Fisher, *Improving Compliance with International Law* (Charlottesville: University Press of Virginia, 1981).

for reasons other than those that lead them to comply with nonlegal prescriptions.

Are legal prescriptions necessarily accompanied by explicit procedures for resolving disputes about their application to specific situations and, in the process, providing authoritative interpretations of their meaning? There is considerable merit to the idea that an intimate relationship exists between law and the resolution of disputes.[28] A critical function of law in human societies is to provide a means for solving problems that arise when the efforts of individual actors to pursue their own interests come into conflict. There is, as well, a close connection between law and dispute resolution in a more applied sense. It is always possible to interpret specific fact patterns in terms of divergent legal principles, and it is no cause for surprise that the parties to disputes invariably invoke those legal principles that point to outcomes compatible with their own interests. Approached from this perspective, legal systems can be treated as procedural devices for arriving at authoritative judgments regarding the merits of two or more conflicting interpretations of the same fact pattern.[29] It is in this sense that law is often referred to as a method of adjudicating the competing claims of the parties to disputes.

Yet numerous international institutions that virtually everyone would agree to classify as legal regimes are silent on procedures for authoritative interpretation and dispute resolution. The four-nation conservation regime for northern fur seals, negotiated originally in 1911, and the five-nation protective arrangement for polar bears and their habitats, signed in 1973, are widely regarded as landmarks in the field of international wildlife law, for example, yet neither contains explicit provisions dealing with the resolution of disputes.[30] Other regimes refer to dispute resolution without offering much substantive guidance. In a typical formulation, the 1959 Antarctic Treaty exhorts the parties "to consult among themselves" with a view to

[28] Lon L. Fuller, *The Principles of Social Order* (Durham: Duke University Press, 1981). For a probing study of the relationship between law and dispute resolution as well as the connection between legal procedures for resolving disputes and the achievement of justice see Jerold S. Auerbach, *Justice without Law? Resolving Disputes without Lawyers* (New York: Oxford University Press, 1983).

[29] Myres S. McDougal and Associates, *Studies in World Public Order* (New Haven: Yale University Press, 1960).

[30] For a more general account of the evolution of international wildlife law see Simon Lyster, *International Wildlife Law* (Cambridge, Eng.: Grotius Publications, 1985).

agreeing on the means to resolve disputes.[31] But it does not commit the parties to any specific method of dealing with disputes, much less to a system relying on adjudication or arbitration as a means of achieving authoritative interpretations.

How can we account for this seeming paradox? Sometimes specific regimes are silent on the issue of interpretation and dispute resolution because their founders simply assume that specialized mechanisms for dispute resolution embedded in the overarching legal system (courts in most contemporary societies) will be able and willing to handle contentious issues arising in connection with the provisions of specific regimes. Appealing as this way of thinking may sound in the context of municipal systems, however, it does not solve the paradox in the context of international society, which can hardly be said to feature highly developed procedures of a general nature for resolving conflicts.[32] In other cases, it seems reasonable to fall back on some notion of autointerpretation under which individual parties to an international regime use their own domestic procedures to handle disputes regarding the regime's provisions which arise from activities taking place within their own jurisdictions.[33] This makes sense particularly in connection with coordination regimes, such as the polar bear or migratory bird arrangements, in which there is little explicitly transboundary activity and each party assumes responsibility for implementing the relevant provisions within its own jurisdiction. In still other cases, the silence of international regimes regarding dispute resolution reflects a tacit acknowledgment that the parties cannot agree on the terms of formal provisions coupled with an optimistic assessment of the ability of those who become involved in actual disputes over the operation of a regime to agree case-by-case on procedures to arrive at mutually acceptable interpretations that will serve to resolve those disputes.

Legal systems vary widely in the extent to which they feature centralized mechanisms such as courts that are able and willing to render judgments on the conflicting claims of individual subjects concerning

[31] Article XI of the Antarctic Treaty provides also for reference of disputes to the International Court of Justice, but only with the explicit consent of the parties to actual disputes.

[32] This is not meant to denigrate, but merely to recognize the limits of, the International Court of Justice and of the United Nations itself acting under Chapter VI of the Charter dealing with "pacific settlement of disputes."

[33] Richard A. Falk, *The Status of Law in International Society* (Princeton: Princeton University Press, 1970), Part III.

the application of prescriptions to specific situations and, in the process, to add to the stock of authoritative interpretations of the requirements of regime rules in practice. Similarly, successful regimes can and do differ in the extent to which they establish their own procedures to resolve disputes or operate in a social setting in which it is standard practice to resort to more general procedures (for example, courts) to resolve disputes over the application of regime rules to specific situations. Hence it seems that it would be a mistake to distinguish between legal and nonlegal regimes on the basis of a criterion relating to the inclusion of provisions for dispute resolution. Reliance on such a strategy would either divide the universe of cases in an inappropriate and unhelpful manner or lead to an analytic quagmire involving tortuous arguments about implied or tacit provisions for dispute resolution and authoritative interpretation.

Do legal prescriptions differ from other prescriptions because the actions of those responsible for implementing them are subject to judicial review? In some municipal settings, judicial review has emerged as a prominent feature of the legal system. In essence, judicial review provides a formalized procedure through which certain parties—those deemed to have standing—are allowed to use the courts to challenge the actions of those responsible for implementing legal prescriptions or to bring pressure to bear on responsible officials who seem reluctant to take appropriate steps to implement legal prescriptions in the first place. There can be no doubt about the value of judicial review as a means of protecting the interests of various subject groups in their dealings with public authorities.[34] And it is a relatively short step from this appreciation of the value of judicial review to the idea that prescriptions are legal if, and only if, they fall within the purview of the procedures for judicial review operative in a given society.

Yet this criterion, too, has serious drawbacks as a means of differentiating between legal and nonlegal prescriptions in international society. Some widely accepted regimes (for example, coordination regimes such as those dealing with migratory birds or the management of wetlands of international significance) lack judicial review procedures of their own because the actions national authorities take to implement the terms of these regimes within their own jurisdictions

---

[34] On the practice of judicial review regarding environmental laws and regulations in the United States consult Bill Shaw, *Environmental Law: People, Pollution, and Land Use* (St. Paul: West Publishing, 1976), Part II, sections 5 and 9.

are subject to judicial review in the relevant municipal forums. Other international regimes (for example, the cooperative regimes for whaling and the conservation of Antarctic marine living resources) lack judicial review procedures because they are not integrated into a more comprehensive legal system featuring clear-cut and generally accepted procedures of this type. Yet no one would be satisfied with the argument that the prescriptions of these and other effective international regimes are not legal because they are not subject to judicial review at the international level.

An even more fundamental objection to the idea that the existence of judicial review procedures can serve as the basis for differentiating between legal and nonlegal prescriptions arises from the fact that the scope or coverage of judicial review procedures in most societies shifts over time in response to political, economic, and social forces, even when the content of the prescriptions themselves remains otherwise unchanged. In many municipal systems—the evolution of environmental law in the United States offers numerous examples—the scope of judicial review has expanded markedly during the recent past as a result of the loosening of requirements for standing, the shrinking applicability of the doctrine of sovereign immunity, and so forth.[35] Whatever one may think of the desirability of such changes, it would be farfetched to say that prescriptions that had previously been nonlegal became legal through an extension of the scope of judicial review. Hence this argument fails to provide a satisfactory answer to our basic question.

Do legal regimes invariably include rules spelling out procedures to be followed in efforts to alter or abrogate their substantive provisions? Yet another procedural argument suggests that legal regimes differ from nonlegal regimes because they always contain explicit provisions covering withdrawal on the part of individual members, restructuring through the adoption of formal amendments, adaptation through procedures not requiring formal acceptance by the participants, and termination in the event of radical changes in circumstances. In fact, international regimes vary greatly in these terms. The regime for the Svalbard Archipelago set forth in the Spitsbergen Treaty of 1920, for instance, is silent on all these issues. The polar bear regime contains specific provisions governing termination of the regime and withdrawal of

[35] Thomas J. Schoenbaum, *Environmental Policy Law: Cases, Readings, and Text* (Mineola, N.Y.: Foundation Press, 1982), chap. 2.

individual members, but it says nothing about amendments designed to alter the regime's provisions (it envisions an undefined process of adjustment through informal consultations). The 1959 Antarctic Treaty, on the other hand, lays out explicit procedures for withdrawal of individual members, amendments to specific provisions, and possible review of the overall regime following thirty years of operation.[36]

What are we to make of all this? The simple answer is that the inclusion of procedures pertaining to alteration or abrogation is not a good indicator of the extent to which a regime is legal. In municipal settings, institutional arrangements are often silent on such matters because they come under the purview of an overarching legal and political system. There is no need for statutes setting forth the terms of specific regimes to lay out procedures for alteration or abrogation when it is widely understood that such issues are subject to the standard legislative procedures of the overall system. In actuality, some international regimes contain more explicit provisions regarding alteration and abrogation than do domestic regimes, precisely because the encompassing procedures for authoritative decision making that we take for granted at the domestic level are much less highly developed at the international level. The absence of such provisions in an international regime, however, is surely a poor basis on which to declare the regime as a whole nonlegal. Few would be satisfied with a method of distinguishing legal from nonlegal regimes that resulted in the regime for Svalbard being put into the nonlegal category or the regime for polar bears being regarded as somehow less legal than the core regime for Antarctica.

Can international regimes govern human activities that are illegal? Many social practices encompass human activities that are widely regarded as partially or even wholly illegal. Those engaged in such practices often play by the rules in the sense that they adhere to the dictates of well-known prescriptions which, in some cases at least, are enforced through the threat or actual use of sanctions. Notorious examples

[36] Thus Article XII of the Antarctic Treaty authorizes, but does not require, the holding of a review conference at any time after the treaty has been in force for thirty years on the request of any of the Contracting Parties. The treaty entered into force in 1961, and this provision became relevant in 1991. But because there is no way to control the agenda of such a review conference, it is likely that none of the Contracting Parties will act to trigger this provision of the treaty during the foreseeable future.

involving widespread activities such as the international traffic in narcotics or slaves and the activities of terrorists come to mind immediately.[37] But many less dramatic or more mundane activities exemplify this point as well. The activities of poachers and their clients who trade in ivory or alligator skins in violation of the rules of the Convention on the International Trade in Endangered Species of Wild Fauna and Flora, for instance, are highly organized and subject to widely understood rules.[38] So also are the efforts of cartels (for example, the Organization of Petroleum Exporting Countries) that form to manipulate world market prices in violation of the rules of the General Agreement on Tariffs and Trade and similar governance systems intended to encourage free and competitive trade at the international level.[39]

Regimes involving illegal activities are particularly common in social settings in which socioeconomic or cultural diversity coexists with political asymmetries that allow certain groups to dominate the process of defining the content of the legal system. Under such conditions, social practices that are widespread among subordinate groups are apt to be branded as illegal, especially when they run afoul of institutional arrangements promulgated by the dominant strata of society. The problems that indigenous peoples in many parts of the world encounter with respect to the operation of international wildlife regimes provide striking illustrations of this phenomenon. Northern hunters and gatherers harvesting migratory birds and their eggs in the traditional manner, for instance, have gotten into trouble for actions that violate the prescriptions of the international migratory bird treaties in force for Canada, Japan, Mexico, Russia, and the United States.[40] Similarly, indigenous whalers whose activities are guided by widely understood cultural norms have sometimes found themselves at odds with the requirements of the international whaling regime that has evolved under the terms of the International Convention for the Regulation of Whaling and that relies on formal manage-

---

[37] Nadelmann, "Global Prohibition Regimes."

[38] See Marc Reisner, *Game Wars: The Undercover Pursuit of Wildlife Poachers* (New York: Viking, 1991). For data on the extent of international trade in wildlife, legal and illegal, see the *TRAFFIC Bulletin*.

[39] Daniel Yergin, *The Prize: The Epic Quest for Oil, Money, and Power* (New York: Simon and Schuster, 1990).

[40] For relevant background consult Ralph Osterwoldt, "Implementation and Enforcement Issues in the Protection of Migratory Species," *Natural Resources Journal* 29 (Fall 1989), 1017–1049.

ment tools, such as quotas and moratoria, adopted through a voting procedure.[41]

The basic point remains unaltered, however; the fact that regimes can and do govern illegal activities suggests a worthwhile line of analysis for those seeking to distinguish between legal and nonlegal regimes in international society. Even so, there are good reasons not to be push this argument too far. Decisions about what to treat as legal and what to brand as illegal inevitably flow from underlying societal values, which can and do vary considerably both from place to place and from time to time. To take a classic example, slavery in the sense of the ownership of some human beings by others has been accepted as legal and regulated through the promulgation of a multiplicity of legal prescriptions in many social settings.[42] The disposal of wastes is another area in which traditional laissez-faire arrangements permitting the members of international society to act with little concern for inadvertent impacts on others are now giving way to more restrictive international regimes dealing with transboundary air pollution, international movements of hazardous wastes, and so forth.[43]

The international agenda at any given time is replete with issues reflecting the efforts of various interest groups to persuade relevant members of international society to delegalize activities currently accepted as legal (though not necessarily moral or ethical) and to legalize other activities, for example, some elements of the drug trade, now treated as illegal. Whatever its merits in specific cases, therefore, this approach to our basic question about the distinction between legal and nonlegal regimes cannot yield answers that are universal in the sense that they apply for all times and places.

Does legal reasoning regarding international governance systems differ from other types of reasoning about the same institutions? There remains the argument that the distinction we are seeking lies more in the nature of the reasoning employed by lawyers and social scientists than in any differences in the character of the institutions or governance systems themselves. It is not immediately apparent that this argument is cor-

---

[41] See Finn Lynge, *Arctic Wars, Animal Rights, Endangered Peoples* (Hanover, N.H.: University Press of New England, 1992). For a broader account of recent developments in the whaling regime see Pat W. Birnie, "International Legal Issues in the Management and Protection of the Whale: A Review of Four Decades of Experience," *Natural Resources Journal* 29 (Fall 1989), 903–934.

[42] Nadelmann, "Global Prohibition Regimes."

[43] Schneider, "State Responsibility."

rect. Neither law nor the various social sciences concerned with international regimes are characterized by consensus regarding the nature of the knowledge claims they seek to establish or the methods to be used in formulating and validating such claims. Both communities, for example, contain exponents both of positivism or neopositivism and of various nonpositivist epistemologies. Nor is it accurate to say that the distinction arises because lawyers are concerned with prescriptive matters, while social scientists generally focus on descriptive concerns. As the sociological jurisprudence of an earlier era and the contemporary law and economics movement both attest, lawyers have a long-standing and influential interest in the uses of descriptive in contrast to prescriptive arguments.[44] And despite the influence of descriptive concerns in recent American scholarship, many social scientists have a deep-seated interest in the development of prescriptive arguments.

Yet there is more to this line of thinking than the preceding paragraph would lead one to believe. The hallmark of legal reasoning, at least in systems influenced by Anglo-Saxon precepts, is a dialectical interaction between fact patterns and general principles.[45] Lawyers, whether they are practicing attorneys, judges, or legal scholars, organize their analytic efforts around the examination of discrete cases. They rely heavily on legal principles to make sense out of the facts of each case, though their views may differ regarding the applicable principles or the proper connection between the principles and the facts. They also use fact patterns presented in a variety of cases to explicate the meaning of legal principles. The result is an interactive form of reasoning that owes as much to literary criticism or hermeneutics as it does to social science methods and that is not reducible to any other well-known form of reasoning. This is why legal training takes place in specialized institutions and why the curriculum offered by law schools places great emphasis on learning to think like a lawyer in contrast to mastering a body of substantive materials that make up the law.

[44] On law and sociology consult Vilhelm Aubert, ed., *Sociology of Law* (Harmondsworth, Eng.: Penguin, 1969); and Robert Paul Wolff, ed., *The Rule of Law* (New York: Simon and Schuster, 1971). For a well-known expression of the law and economics perspective see Richard A. Posner, *Economic Analysis of Law,* 2d ed. (Boston: Little, Brown, 1977).

[45] The organization of virtually every casebook used in American law schools reflects this fundamental perspective. But for some reflections on these matters see J. Roland Pennock and John W. Chapman, eds., *Ethics, Economics, and The Law (NOMOS XXIV)* (New York: New York University Press, 1982).

This argument does not, of course, lead to the conclusion that legal regimes and nonlegal regimes or legal prescriptions and nonlegal prescriptions differ from each other in some easily identifiable and significant way. Rather, it suggests that the difference we should be concerned with lies in the nature of the discourse among students of these phenomena rather than in the phenomena themselves. If this is true, there may be much to be gained from opening up a dialogue between those who approach the same phenomena from different vantage points to gain a fuller picture of the nature and role of institutional arrangements or governance systems in international society. As is true of all situations involving distinct language communities, communication among those belonging to the two cultures is apt to be both difficult and imperfect. Far from regarding these barriers to communication as a deterrent, however, we must make a conscious effort to overcome them. We should, for example, encourage individuals who are able and willing to become conversant with both modes of reasoning, and we should deliberately create opportunities for members of the two groups to interact under favorable conditions.

INTEGRATING THE TWO COMMUNITIES

The term *regime* (not to mention terminological equivalents such as *governance system, treaty system, management system,* or *institutional arrangement*) is in common use in international treaties and conventions, resolutions of the United Nations General Assembly, and declarations emanating from international conferences. A few concrete examples will illustrate the nature and extent of this usage. The 1982 Convention on the Law of the Sea refers explicitly to the regime of passage through international straits (Article 34), the regime for the exclusive economic zone (Article 55), the regime of islands (Article 121), and the regime for the Area or, in other words, the deep seabed (Article 154). The unratified 1988 Convention on the Regulation of Antarctic Mineral Resource Activities stresses in its Preamble that a "regime for Antarctic mineral resources" must be compatible with key provisions of the Antarctic Treaty of 1959. The United Nations General Assembly, in expressing its views on the "Question of Antarctica," has stated explicitly that negotiations leading to the formation of "any regime . . . for the protection and conservation of the Antarctic environment" should involve "all members of the international community" (UNGA 44/124).

If anything, jurists, legal scholars, and publicists have shown an even even more striking propensity to use the language of regimes in their efforts to describe both the institutional arrangements established under the terms of treaties and conventions and the established practices that have evolved more informally in international society. It will come as no surprise that some of the most articulate contributions to this discourse are associated with the work of North American scholars. Oscar Schachter, an American with a long and distinguished record of service to the United Nations, has spoken at length about "managerial regimes for ocean resources."[46] L. F. E. Goldie, a well-known Canadian legal scholar, has written extensively about regimes for marine resources or, as he puts it, "regimes for structuring the maritime environment."[47] Nor is the term used in a purely descriptive fashion. Michael Riesman, for instance, has sought to shed light on processes of lawmaking in international society through a study of the "regime of straits."[48] And addressing issues relating to the effectiveness of international institutions once they are in place, Abram Chayes and Antonia Chayes have contributed to our understanding of "adjustment and compliance processes in international regulatory regimes."[49]

The concern with international regimes, however, is not limited to North America, and some of the most eloquent and insightful discussions are to be found in the work of jurists and scholars from other parts of the world. Nagendra Singh, a distinguished Indian lawyer and member of the International Court of Justice, spoke forcefully in an introduction to the work of the Experts Group on International Law of the World Commission on Environment and Development

[46] Oscar Schachter, *Sharing the World's Resources* (New York: Columbia University Press, 1977), Part II.

[47] L. F. E. Goldie, "The Management of Ocean Resources: Regimes for Structuring the Marine Environment," in Cyril E. Black and Richard A. Falk, eds., *The Structure of the International Environment*, Vol. 4 of *The Future of the International Legal Order* (Princeton: Princeton University Press, 1972), 155–247.

[48] L. Michael Riesman, "The Regime of Straits and National Security: An Appraisal of International Lawmaking," *American Journal of International Law* 74 (January 1980), 48–76.

[49] Abram Chayes and Antonia H. Chayes, "Adjustment and Compliance Processes in International Regulatory Regimes," in Mathews, ed., *Preserving the Global Environment*, 280–308.

about "why a legal regime is needed" to govern international commons or "extraterritorial spaces."[50] The Australian legal scholar Gillian Triggs has assembled a symposium volume on Antarctic issues titled *The Antarctic Treaty Regime*.[51] And Francisco Orrego Vicuna, a prominent Chilean legal scholar, explores the "living resources regime," the "regime for the high seas," the "legal regime relating to ice," and, more broadly, "the general regime of the Law of the Sea" in his extensive study of issues relating to minerals in the Antarctic region.[52] William Butler, a leading British expert on Soviet thought and practice in the field of international law, includes a lengthy discussion of the "legal regime for Arctic waters and straits" in his work on the legal status of the Northeast Arctic Passage.[53]

There is little indication, however, that lawyers and legal scholars have made a conscious effort to examine, much less debate, the conceptual and theoretical issues raised by their reliance on the idea of regimes or legal regimes in international society. Legal scholars have occasionally collaborated with political scientists in studies of international regimes that pay some attention to conceptual and theoretical issues. Prominent examples include the participation of Edith Brown Weiss in the book *Regimes for the Ocean, Outer Space, and Weather* prepared under the auspices of the Brookings Institution in the 1970s[54] and of Michael M'Gonigle in a volume titled *Pollution, Politics, and International Law,* also written during the 1970s under the auspices of the University of British Columbia and the London School of Economics.[55] But a preliminary search has failed to turn up much evidence of an interest on the part of legal scholars in reflective or interpretive examinations of issues surrounding the use of the concept of regimes in discussions of institutional arrangements or governance systems at the international level.

[50] Nagendra Singh, "Foreword," in Experts Group on Environmental Law of the World Commission on Environment and Development, *Environmental Protection and Sustainable Development: Legal Principles and Recommendations* (London and Dordrecht: Graham and Trotman/Martinus Nijhoff, 1987), xix–xx.

[51] Gillian D. Triggs, ed., *The Antarctic Treaty Regime: Law, Environment and Resources* (Cambridge, Eng.: Cambridge University Press, 1987).

[52] Francisco Orrego Vicuna, *Antarctic Mineral Exploration: The Emerging Legal Framework* (Cambridge, Eng.: Cambridge University Press, 1988).

[53] William E. Butler, *Northeast Arctic Passage* (Alphen aan den Rijn: Sijthoff and Noordhoff, 1978).

[54] Seyom Brown, Nina W. Cornell, Larry L. Fabian, and Edith Brown Weiss, *Regimes for the Ocean, Outer Space, and Weather* (Washington, D.C.: Brookings Institution, 1977).

[55] R. Michael M'Gonigle and Mark W. Zacher, *Pollution, Politics, and International Law: Tankers at Sea* (Berkeley: University of California Press, 1979).

Whatever the proper interpretation of this situation may be (and there are several possibilities), it contrasts sharply with recent debates among theoretically inclined political scientists and economists interested in international institutions. In such quarters, regime analysis, described by some as the "latest wave" in international relations theory,[56] has become the focus of a lively exchange of views encompassing not only substantive issues relating to the identification, formation, and effectiveness of regimes but also epistemological questions concerning the proper methods for studying international regimes. Although it is surely premature to predict the ultimate fate of this latest wave in the development of theories about international relations, it is beyond doubt that regime analysis has already had an impact on the way social scientists think about institutional arrangements in international society.

This asymmetry makes it difficult to engage in direct comparisons regarding conceptual and theoretical matters between the literature on international governance systems that social scientists have produced and the analogous literature produced by legal scholars. The point is not that the legal scholars have little to contribute to the development of regime analysis in conceptual and theoretical terms or that an effort to compare and contrast the intellectual foundations of the work of the two communities would be of no interest; far from it. Rather, we need to devise a means for exploring this subject that is not hindered by the asymmetry that marks the two bodies of literature.

One promising avenue, I now believe, is a strategy that begins with an effort to identify important topics in regime analysis of interest to the members of both intellectual communities and proceeds to envision or invent ways for the two groups to join forces to shed light on the conceptual and theoretical content of these issues. To conclude this chapter and to reprise the central themes of this volume, I initiate such an effort in the following paragraphs, suggesting issues that strike me as promising and offering some indication of how legal scholars and social scientists working together on these topics can broaden and deepen our understanding of international governance systems.

First, international regimes operate within a changing social sys-

---

[56] James F. Keeley, "The Latest Wave: A Critical Review of Regime Literature," in David G. Haglund and Michael K. Hawes, eds., *World Politics: Power, Interdependence and Dependence* (Toronto: HBJ-Holt College Publishers of Canada, 1990), 553–569.

tem. The international system has changed rapidly in recent years in the number and variety of its member states; the scope of the economic, political, and social inequalities among member states; the roles played by nonstate actors (including individuals as well as intergovernmental organizations, nongovernmental organizations, and multinational corporations); the level of interdependence among its members; the distribution of power (in the material sense) among the members of this social system, and the emergence of new issues on the international agenda (for instance, problems of global environmental change).[57] But what are the implications of these changes, taken together, for the formation of international governance systems or regimes, the effectiveness of these systems once they are in place, and the evolution or transformation of regimes over time? This is an area in which both legal scholars and social scientists, starting from their own analytic premises and using their own methods, have much to contribute. What is needed now is a sustained effort to integrate these streams of analysis in the interests of pushing our understanding to a level beyond that reachable by either group operating alone.

Turning to more specific topics, there is much to be said for encouraging work that focuses on the distinctions among different types or sources of obligation and on the interactions among them. Subjects may feel obligated to comply with a regime's prescriptions for moral, normative, contractual, utilitarian, or legal reasons. But can we sharpen these distinctions and use them as the basis for an inquiry into interactions among the different sources of obligations? Lawyers and legal scholars refer frequently to legal norms and the legal character of contractual obligations as well as to prescriptions that are legally binding because they are authoritative. Yet they are likely, at the same time, to emphasize the distinction between what is legal on the one hand and what is ethical or moral, fair or just, on the other.[58] Social scientists have referred regularly in their analyses of regimes to rules, norms, conventions, principles of rectitude, and so forth with little effort to distinguish clearly among them.[59] A move by both groups to

---

[57] Compare, for example, the account in Bull, *Anarchical Society*, prepared in the mid-1970s with the account in Zacher, "Decaying Pillars of the Westphalian Temple," which reflects the concerns of the early 1990s.

[58] Alan Gewirth, "Obligation: Political, Legal, Moral," in Pennock and Chapman, eds., *Political and Legal Obligation*, 55–88.

[59] Stephen D. Krasner, "Structural Causes and Regime Consequences: Regimes as Intervening Variables," in Krasner, ed., *International Regimes*, 1–21.

make common cause in dealing with these conceptual complexities would not only avoid unnecessary confusion but also open up a promising line of analysis concerning the conditions under which distinct types of obligations reinforce or contradict each other in international society.

Factors that determine the extent to which subjects do, in fact, comply with the prescriptions embedded in international regimes should be approached similarly. Although the topic is rife with misunderstandings, both legal scholars and social scientists have a long-term interest in questions concerning the links between enforcement and compliance in international society. To what extent does compliance in international society or, for that matter, in any other social setting really depend on the threat or actual use of sanctions on the part of some central authority or certain agents authorized to act in the name of society? What is the role of transparency in the pursuit of compliance, and how can transparency be maximized by exercising of care in crafting prescriptions to be incorporated into international regimes?[60] What has been the experience with decentralized compliance mechanisms, including various forms of self-help, in international society and in other societies lacking centralized structures of authority? It is hard to think of questions that are more critical to our understanding of the nature of international institutions and that are, at the same time, better suited to collaborative study on the part of legal scholars and social scientists.

The topic of dispute resolution lends itself to similar treatment. In thinking about the handling of disputes or conflicts in international society, legal scholars have tended to direct their attention to procedures such as arbitration and adjudication that yield binding decisions, while social scientists have been more interested in bargaining or negotiation and the activities of mediators in assisting negotiation. In the extreme, these practices lead to a deep division between lawyers issuing calls for increased reliance on the International Court of Justice and social scientists preoccupied with devising bargaining tactics intended to produce victory for one side or the other in specific

[60] A new wave of work on compliance with international prescriptions, stressing such factors as transparency in contrast to sanctions, is now under way. For a general account see Abram Chayes and Antonia Handler Chayes, "On Compliance," *International Organization* 47 (Spring 1993), 175–205. Several of those engaged in this work (for example, Philipp Hildebrand, Ronald Mitchell, and David Victor) have strong interests in environmental regimes.

disputes.[61] But even in its more moderate forms, this division of labor is misplaced. There is, in fact, a continuum of procedures for handling international disputes, ranging from use of good offices and imaging exercises at one end to formal court proceedings at the other.[62] What we need now is a better understanding of the conditions under which each of these techniques can be used to good advantage in a social setting of the type prevailing in international society coupled with a sophisticated appreciation of how to shift back and forth among these techniques as the need arises. Surely, these are matters for legal scholars and social scientists to tackle collaboratively using the full range of concepts and analytic procedures at their disposal.

Yet another topic of mutual interest arises from the distinction between legal and illegal practices and, more specifically, from a study of the processes through which activities once accepted as legal in international society become objects of prohibition regimes branding them as illegal and vice versa. Do these processes involve distinct phases or stages as some observers have suggested?[63] Are they always unidirectional in the sense that they move steadily toward prohibiting practices (for example, international commerce in slaves or various animal species) initially regarded as legal? Or can they lead toward the legalization of practices considered illegal in earlier times? This topic clearly calls for an analysis of interactions between ideals and actions, a subject of continuing interest both to legal scholars and to social scientists. Students of law and society have often employed the idea of a "normative gap" to analyze the role law plays, at one and the same time, as a regulator of actual behavior and as a force for social change.[64] Social scientists have long been interested in the gap between the ideal and the actual with regard to human behavior, an interest that has led both to a search for the determinants of this gap and an effort to predict the consequences of a widening or narrowing

---

[61] To Illustrate, compare the perspectives underlying Shabtai Rosenne, *The World Court: What It Is and How It Works* (Dobbs Ferry, N.Y.: Oceana Publications, 1973), and Thomas C. Schelling, *The Strategy of Conflict* (Cambridge, Mass.: Harvard University Press, 1960).

[62] F. S. Northedge and M. D. Donelan, *International Disputes: The Theoretical Aspects* (New York: St. Martin's Press, 1971), Part III.

[63] Nadelmann, "Global Prohibition Regimes," 484–486.

[64] Urban G. Whitaker, Jr., *Politics and Power: A Text in International Law* (New York: Harper & Row, 1964), chap. 2.

of the gap.[65] What is needed now is an initiative designed to pool the insights of the two communities on this topic.

Finally, however, it seems likely that the most important thing the legal community and the social science community have to offer each other in broadening and deepening our understanding of international governance systems or regimes is their distinctive modes of reasoning. The evaluation of this proposition is complicated because neither community enjoys consensus regarding the nature of its knowledge claims and the procedures for formulating and validating them. Yet the dialectical processes through which lawyers move back and forth between fact patterns and legal principles surely differ fundamentally from what most social scientists do, whether or not they subscribe to a positivist or neopositivist epistemology. The difference is not merely a matter of adherence to divergent paradigms. It involves a deeper division concerning not only what we know and how we come to know what we know but also what there is to know and what we want to know. The depth of this division makes it easy to understand why legal scholars and social scientists are often puzzled, and sometimes mystified, by each other's discourse. But this only increases the importance of the challenge before us. There are good grounds for concluding that the development of a more effective working relationship between the legal community and the social science community is a necessary condition for the articulation of a comprehensive and fully satisfactory account of the nature and roles of regimes or governance systems in international society.

[65] Marion J. Levy, Jr., *Modernization: Latecomers and Survivors* (New York: Basic Books, 1972).

Index

Cornell Studies in Political Economy

EDITED BY PETER J. KATZENSTEIN